Boatowner's
Energy
Planner

Boatowner's Energy Planner

How to Make and Manage
Electrical Energy on Board

KEVIN JEFFREY
with **NAN JEFFREY**

International Marine/Seven Seas
Camden, Maine

Published by Seven Seas

10   9   8   7   6   5   4   3   2   1

Copyright © 1991 Seven Seas, an imprint of TAB
BOOKS. TAB BOOKS is a division of McGraw-
Hill, Inc.

Library of Congress Cataloging-in-Publication Data

Jeffrey, Kevin, 1954–
    Boatowner's energy planner / Kevin Jeffrey
      with Nan Jeffrey.
          p.   cm.
    Includes index.
    ISBN 0-915160-63-3
    1. Boats and boating—Electric
equipment.   I. Jeffrey, Nan, 1949–
II. Title.   III. Title: Boat owner's energy
planner.
VM325.J43   1991
623.8′503—dc20   91-4071
                                           CIP

TAB BOOKS offers software for sale. For information and a catalog, please contact TAB Software
Department, Blue Ridge Summit, PA 17294-0850.

Questions regarding the content of this book
should be addressed to:

Seven Seas
P.O. Box 220
Camden, ME 04843

Typeset by A & B Typesetters, Inc., Bow, NH
Printed by Arcata Graphics, Fairfield, PA
Design by Patrice M. Rossi
Illustrated by Chuck Steacy
Edited by Jonathan Eaton, Eivind Boe,
Thomas P. McCarthy
Production by Janet Robbins

Acknowledgments

We would like to thank the many boatowners and marine energy professionals who contributed their expertise and support to this book. In particular we would like to thank Jack Csenge, Hamilton Ferris, Dane Goodson, Richard Gottlieb, Michael Hoffman, Robert La-Chapelle, Bill Montgomery, Richard Neilson, Bill Owra, and Robert Weller.

Contents

Prologue

Think of a boat as a group of systems working toward the common goal of providing safe and enjoyable passage on the water. This book explores in depth the electrical energy systems of boats, including methods of producing, storing, and distributing electricity.

Boat owners inherit a unique opportunity to make and manage electrical energy. Once away from the dock they have only their on-board generating systems to provide adequate power for lighting, communications, navigation, refrigeration, and appliances. With proper preparation, meeting this challenge can be a highly satisfying experience.

We've divided the subject into parts and chapters. Part I, An Introduction to Energy Systems, is a brief, annotated roster of the simple concepts and devices that will be examined in greater detail later in the book. It contains the following:

- **Chapter 1 — Understanding Energy:** Chapter 1 first explores the role electrical energy plays for the modern boater. Many of the other systems found on boats depend on a reliable source of electricity. The chapter then examines energy itself. It is helpful to ask ourselves, What is energy? What different forms does it have? How is it produced? The answers to these and other questions help lay the groundwork for what follows.

  Also included in this chapter are some reasons why clean, renewable sources of electrical energy make sense for today's boater. Solar, wind, and water generators have recently come into their own and are now widely available for use in the marine environment.

- **Chapter 2 — Methods of Charging Batteries: What Is Available?:** This chapter provides a quick overview and comparison of all types of electrical energy–producing equipment for boats, including alternators, from standard through the high-output variety; small portable generators and battery chargers; small solar trickle chargers and large, high-capacity solar panels; small, permanently mounted wind generators and large propeller units suspended in the rigging; and water generators, including the trailing-log and outboard-leg types. In-depth looks at all these are given in Parts III and IV.

- **Chapter 3 — Other System Components: What Is Available?:** Chapter 3 introduces the other components that, together with the charging source, make up a complete energy system. These devices store, regulate, and monitor the energy you produce, and make the system safer and more reliable.

The chapters in Part II, Electricity and Batteries, are as follows:

- **Chapter 4 — Basic Electricity for Boaters:** Here we look at the instruments and meters used for keeping track of electrical energy and diagnosing problems in the system. A simple electrical circuit is described, then used as a basis for understanding a boat schematic. Examples are given to illustrate the most common schematic arrangements.

- **Chapter 5—Of Batteries and Charging:** Here batteries are discussed in detail, since they are the sole means of storing electrical energy for later use. Batteries are often neglected and improperly charged and therefore frequently the source of electrical energy–system failure. Types of batteries, sizes and charging characteristics, and proper maintenance and safety precautions all are covered.

Part III, Gasoline- and Diesel-Fueled Charging Systems, contains the following chapters:

- **Chapter 6—Engine-Driven Alternators:** Standard marine alternators, those typically fitted to inboard and outboard engines, are covered in the first part of this chapter. They operate and are controlled much like the alternators in automobiles. An automobile alternator and controls are fine for a boat with a low electrical demand or one that uses its engine frequently. Most boaters, however, do not use their craft like an automobile, with the engine running and little demand for electricity. Since boats often sit quietly at anchor or on a mooring or use sails for propulsion, their electrical needs are much greater. Some relatively new products, including high-output marine alternators and special alternator controls, provide more electrical power while reducing engine running time.

- **Chapter 7—Small Portable Generators and Battery Chargers:** Small portable gasoline- and diesel-powered generators can be a valuable addition to your energy-equipment inventory and are available in a variety of sizes and outputs. Most portable units are AC-DC hybrids, but a few have a strictly DC output. All are reviewed in this chapter, with tips on installation, operation, and troubleshooting. AC-to-DC battery chargers are covered here, since they make for an efficient DC charging system when coupled with a portable generator.

In Part IV, Renewable-Energy Charging Systems, you'll find the following:

- **Chapter 8—Photovoltaic (PV) Solar Panels:** A photovoltaic solar panel is probably the most benign electrical generator in the world. Sunlight striking its surface will create electricity, and no noise or moving parts are involved. Chapter 8 covers solar-cell theory and panel construction and selection. Solar panels vary in size, weight, output, and suitability to the marine environment. We review all available solar panels, along with other components necessary for a complete system.

- **Chapter 9—Wind Generators:** Marine wind generators come in two basic types, those with small-diameter propellers that resemble farm water-pumping windmills, and those with two-or three-bladed large-diameter propellers. The factors that determine which is right for you are discussed in this chapter.

- **Chapter 10—Water Generators:** Water generators on a boat are really just another form of wind power. The motion of a sailboat through the water provides power, which is converted into electricity by one of five types of units: trailing log, short flexible lead, outboard leg, auxiliary prop through the hull, and generator on a freewheeling shaft. They can operate anytime the boat is under way, and some come as part of a wind-water combination generator.

The following chapters are contained in Part V, Marine AC Electrical Systems:

- **Chapter 11—DC-to-AC Inverters:** Inverters that change direct current from your batteries to alternating current for power tools and other appliances are now efficient and affordable. They come in a wide range of power ratings, and some are set up to work in reverse as a convenient battery charger if AC is available.

- **Chapter 12—Direct AC Power Systems:** Sometimes it is more convenient to supply AC power directly instead of through an inverter. Direct AC power can be provided on board by connecting to shore power at a dock, by running a large portable generator or a gen-set, or by using a special auxiliary engine–driven AC generator. These three options are covered in detail.

And finally, Part VI, Sizing and Selecting Your System, contains these chapters:

- **Chapter 13—Estimating Your Electrical Load:** This chapter allows you to calculate easily the daily electrical load on your boat. From this you can find the total generation capacity you require. Lighting, refrigeration, autopilots, and other marine appliances are covered, with helpful recommendations for reducing your daily load. Examples are given for boats with light, medium, and heavy electrical loads.

- **Chapter 14—Selecting Your System:** The size and type of generating equipment you choose to have on board will depend not only on your electrical oad, but also on what type of boat you have and how and where you use it. Chapter 14's recommendations match requirements with available equipment. With this chapter and those that precede it, you can design the ideal electrical energy system for your needs.

We hope that this book will give you the confidence and skills to make and manage your energy supply effectively.

Kevin and Nan Jeffrey
Barnstable, Massachusetts
January 1991

Boatowner's
Energy
Planner

1

Understanding Energy

===

THE ROLE OF ELECTRICITY ON A MODERN BOAT

On board a boat you become the manager of your own electric utility company. You are free to determine how, when, and in what quantity electrical energy is produced, how much is used right away, and how much is stored for later use. A liberating feeling of self-sufficiency comes from supplying your own electrical energy needs.

As a utility manager you also become responsible for the maintenance and safe use of the generating equipment. In the event of a power failure there is no utility crew to get you "on line" again free of charge. Considerations of equipment size and weight; the noise, smells, or vibrations it might produce; and the physical energy you must expend to operate it become important to you. This book will help you prepare for potential problems and evaluate the advantages or disadvantages of each system.

You probably consume much less electricity on your boat than you would use in a house. This is just as well, since a boat's energy system lacks a land-based utility's advantages of scale, and the unit price of the energy you produce on board will inevitably be higher. This is not to say that you will have large energy costs on a boat. Through simple acts of conservation and improvements in efficiency, you should be able to enjoy modern conveniences while also saving money. As a bonus you will be able to use what you learn on the water to help you live more efficiently on land.

Some boaters prefer to eliminate the need for electricity altogether, particularly those with either an outboard engine or no engine at all. While this way of thinking has a great deal to recommend it, eliminating electricity does not necessarily make life aboard simpler or less expensive. Interior lighting can be supplied by kerosene, and the soft, warm glow provides a soothing, romantic atmosphere. Our Tilley lantern often lights and warms the cabin on cool nights. The burning of a fuel, however, produces moisture and fumes that can be annoying and harmful if the cabin is not well vented. On a hot night the extra heat from kerosene lamps is most unwelcome. Lamps must be trimmed, tinkered with, and lighted each time you move to a different part of the boat. With children on board, kerosene cabin lighting can be downright dangerous.

Lighting above decks, including running lights and the anchor light, can also be accomplished with kerosene, but considerations of cost and maintenance still apply. It is possible to use disposable batteries to operate lanterns for spot lighting and radios for music and weather reports. Disposable batteries are not inexpensive, though, and when their useful life ends they become an insult to the environment.

If simplicity and low cost are really the objectives, a better approach might incorporate a small solar panel and a low-cost 12-volt battery (if you don't already have one for your engine). With these you can run a few fluorescent cabin lights, a low-drain anchor light, and a weather radio, and use the kerosene lamps occasionally as desired. You can even use the 12-volt battery to recharge ni-cad batteries for flashlights and other equipment. This system is simple and safe, and still leaves plenty of scope for roughing it. At around 100 watt-hours per day, you are using less than one percent of the daily power required by the average American home. With a twenty-year or more lifespan, the solar panel will probably save you money in the long run.

It is more common for boaters to want a few conveniences on board. Truly, some of the finer aspects of modern life are powered by electricity, including good lighting, music and entertainment, weather reports and communication, and simple refrigeration (keeping a modest amount of food cold in a well-insulated box). These amenities use relatively little electricity, and it is easy to supply power for them from an on-board energy system. At around 1,000 watt-hours per day, you'd be using about five percent of the power required in the average American home.

Once an energy system is provided, it is tempting to add other conveniences and safety items to the electrical load. These might include electronic instruments and navigational aids, with depth sounder, radio direction finder, radar, Loran, and satnav as just a few of the possibilities. You might wish to upgrade from simple refrigeration to a system with more capacity and a freezer compartment. You may have electric motors in cabin fans, autopilot, windlass, or pumps. Or you might have power tools, galley aids such as blenders, microwave ovens and coffee/grain mills, or other appliances that you want to use on board. Recently an electrically powered onboard system for making fresh water has become practical, and it's not unusual these days to carry a personal computer for work, navigation, or just for fun. At this level you will have to be a careful energy manager. An electrical load of 2,000 watt-hours of power consumed per day—a heavy electrical load for a boat—is equivalent to about ten percent of the daily demand of the average American home.

WHAT IS ENERGY?

The electrical energy used on a boat, or for that matter in a home, must be "manufactured" from other forms of energy. It is thus said to be high-grade energy, and should be reserved for things that only electricity can do. Tasks such as cooking, drying clothes, and heating homes or water can all be accomplished more efficiently with lower grades of fuel energy. In setting up a safe and efficient electrical energy system, it is helpful to take a closer look at what energy is, what different forms it can have, and how we can make it work for us.

One definition of the word *energy* is "the ability to do work and overcome resistance." Primitive man survived using what food he ate to create internal energy for his daily tasks and using the sun's energy to provide warmth and light. The discovery of fire led to an ability to do more work, overcoming the "resistance" of darkness and cold temperatures.

The domestication of animals revolutionized man's ability to do work, with dramatic changes in his ability to produce food, transport goods, and secure raw materials. Later on in his development he also came to appreciate the work he could perform by harnessing the energy of moving water and the wind. Windmills, waterwheels, beasts of burden, and wood fires remained man's sources of energy until quite recently, when the development of steam and then internal-combustion engines created a second energy revolution.

Scientific discoveries early in this century eventually led to the splitting of the atom during World War II. Since then we have been harnessing the energy released during this process for the production of electricity. The newcomer to man's energy arsenal comes not from splitting but from slamming together or fusing atoms. Fusion energy has tremendous promise, but harnessing it to produce electricity remains a distant prospect.

During this century man has also become more sophisticated in his use of energy from the sun, wind, and moving water. Solar-electric generating plants, electricity-producing wind generators, and modern hydroelectric dams are all contributing to the satisfaction of man's energy needs.

What Forms Does Energy Take?

Energy, or the ability to do work and overcome resistance, comprises different forms. It can be mechanical, electrical, or chemical, or it can exist as heat or radiation. It can be in motion (kinetic energy) or at rest (potential energy). Theoretically, energy can be converted from one form to another without loss. This is known as the law of conservation of energy. In practice, however, the usable energy we get when converting energy from one form to another is almost always diminished, since some escapes during conversion, usually as heat. How much is lost depends on something we call the conversion efficiency.

The human body is a good example of efficient energy use. We eat food and convert it to chemical energy, some of which is stored for use on demand. The central nervous system then converts potential energy to electrical energy, sending impulses to our muscles. The muscles in turn generate kinetic energy, allowing us to walk, run, and work. The heat lost in the conversion from one form of energy to another keeps our bodies at a comfortable and critical 98.6 degrees Fahrenheit. The human body is an elegant, perfectly balanced energy system.

Firewood, oil, and coal are reservoirs of potential chemical energy. When burned they emit heat and radiation energy. Rushing water or moving air has kinetic energy. If the water or wind is used to turn a gristmill, that energy remains as mechanical energy in a rotating shaft. If the water or wind is used to turn electrical generators, it is either converted into electrical energy for immediate use or, in small systems, stored in batteries as potential chemical energy.

Gasoline and diesel fuels are refined petroleum products whose potential chemical energy is converted by the internal combustion engine of a car or a boat into the mechanical energy of a rotating shaft. Some of this kinetic energy may be taken away, by means of belts and pulleys, to turn an alternator shaft. The alternator spins and produces a somewhat lesser amount of electrical energy that, if stored in a battery, becomes potential chemical energy again! When an appliance aboard your boat is turned on, the energy leaves the battery as electrical energy. It changes form one final time as it is used to provide light (visible radiation and heat), run a cabin fan (mechanical energy), or operate a VHF radio (mechanical sound energy and transmitted radiation energy). Each time energy changes form, a little is dissipated. The fewer changes you require it to undergo, the more usable energy remains, and the greater the end-use efficiency.

Just as public utility companies must choose which energy sources they will use to generate electricity, so too must you. Listed below are all present-day sources of energy—renewable and nonrenewable—used for producing electricity. Nonrenewable sources are mined from the earth and make up the bulk of our current fuel for generating electricity. Of these, only fossil fuels are suitable for boats. The renewable energy sources all, in one way or another, result from sunlight hitting the Earth.

Nonrenewable Energy Sources

Fossil fuels.   Fossil fuels contain chemical energy created by organic matter trapped underground millions of years ago and gradually converted into oil, coal, and natural gas by intense pressure and temperature. Forty-two gallons of crude oil is equivalent to one-quarter ton of coal or 5,700 cubic feet of natural gas. Crude oil is refined into products such as kerosene, gasoline, and diesel fuel, which are burned to heat homes, to make steam to drive large electrical generators, or to produce mechanical energy, as in the internal combustion engines of cars, boats, and portable generators.

Although coal was originally used for the same purposes as oil, its use is now limited primarily to coal-fired electrical power plants, together with the occasional coal furnace in a home or coal stove in a cozy ship's saloon. Natural gas is burned either for space heating or cooking or to create steam for producing electrical or mechanical energy.

Nuclear fission.   Nuclear fission produces energy by breaking up uranium atoms, releasing huge amounts of heat. The uranium must first be enriched in a sophisticated process that makes it fissionable, or fissile. A pound of ordinary uranium yields almost three million times the energy supplied by a pound of coal. A special form of nuclear reactor—the breeder reactor—converts some of the uranium to plutonium while it is undergoing ordinary fission. Plutonium is also an effective fissile fuel, and therefore the reactor "breeds" one type of fuel while consuming another.

Synthetic fossil fuels.   Fossil fuels locked up in solid sedimentary formations can be "synthesized" to a more usable, more transportable form. Examples include extracting petroleum from oil-shale rock formations, gas from coal (coal gasification), and liquid fuel from coal (coal liquefaction).

Geothermal energy.   The natural radioactive decay of rocks below the surface creates heat, which when extracted can be used to drive electrical generators. This form of energy, while not renewable, will be available for use into the very distant future.

Renewable Energy Sources

Solar energy.   What we think of as solar energy is actually the result of a self-sustaining nuclear fusion reaction of the star, 93 million miles away, that we call our sun. This is the same fusion reaction we are now trying to simulate under controlled laboratory conditions. The energy released from the sun is constant, even though the usable energy reaching a particular place on the Earth is affected by clouds, smog, and the tilt and rotation of the planet. Objects on Earth that absorb the sun's rays—in part, radiant heat and light energy—convert those rays to sensible heat (the heat that we can feel and measure). This is the principle used in solar collectors to produce heat and hot water for homes, and in the large, concentrating steam generators used for producing electricity. Sunlight can also be changed directly into electrical energy by the photovoltaic cell.

Wind energy.   Wind, the movement of air caused by temperature variations induced by the uneven solar heating of the Earth and its atmosphere, carries mechanical energy. This energy has been harnessed for centuries by sailors to propel their ships. Windmills have long been used to grind grain, pump water, or turn machinery; today windmills use the wind to drive generators, creating electricity.

Water energy.   Think of the moving water in a river or stream as a type of solar energy. The sun evaporates water from the Earth's surface, and the water returns as rain or snow. The rain or snowmelt flows downhill until it reaches the ocean, its state of lowest potential energy. The natural flow of rivers and streams can be harnessed to drive turbines that turn electrical generators. The steady movement of ocean waves or tides also can be used to produce electricity. A water-powered electrical generator for a sailboat harnesses the motion of the vessel to turn a propeller through the dense and relatively motionless water.

Biomass.   Surplus or otherwise unusable organic matter can be used to produce energy. Wood, organic wastes, plants, peat, or like materials produce usable energy in three ways. They can be converted to heat by burning, and the heat can be used to create steam for generating electricity. Biomass also can be fermented and then distilled to produce ethyl alcohol, a liquid that has promise for replacing fossil fuels in car and boat engines. Finally, biomass can be converted to methane gas, a fuel, by anaerobic digestion. While there are electricity-generating biomass facilities operating today, these should not be confused with garbage-to-energy plants, since those facilities also burn plastics and other materials that create toxic fumes and residues.

Ocean thermal energy conversion (OTEC).   The substantial differences in temperature between the surface of the ocean, which is warmed by the sun, and the deeper, colder water below can be harnessed to produce energy. Simply put, the warm water vaporizes a low-boiling-point liquid (transferring its energy to the liquid), which in turn drives a turbine generator to produce electricity. During this process, the vapor loses much of its own heat energy. It is further cooled back to a liquid by the colder water below, and is ready for a new cycle. This system operates most efficiently in the tropics, where the surface water is warmest.

THE CASE FOR RENEWABLE ENERGY SYSTEMS ON BOARD

With a better understanding of energy and the sources available for generating electricity, you must now investigate a wide array of marine generating equipment and select an appropriate system.

Renewable marine energy systems using solar, wind, or water generators were introduced about 15 years ago. Since then they have been tested in all sea conditions, on almost every type of vessel afloat. The equipment available today is no longer just a curiosity. It is well engineered for the marine environment and deserves serious consideration when you choose your system.

Renewable energy systems vary in several ways from their gasoline- and diesel-fueled counterparts. Energy changes form fewer times in a renewable energy system. The "fuel" to power renewable energy systems is not purchased at marinas and does not require storage in a fuel tank. Instead, it is available for the taking, in varying quantities, anywhere in the world. Renewable systems are quiet and give off no fumes or smells. They are also typically easy to maintain.

Solar, wind, and water generators are innately simple. We recently received a letter from a man who sailed across the Atlantic from the Canary Islands to the British Virgin Islands. He left port with two engine-driven alternators and a 7.5-kilowatt generator to supply electricity. Within a few days all three of these sources of power were inoperative. His last resort was a water generator he planned to use as a backup, which allowed him to complete the trip with enough electricity for lighting, instruments, and even an electrically operated refrigerator-freezer. He now considers renewable generators as his primary source of electricity, and the engine-driven sources his backup.

Although this, of course, is an isolated incident, I have heard many similar accounts, all of which illustrate the proven maxim that on a boat a simple piece of equipment has a better chance of functioning when you need it than a more complex one. A marine alternator is itself simple, but it depends on a gasoline or diesel marine engine, which is considerably more complicated. The reliability of renewable energy systems has made them favorites with offshore cruisers and racers. They also make sense where it is impractical to carry enough gasoline or diesel fuel to generate electricity on an extended voyage.

Renewable systems do have drawbacks. They are usually not as convenient to operate. Instead of generating electricity when you choose, you must generate when the sun is out, the wind is blowing, or the boat is under sail. Renewable systems also require a bit more effort on your part than gasoline- or diesel-fueled systems. Solar panels should be kept facing into the sun without being shaded by other parts of the boat. Some wind generators must be shut down in high winds to prevent damage. Water generators should be checked periodically to make sure the propeller is not fouled. Renewable systems, except for water generators, are probably going to take up more space on your boat. Solar-panel mounting must be creative to keep from monopolizing valuable deck space.

Your demand for electricity, the type of boat you have, and how and where you use it are all going to help determine what part renewable energy plays in your total system. While cruising in the Bahamas on our catamaran, one 35-watt solar panel satisfied our small electrical needs of six fluorescent cabin lights, one low-drain anchor light, a cassette tape deck, and VHF and shortwave radios. Night sailing sometimes required the use of our wind/water generator to handle the additional load of running lights. We had optimum conditions for using solar energy: a light electrical load, wide decks for placing solar panels, and a sunny climate. A heavier electrical demand, a different boat, or a different cruising ground would have changed our conditions and most likely the size or type of energy system we employed.

You too can benefit from using one or more renewable energy system, whether as your primary means of producing electricity or as a backup to a gasoline- or diesel-fueled system. These systems even make sense for powerboats, keeping the batteries topped up when at the dock or on a mooring. For more specific information on solar, wind, and water energy systems for marine use, refer to Part IV of this book.

2

Methods Of Charging: What Is Available?

The generator is the most important—and often the least understood—part of an energy system on board. Generators for boats vary widely in the fuel they use and how they operate. This chapter offers a chance to become familiar with the readily available marine charging systems. For a detailed discussion of each system, refer to Chapters 6 through 10. A listing of marine generator equipment manufacturers and suppliers appears in Appendix C.

In this book, *generator* is a generic term designating any electricity-producing piece of equipment. It does not distinguish units that produce direct current (DC) electricity from those that produce alternating current (AC). In other contexts, the word generator refers only to a direct current–producing device, resulting in some cause for confusion. The DC generator is used in many wind and water units and will be discussed in later chapters.

Some of the equipment listed here is intended only for marine use, while some is marketed for marine and RV use. Still other equipment may be used primarily on land but might also be suitable for use on a boat. There is nothing wrong with having "standard land use" or "automobile" equipment on board, provided it adheres to marine safety regulations, and you know how it differs from its marine counterparts, and you make sure it is used appropriately. To help sort out available charging systems, this chapter will include equipment comparisons according to the following criteria:

- suitability for marine use

- performance

- efficiency

- reliability

- power output

- cost

- size

- weight

- noise and vibration

- appearance

- ease of installation

- ease of operation

- ease of maintenance and repair

- storage

- safety

STANDARD MARINE ALTERNATORS

Standard marine alternators—alternators that come as standard equipment on most marine engines—have for the past 25 years been the most common way to generate electricity, and will probably remain in the energy-equipment inventory for many years to come. They are mass-produced for the marine market, and in most ways are identical to the alternator in your car. "Marine" alternators are certified not to ignite propane and gasoline fumes. They are small, simple devices that take some of the available power from the main engine, by way of pulleys and belt(s) off the rotating main shaft, and turn it into electrical energy. We should reiterate that some of the power produced by your engine is depleted in driving an alternator, the amount lost being proportional to the current generated.

A standard marine alternator is shown in Figure 2-1. Alternators initially produce alternating current, which is converted (rectified) to direct current before leaving the unit, and the device is rated according to the amount of direct current it can produce. Usable energy is lost as heat when an alternator converts the mechanical energy of its rotating shaft into electrical energy. Thus, actual output is somewhat less than the rated value, decreasing with increasing temperature. All standard marine alternators come with a voltage regulator to protect the batteries from overcharging. The regulator is either internal (attached at the rear of the unit or mounted within) or external (mounted separately from the alternator).

There are many alternator manufacturers, including Delco, Motorola, Leece-Neville, Prestolite, Mitsubishi, and Bosch. Manufacturers often change the name of their product to that of the engine on which it is mounted, such as Volvo, Yanmar, Perkins, Universal, or Westerbeke. See Chapter 6 for more specific information on alternators.

- *Suitability for marine use*—Standard marine alternators work well in a standard engine compartment.

- *Performance*—Output is greatly affected by temperature. You should

FIGURE 2-1 (left). **Standard marine alternator. (Courtesy Lucas/CAV Ltd.)**
FIGURE 2-2 (right). **High-output alternator. (Courtesy Ample Power)**

count on only about 85 percent of rated value when the units are hot.
They should be operated at about 60 to 70 percent of rated capacity if
running long periods. Internal tolerances and airflow cooling characteristics are fair. Alternators can be operated in any conditions that facili-
tate engine running.

■ *Efficiency*—The alternators themselves are about 70 percent efficient in
terms of converting mechanical energy into electrical energy. Overall
system efficiency of around 5 to 10 percent takes into account efficiency of main engine and drive system. Efficiency drops as current is
limited by a standard voltage regulator.

■ *Reliability*—Simple and reliable, but dependent on the reliability of
marine engine and voltage regulator.

■ *Power output*—Wide range available, from 15-ampere small-output
units, to 35- to 50-ampere medium-output units, to 100-ampere (and
more) large-output units.

■ *Cost*—Standard equipment on marine engines. Relatively low replacement cost. Cost of operation includes wear on main engine and increased fuel consumption.

■ *Size*—Small, cylindrical shape takes up little room in engine compartment. No additional space required on boat. Typical size is 5 to 7
inches in diameter, 6 to 9 inches long.

■ *Weight*—Relatively light for amount of power generated. Typical weight
about 15 to 20 pounds.

- *Noise and vibration*—Very little associated with alternator, but amount from main engine can be substantial.

- *Appearance*—Not applicable, since located out of sight in engine compartment.

- *Ease of installation*—Most engines come with an alternator already mounted. Replacing a faulty alternator with a new unit is easy, provided a clear wiring diagram is available. Output and battery voltage should be monitored.

- *Ease of operation*—Very easy to operate. They are on whenever main engine is running.

- *Ease of maintenance and repair*—Easy to maintain by checking for proper belt tension and keeping track of current output to make sure voltage regulator is working. While troubleshooting and minor repairs can be performed by the owner, most alternators are serviced by professionals.

- *Storage*—Not applicable.

- *Safety*—Very safe provided they are marine-certified units, which are spark-suppressed to reduce the risk of igniting explosive fumes. Especially important on boats with a gasoline-fueled main engine, but also a concern when using propane- or gasoline-fueled portable generators. If alternator diodes short out during operation, a potentially hazardous situation results unless external isolating diodes are used.

HIGH-OUTPUT ALTERNATORS

The classification *high output* does not refer just to a large-capacity standard alternator. It denotes an alternator that has been carefully designed and built to provide high current at relatively low RPMs, without excessive wear or heat production. These units are ideal for boats that spend most of their time at anchor, on a mooring, or under sail, since they significantly reduce the time required for running the main engine to charge batteries. They are also useful on boats that have a high electrical demand. Battery capacity must be sufficient to take advantage of high-output alternators. Figure 2-2 shows a typical high-output alternator. The units come with internal or external voltage regulators. For more information on high-output alternators, refer to Chapter 6.

- *Suitability for marine use*—Highly suited to a marine environment. Materials have been upgraded for better resistance to galvanic and stray current corrosion.

- *Performance*—Perform well at the lower RPMs experienced while using the main engine solely for charging batteries. Built to withstand high temperatures during sustained high output. Due to construction, temperatures produced are less than those for similarly rated standard alternators. Best performance requires sufficiently large battery capacity.

- *Efficiency*—Maximum efficiency of alternator is reached at lower RPMs than standard units, typically corresponding to engine idling speeds. There is a higher overall system efficiency of around 8 to 15 percent, since the power of the main engine is better used during running time.

- *Reliability*—Special construction materials and techniques greatly increase the reliability of high-output alternators.

- *Power output*—Commonly have output ratings from 50 to 190 amperes. Higher-rated units available.

- *Cost*—High-output units cost more, but the savings in fuel and main engine wear, plus the longer life of the alternator, will offset the initial price difference. Typical cost with standard regulator: $300 to $600.

- *Size*—These units are about the same size as standard marine alternators.

- *Weight*—About the same weight as standard units; very good weight-to-energy output ratio.

- *Noise and vibration*—Closer internal tolerances than those of standard marine alternators mean less audible noise, and also less electromagnetic "noise" that can disrupt operation of electronic equipment. Noise and vibration of main engine is still a factor, but running time is reduced.

- *Appearance*—Similar to standard units.

- *Ease of installation*—Easy to install provided clear wiring diagrams are available and provided there is proper clearance for new unit. Check whether high-output unit is small- or large-case, then compare size with existing unit.

- *Ease of operation*—Very easy to use: simply turn on the main engine.

- *Ease of maintenance and repair*—Same as with standard units.

- *Storage*—No additional storage required.

- *Safety*—These units are certified for marine use (spark-suppressed) and high operating temperature (kkk rating). Potential for hazardous situation exists if diodes short during operation, unless external isolating diodes are used.

Standard and high-output marine alternators are typically supplied with inexpensive automotive-type voltage regulators that protect your batteries from overcharging. These standard regulators work well in automobiles, where the initial starting current is rapidly replaced, following which minimal current is supplied during the remaining engine running time. They do not, however, make the most efficient use of the limited engine running time on a boat. It is desirable to "override" temporarily the existing standard voltage regulator, or to provide an automatic fast-charge regulator to take best advantage of the alternator and battery capabilities.

Several varieties of manual alternator controls are available. Shown in Figure 2-3 is the AutoMAC by Weems and Plath (formerly Spa Creek Instruments). This unit is designed for use with your existing voltage regulator. Instead of tapering off current from the alternator soon after charging begins, the control allows you to maintain a manually selected current level until it senses that the battery is charged, when it automatically shuts off and the standard regulator takes over.

Other "fast-charge" alternator controls include the Balmar ABC and Weems and Plath's

---

FIGURE 2-3. **The AutoMAC alternator control, a voltage regulator bypass device. Such devices are installed parallel with the existing voltage regulator, leaving all wiring in place. See Chapter 6 for more details. (Courtesy Weems and Plath)**

AutoCharge controllers, which temporarily bypass the voltage regulator; and the 3-Step Deep Cycle regulator by Ample Power Company and the Quad-Cycle Regulator/Monitor by Cruising Equipment Company, which take the place of a standard regulator and automatically give a fast, complete charge to your battery. For more information on fast-charge alternator controls, refer to Chapter 6.

- *Suitability for marine use*—Fast-charge alternator controls are suitable for marine and RV use. Typically the control, along with a current monitor and on-off switch, can be bulkhead mounted similar to an electric control panel.

- *Performance*—These units work well provided there is sufficient battery capacity to take advantage of the increased current output. The manual controls do not perform as accurately and require more careful monitoring than the automatic variety.

- *Efficiency*—These units can greatly increase the efficiency of the complete charging system, since engine running time is reduced.

- *Reliability*—The manual controls are less complex and thus perhaps more durable than the automatic controls, but reliability of a unit depends most on how it is operated; incorrect use may lessen both performance and reliability.

- *Power output*—Manual controls are available for 50-ampere to 150-ampere alternator outputs, and automatic controls can handle up to a 200-ampere alternator output.

- *Cost*—Manual controls cost around $150, while automatic controls can be as much as $500 when they incorporate ancillary, useful monitoring functions. The automatic controls may add to the life of your batteries by charging them correctly through all stages of charge (see Chapter 5).

- *Size*—About the size of an electrical panel.

- *Weight*—Just a few pounds.

- *Noise and vibration*—No noise or vibration generated by the controls themselves. They reduce engine time, and thus engine noise and vibration.

- *Appearance*—Most units are attractive and have a low profile.

- *Ease of installation*—These units can be owner-installed with the proper instructions. Easiest installation with externally regulated alternators. Some suppliers will wire your alternator for you for a nominal fee.

- *Ease of operation*—Manual controls are fairly easy to operate, but care must be taken not to overcharge the battery. Automatic controls require no owner operation except for selecting monitoring function.

- *Ease of maintenance and repair*—Units require no maintenance and can either be owner-repaired or sent back to manufacturer for service.

- *Storage*—No additional storage is required.

- *Safety*—All of today's production varieties have automatic shutoff to keep batteries from overcharging. Other safety considerations similar to standard voltage regulators.

SMALL PORTABLE GENERATORS

When you use your main engine solely to charge batteries, you are tapping only a small part of the engine's potential power. Portable generators use the full capacity of a small engine, spinning an alternator or generator to produce electricity. The term *small portable generator* refers to a generator that can be carried and moved around, weighing less than 75 pounds.

Portable generators come in a wide range of sizes and power output. Most units produce alternating current and a smaller amount of direct current for charging batteries. They are useful for operating power tools and other high-demand AC appliances; for providing alternating current to run a battery charger; or for charging batteries directly. The Kawasaki GD-700A shown in Figure 2-4 is a gasoline-fueled portable generator. It produces 600 watts of continuous AC power, while simultaneously producing about 100 watts of DC power. This dual output is a nice feature; with many portable generators you must choose either AC or DC.

Some small generators produce only direct current. Balmar has taken this approach with its Power Charger, shown in Figure 2-5. A 4-horsepower Yanmar diesel engine is mated to a high-output alternator, and is rated at about 1,200 watts of DC power for charging batteries.

FIGURE 2-4.   **Kawasaki GD-700A portable generator. (Courtesy Hamilton Ferris)**

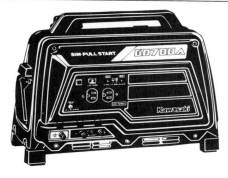

FIGURE 2-5.   **The Balmar Power Charger, a DC-producing small generator.**

The lightweight Tanaka QEG-250 shown in Figure 2-6 also has no AC capability, but produces almost 250 watts of DC power for charging batteries or operating DC equipment directly. Refer to Chapter 7 for more information on small portable generators.

- *Suitability for marine use*—Small portable generators are suitable for marine or land use.

- *Performance*—Perform well in most conditions, but generally should not be operated in rough sea conditions. Standard gasoline-fueled units must be coupled with an AC-to-DC battery charger for efficient DC battery charging. Units should be securely fastened for times at sea. Exhaust must be well vented for safety, making above-deck use mandatory. Some of the diesel-fueled units can be run below decks if well vented.

- *Efficiency*—Much more efficient use of fuel than running main engine for charging batteries or for direct AC loads. Overall system efficiency varies between 10 and 20 percent.

- *Reliability*—Moderately reliable, since still dependent on gas- or diesel-fueled engine.

- *Power output*—Alternating or direct current at wide range of power output. AC output anywhere from 300 up to 2,000 watts.

- *Cost*—Ranges from low to high. Tanaka units around $350; 600-watt standard gasoline-fueled type around $550; Power Charger and other higher-output models over $2,000.

- *Size*—Sizes also vary, with the small units under one cubic foot, medium units and Power Charger from 1.5 to 2 cubic feet, large units up to 5 cubic feet.

- *Weight*—Tanaka gets the best rating at only 19 pounds; medium units are in the 40- to 50-pound range; larger units up to 75 pounds.

- *Noise and vibration*—All portable generators are noisy and cause vibration, some less so than others. Generally, the lower the output, the less noise produced. Four-cycle engines are usually quieter than two-cycle engines. Air-cooled diesel engines are noisier than water-cooled versions. The noise will affect you as well as neighboring boats, especially when the portable generator is used in the cockpit or on the foredeck. Diesel-fueled vented units can operate below without disturbing the neighbors. Vibration through the deck to below can be dampened but is still a consideration.

- *Appearance*—This is not much of a factor, since the units are brought out only occasionally, then stored again.

- *Ease of installation*—No installation required. Simply run cables to batteries for charging, or plug in tools and appliances directly.

- *Ease of operation*—Very easy to operate. Simply remove and return to storage, pull-start (some units have electric start), and maintain fuel level.

- *Ease of maintenance and repair*—Moderate level of skill required to maintain engine, similar to lawn mower care.

- *Storage*—The amount of space required is related to power output and weight.

- *Safety*—Units using gasoline are potentially hazardous. Good venting is absolutely necessary to make sure exhaust fumes do not collect in cabin areas.

AC-TO-DC BATTERY CHARGERS

Although many types of equipment can "charge batteries," the term *AC-to-DC battery charger* is reserved for a device that converts AC power into DC and sends it to the batteries. Battery chargers don't actually produce electricity, they only change it from one form to another. These units come in a variety of sizes, outputs, and levels of regulation ranging from unregulated automotive chargers to units with moderate regulation to completely automatic units for charging deep-cycle batteries.

A battery charger can be used dockside with a shore power hookup or coupled with a portable generator or gen-set. The well-constructed Dynamote Super Charger is shown in Figure 2-7. Other marine units include models from Todd Engineerng, Ample Power Company, Newmar, Professional Mariner, and Ray Jefferson.

- *Suitability for marine use*—Very suitable, as long as there is an isolation transformer to separate incoming AC power from boat DC circuits. All marine battery chargers incorporate an isolation transformer, but some inexpensive automotive-type units do not. These should not be used on a boat unless an isolation transformer has been fitted to the boat's shore power receptacle.

- *Performance*—Depends on the unit and its regulation system. Even some "automatic" units can overcharge or undercharge a battery. Unregulated chargers perform well for short periods when coupled to a portable generator or gen-set. Safe regulation devices for unregulated or poorly regulated battery chargers can be added separately.

- *Efficiency*—Varies with type of charger. Overall system efficiency, taking into account efficiency of the production of AC power, is around 20 percent.

- *Reliability*—In general, a simple and highly reliable piece of gear.

FIGURE 2-7. **Battery charger. (Courtesy Dynamote Corp.)**   **19**

- *Power output*—Starts at 10 amperes for small units and goes up to over 100 amperes for large battery chargers. A range of 20 to 40 amperes is common for pleasure boats.

- *Cost*—Automotive types start at under $100. The average price of marine units is $200 to $300; units that are more efficient and have higher outputs cost more.

- *Size*—Battery chargers are relatively small and can be easily stowed or permanently mounted.

- *Weight*—Weight is usually proportional to rated output, but averages about 20 pounds.

- *Noise and vibration*—None.

- *Appearance*—Not much of a concern, since they are typically out of sight. Some units have attractive housings for high-visibility installations.

- *Ease of installation*—Units can be permanently wired into your electrical system or left for portable use. Permanent installation is relatively easy, although probably best left to a professional.

- *Ease of operation*—Easy. No owner input necessary for most automatic units; battery monitoring required with unregulated models.

- *Ease of maintenance and repair*—Nothing to maintain, and usually no owner-serviceable parts.

- *Storage*—Easy to store, either mounted or left for portable operation.

- *Safety*—Care should be taken with this type of charging system because of the presence of high-voltage alternating current on board. Exercise the same precautions as for DC-to-AC inverters, AC generators, and gen-sets.

PHOTOVOLTAIC (PV) SOLAR PANELS

Solar panels capture radiant energy from the sun. Some use black surfaces to absorb the radiant energy, transferring it as heat to water or air. We will explore another type of solar panel, the photovoltaic solar panel, which transforms the radiant energy from the sun directly into electricity, with no noise or moving parts.

In each panel a number of very thin photovoltaic solar cells are connected to achieve the desired electrical output. Output is determined by surface area, which is why all panels are thin. Higher-output panels have relatively large surface areas. Figure 2-8 shows an Arco panel rated for an output of 47 watts.

Some solar panels are made for marine use, and others are less expensive "land-use" panels that also can be used on a boat. Manufacturers of solar panels include Arco, Hoxan, Kyocera, Solarex, Solec, and Sovonics. Panels differ in size, output, efficiency, and construction materials. For more information refer to Chapter 8.

- *Suitability for marine use*—All panels are suitable for a marine environment. Standard panels have a rigid, tempered glass cover that is strong but can break when abused repeatedly. They also have a deeper frame for potential rack mounting. Marine panels are thin, usually have an unbreakable cover, and are flexible for mounting on curved surfaces.

FIGURE 2-8.   **An Arco solar panel rated for 47 watts of output. (Courtesy Jack Rabbit Marine)**

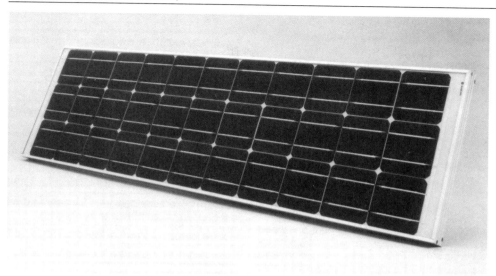

FIGURE 2-9.   **Solarex 18-watt marine panels in use.**

- *Performance*—The performance of a panel is greatly affected by the angle at which it faces the sun, and by shade (such as from sails or rigging); it is affected to a lesser degree by temperature. Sovonics panels are not as sensitive to partial panel shading as other types. Panels produce electricity only during daylight, but may perform, though at a reduced level, during periods of clouds or high overcast.

- *Efficiency*—A solar panel can be anywhere from 5 to 14 percent efficient at converting sunlight to electricity, depending on cell construction. Sovonics and other "thin film" solar cells have the lowest ratings.

- *Reliability*—Very good, since there are no moving parts. Estimated 20-year or longer lifespan on land, but somewhat less on board a boat, where there is more wear and tear.

- *Power output*—Single-panel output varies from 1 or 2 watts up to nearly 100 watts.

- *Cost*—High initial cost for the power produced (see, for example, the case studies in Chapter 14), but fuel savings and reduced engine wear can be significant.

- *Size*—Solar panels are thin but need a large surface area for high output. Boatowners must be resourceful in finding mounting locations on board.

- *Weight*—Panel weight depends on output, and will be anywhere from 3 to 25 pounds.

- *Noise and vibration*—None.

- *Appearance*—Subject to individual taste. Most boatowners agree that they don't significantly affect overall boat appearance. Panels can be trimmed in wood or other materials.

- *Ease of installation*—Easiest installation is to leave panel loose for directing into sunlight. In this case, panel must be secured or stored when under way. Permanent mounts are relatively easy on a rack off the stern, over the cockpit, on the deck, or sewn into dodgers and sun covers.

- *Ease of operation*—Should keep panels faced into unshaded sunlight for most efficient operation. Otherwise just monitor output.

- *Ease of maintenance and repair*—If problem is in external wiring or panel junction box, repair is easy. Panels with internal problems must be returned to manufacturer.

- *Storage*—Either in a permanent mount or below decks. Solar panels do require a fair amount of space.

- *Safety*—Maximum solar panel voltage is only around 20 volts DC, so they are very safe. The only hazard associated with solar panels is the potential for crew slipping on deck-mounted units.

WIND GENERATORS

The energy of moving air can easily be captured and transformed into electricity on board a boat. There are several types of wind generators available for marine use. European manufacturers fabricate small, permanently mounted generators that can be left up in any wind condition. Their multibladed props resemble windmills used for pumping water on farms. Their electrical output is modest due to their small propeller size and low efficiency. American manufacturers offer larger wind generators with two- or three-bladed propellers, similar to the props used on airplanes.

Some wind units produce electricity with DC generators, in which an armature (comprising a series of coils mounted on a rotor) spins inside a set of permanent magnets. They have brushes, or metal contacts, to conduct the current away from the spinning commutator on one end of the armature. Other units resemble an alternator in that a permanent-magnet rotor spins inside a set of coils in which alternating current is generated and then rectified to DC. These units require no brushes unless equipped with slip rings in the mount so that the generator may turn to seek the wind.

Currently there are three major American-made marine wind generators, the Windbugger by Bugger Products, the Fourwinds II by Everfair Enterprises, and the Neptune Supreme by Hamilton Ferris Company. These units can be mounted on a pole at the stern of the boat, as shown in Figure 2-10, suspended in the foretriangle as shown in Figure 2-11, or permanently mounted to the upper forepart of a mizzenmast. The European units include the Ampair 100 (shown in Figure 2-12), the Aquair, the Rutland, the LVM, and the Windbat. They are usually mounted on a pole at the stern or at the masthead.

A few of the wind units set up for rigging suspension, namely the Neptune Supreme, the Fourwinds, and the Aquair, can convert into water generators for use under way. Pole-mounted units and mizzenmast units will work while under way. Wind generators are for use only on sailboats, or on powerboats at a dock or on a mooring. For more information, refer to Chapter 9.

- *Suitability for marine use*—All wind generators are constructed for the marine environment.

- *Performance*—Depends on wind speed, prop size, and efficiency of the generator. Winds are often fluky in protected anchorages, resulting in lower output; open waters are best. Performance also increases with

FIGURE 2-10 (left).   **Pole-mounted Windbugger. (Courtesy Windbugger)**
FIGURE 2-11 (right).   **Rigging-suspended wind generator. (Courtesy Hamilton Ferris)**

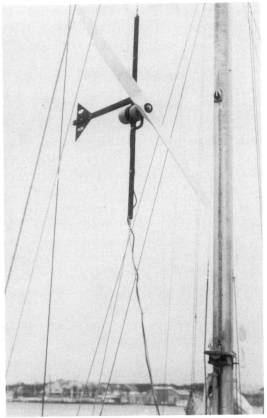

height off the water. Sailing downwind greatly reduces apparent wind speed and performance.

- *Efficiency*—Good wind generators are about 40 percent efficient at extracting the maximum power available. European models have lower efficiencies due to their blade configuration.

- *Reliability*—All wind generators are reliable. They are made to last and have few moving components.

- *Power output*—Varies according to wind speed for a given propeller size and unit efficiency. American units can produce up to 180 watts in 20 knots of wind. European units can produce up to 60 to 100 watts in 20 knots of wind.

- *Cost*—Expect to pay around $1,000 for the larger units, and around $500 to $800 for the smaller-prop types.

- *Size*—Propeller diameter varies from 2 feet up to 6 feet. Size of the alternator or DC generator used is about that of an engine alternator.

- *Weight*—Typically around 20 or 30 pounds without mounting hardware.

- *Noise and vibration*—Most units are fairly quiet. The amount of noise depends on propeller and balance—the faster the prop RPMs, the more potential for noise. Small-bladed models don't rotate as fast for a given wind speed and therefore produce less noise. As wind speed increases so does the noise from rigging and seas, which helps to mask wind-generator noise.

- *Appearance*—Varies. Take time to pick the unit best suited to your tastes and boat.

- *Ease of installation*—Setting up a rigging-suspended unit involves fussing with proper line lengths and configuration. Pole-mounted units need some skill for the securing and bracing of the pole and struts.

- *Ease of operation*—Large-bladed units require an air brake or manual shutdown in high winds; small-bladed units do not. Rigging-suspended units must be raised when in port and lowered before going to sea.

- *Ease of maintenance and repair*—Wood propellers require occasional maintenance, and generator brushes may need changing. Some alternator or generator repair can be performed with appropriate tools and skill level. Other repairs are best done by the manufacturer.

- *Storage*—Rigging-suspended wind units require storage when under way. They take up about the same amount of room as a pair of dinghy oars.

- *Safety*—Large-prop wind generators are potentially hazardous and must be operated with proper care. This is not hard to do, but without caution serious injury to crew and guests can result, especially with children on board. Large-prop units can easily be mounted out of reach. Small-prop wind units are much safer, especially when mounted at the masthead.

WATER GENERATORS

Water generators indirectly use the power of the wind, captured by sails, to produce electricity. A small portion of the energy propelling a sailboat through the water is "borrowed" to turn a water generator propeller towed behind the boat. These generators make sense only for boats under sail. It is much more efficient on a powerboat or a sailboat under power to use the engine directly to produce electricity.

There are three varieties of water generators. The most common is the "trailing log," shown in Figure 2-13, which employs an outboard engine propeller mounted backward on a length of stainless steel rod. This prop assembly trails behind the boat on 50 to 100 feet of braided nylon line, and is attached to a swivel-mounted generator at the stern of the boat. As the prop is pulled through the water, it spins rapidly, which, by way of the braided line, spins the shaft of the generator. Jack Rabbit Marine, Hamilton Ferris Company, and Everfair Enterprises offer trailing logs.

The second type, shown in Figure 2-14, is the Power Log manufactured by Greenwich Corporation. Here the generator is attached to the propeller and the entire assembly is towed just behind the boat. The tow cable, called a "short flexile lead," does not spin and thus can transfer electricity to the batteries. (Power Log can also operate in the "trailing log" mode with a longer tow cable, which still does not spin.)

FIGURE 2-14.   **The Power Log. (Courtesy Greenwich Corporation)**   **27**

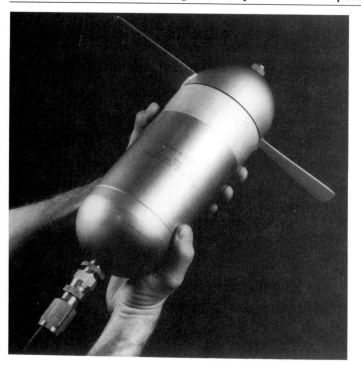

The "outboard leg" generator mounts off the stern of the boat (Figure 2-15), resembling an outboard motor. Power is transferred to the generator through a spinning shaft, which sits well above the waterline. For more information on water generators, refer to Chapter 10.

- *Suitability for marine use*—Water generators are well suited to the marine environment. On trailing-logs the stern-mounted generator shaft has a seal that should be waterproof to protect internal parts. This is not a problem on the Power Log, since the entire unit is submersible.

- *Performance*—Water generators create a small amount of drag on a boat and may not be suitable in some conditions. High boat speeds can cause a trailing-log prop to skip out of the water, greatly affecting performance. Hamilton Ferris Company has a "diving plane" for fast boats, which helps to keep the prop submerged. The Power Log trails on a short length of flexible cable and remains submerged in most conditions.

- *Efficiency*—Overall efficiency at converting the water stream into electricity is about 30 percent, less than that for wind generators, which use the wind directly and have more efficient props. Downwind, how-

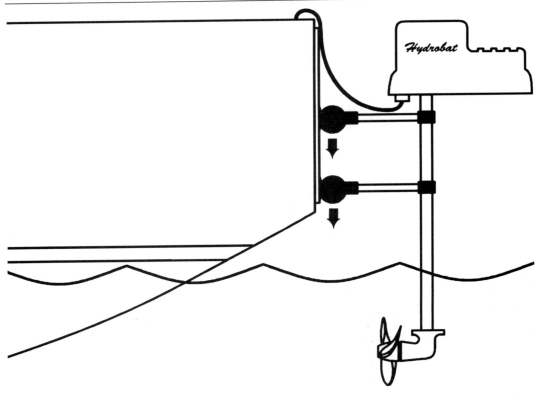

ever, water generators are more efficient than wind generators because
there is no decrease in the apparent speed of the moving fluid.

- *Reliability*—Very reliable because of the simplicity of the system. Props
  on trailing-log units have become meals for large fish, though this is
  not frequent. The Aquair unit uses a permanent-magnet alternator that
  does not require brushes to transfer power or field current. The Power
  Log unit also uses a permanent-magnet alternator, but it is continu-
  ously submerged. Though well sealed and protected, this heightened
  exposure may offset any increase in long-term reliability conferred by
  the elimination of brushes.

- *Power output*—Varies with speed of boat, from 2 to 4 amperes at 4
  knots, to 9 to 11 amperes at 7 knots.

- *Cost*—The Power Log is a well-crafted unit, and the most expensive at
  about $1,500. Most units are priced at around $750.

- *Size*—Trailing-log units are about the size of a standard marine alternator, not including the prop, shaft, and line assembly. Power Log has no shaft or long line. The outboard-leg type is similar in size to a small outboard motor.

- *Weight*—Approximately 20 pounds.

- *Noise and vibration*—Water generators make little noise for the most part, although noise and vibration from a poorly supported outboard-leg generator can be annoying. Vibration of the spinning line on a trailing-log type is noticeable at high boat speeds. Power Log has no noticeable noise or vibration.

- *Appearance*—Outboard-leg units are most noticeable, and therefore potentially the least attractive. Of the trailing-log types, the Hamilton Ferris Neptune Supreme and Aquair units are well designed and attractively mounted on the stern of the boat.

- *Ease of installation*—Installation requires only mounting the bracket for a swiveling generator or outboard-leg unit on the stern. The Power Log requires a below-waterline strut attached to the stern. Wiring is easy; most units come with appropriate wiring schematics.

- *Ease of operation*—The outboard-leg generators are probably the easiest to operate, since they slide in or out of the water on a track similar to an outboard motor. The Power Log requires retrieval from the water when not in use. Trailing-log units require retrieval of the prop, shaft, and line assembly when the boat slows down or during adverse sea conditions.

- *Ease of maintenance and repair*—Similar to wind generators. Spare props and generator parts are easy to carry on board.

- *Storage*—Some space is required, although when the unit is stowed at the stern it scarcely intrudes on deck space.

- *Safety*—The Power Log is probably the safest unit, with an outboard-leg generator a close second. Due to the spinning line and prop, care must be taken when operating and retrieving a trailing-log unit. For safer and easier retrieval, Hamilton Ferris offers a funnel that slides over the towline, enclosing the prop to stop it from spinning. The Aquair unit includes a safety "break link" that protects the alternator if the prop becomes snagged.

3

Other System Components:
What Is Available?

The generator is only the beginning of a complete energy system on a boat. There are myriad other components on the marine market to make your system more efficient. This chapter describes those components and outlines how they can be used. Your selection will depend on your system; no group of components is right for every situation. Refer to Chapter 14, Selecting Your Energy System, for appropriate combinations.

BATTERIES

Batteries, which store electricity for later use, may well be your second largest expense. Their useful life is directly related to how they are cared for and the charging and discharging techniques employed. Batteries come in a variety of sizes and storage capacities, and are constructed according to intended use. Starting-and-lighting batteries (like those used in automobiles) provide high cranking power for engine starting, and can power some lights and other small appliances when the engine is off. Hybrid deep-cycle batteries, the usual choice for boats, offer sufficient (albeit lesser) cranking power along with deep-cycling ability for operating heavier loads. True deep-cycle batteries have yet lower cranking power but can be repeatedly and deeply discharged. See Chapter 5 for a fuller explanation.

High-quality lead-acid marine-battery manufacturers include Surrette of Tilton, New Hampshire; Rolls Engineering of Salem, Massachusetts; GNB of St. Paul, Minnesota; and RAE of Berlin, Connecticut. Some marine batteries are called "sealed" or "maintenance free." They don't require the periodic addition of distilled water. A relative newcomer, the Sonnenschein Prevailer battery (shown in Figure 3-1) uses a gelled electrolyte and promises to help set the standard for future battery engineering. Prevailer batteries are totally sealed and can be installed in any position. The battery's state of charge can be checked remotely by voltage measurement, so they can easily be stored in hard-to-reach places. High-quality marine bat-

FIGURE 3-1. **Gelled-electrolyte battery. (Courtesy Sonnenschein Batteries, Inc.)**

31

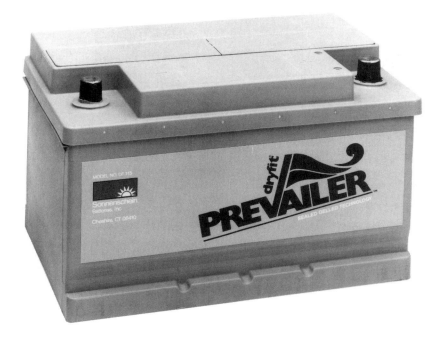

teries cost around $2 per ampere-hour of capacity. An average 120-ampere-hour battery takes up about 0.65 cubic foot and weighs approximately 85 pounds. Refer to Chapter 5 for more detailed battery information.

Low-Battery Alarm/Disconnect Switch

The life of a deep-cycle battery can be substantially increased if it isn't deeply discharged before recharging. A simple low-battery-disconnect switch prevents current from being drawn below a preset battery voltage. An audible and/or visible alarm tells you that it is time to recharge that battery bank.

Weems and Plath has a simple low-battery alarm that resets when the electrical load is switched to another battery bank or when electricity use is discontinued. Manual switching of the electrical load is required. Weems and Plath also offers the Intelli-Switch, which automatically turns on a warning light and switches to another battery bank, or disconnects the circuit, when voltage is low. Professional Mariner has an audible and visible alarm, shown in Figure 3-2, that alerts on either low or high voltage. Hamilton Ferris offers the LVD (low voltage disconnect), which automatically disconnects a load until the battery begins recharging. It comes in 8-ampere and 16-ampere versions. Low-battery-disconnect/alarm devices are also included on many inverters and voltage regulators.

FIGURE 3-2 (left).   **Low-voltage battery alarm with light and audible tone. (Courtesy Professional Mariner)**

FIGURE 3-3 (right).   **Catalyst battery caps. (Courtesy Hydrocap Corp.)**

Battery Caps (Catalyst)

Part of the chemical reaction taking place during proper charging of a lead-acid battery is the breakdown of water (H_2O) into hydrogen (H_2) and oxygen (O_2). These gases escape through vents in the top of each battery cell, requiring periodic "re-watering" of the battery. Catalyst (or gas-recombinant) battery caps recombine the hydrogen and oxygen before they have a chance to escape. This greatly reduces the amount of replacement water necessary, while virtually eliminating the possible accumulation of explosive hydrogen in the battery compartment. All battery compartments should be well vented, but catalyst battery caps provide an additional measure of safety. The top of the battery also stays cleaner, increasing its life, since the fine mist of electrolyte that normally accompanies the outgoing gases is dramatically reduced.

When the battery starts gassing during final charging, the catalyst battery caps get warm to the touch as they recombine the hydrogen and oxygen. This feature provides some useful information about your energy system. First, it lets you know at what voltage the battery begins to gas, suggesting a good set point for the voltage regulator. Second, if all the caps begin to get hot, the system is overcharging, and the final charging current should be reduced. Finally, if one cap remains cool while the others heat up, it signals a weak cell and a need for equalizing the battery (explained in Chapter 5). If one cell gets hot while the others are just warm, that cell should be checked.

Hydrocap Corporation offers catalyst battery caps, shown in Figure 3-3, for almost any type of nonsealed lead-acid battery. (Sealed batteries do not have battery inspection/vent caps.) Before replacing your standard caps, however, allow the company to review your complete charging system and make a recommendation. These caps are available through many marine energy equipment suppliers, or directly from Hydrocap Corporation, for about $40 for a set of six. They should last the life of your battery or longer. See Chapter 5 for additional catalyst battery-cap information.

Battery Equalizer

This device is geared for boats that have a split 12-volt/24-volt system (see Chapter 5). Such a system may have a 24-volt alternator and 12-volt battery banks connected in series to provide 24-volt service. The Vanner battery equalizer shown in Figure 3-4 allows 12-volt appliances to be run from a 24-volt source, equalizes the battery discharge rates when 12-volt and 24-volt loads are present, and supplies charging current equally to all batteries.

FIGURE 3-4A.   **A battery equalizer for use with a system that provides both 12- and 24-volt service. (Courtesy Vanner, Inc.)**

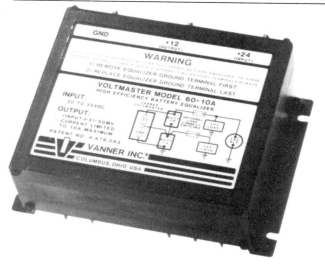

Battery Isolators (Charging Diodes)

Batteries that are being used independently most often have different states of charge, and therefore different charging requirements. Battery isolators (also called splitters or charging diodes) are ideal for charging two or more battery banks simultaneously. Isolators allow a proper charge to be allocated to each bank as needed, and since batteries remain isolated from each other, a discharged battery won't steal current from a charged one.

Isolators vary in type and size. They consist of diodes—one for each battery to be isolated—that allow current to flow in only one direction. Each diode must be sized for the

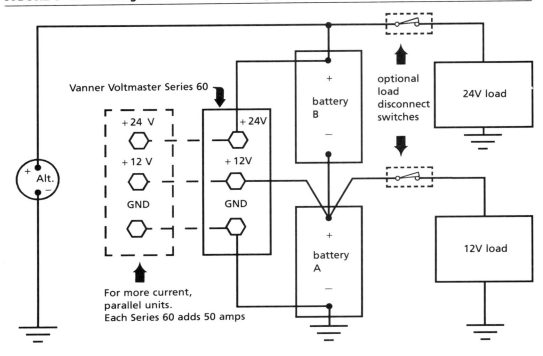

amount of current that will pass through it. Make sure that each diode in an isolator is rated higher than the full amount of expected current. Since some heat is dissipated as current flows through a diode, a metal heat sink is usually incorporated. The larger the current rating, the larger the heat sink. Isolating diodes can be purchased and wired separately, or in assembled units that can charge two or three battery banks.

Charging diodes are required for solar, wind, and water generators. The diode prevents battery current from reversing back through the generator when it is not in operation. Isolators can also prevent high current surges in the wiring and eliminate the risk of fire should an alternator fail and short-curcuit the battery.

There is a slight voltage drop through an isolating diode, usually about 0.5 to 1.0 volt, which means that the voltage measured at the battery will be less than that measured at the generator output. If this is not compensated for, batteries never become fully charged. See Chapter 5 for proper methods of compensation.

Assembled battery isolators, like those from Ample Power shown in Figure 3-5, are available from marine energy equipment suppliers for two- or three-battery systems, various current ratings, and one- or two-alternator setups. Isolators cost from $75 to $250 and can easily be wired in.

FIGURE 3-5. **A selection of four battery isolators from the Ample Power Company. See Figure 6-2 for a schematic view of the isolator location in the charge-system wiring.**

Battery Selector Switches

When using more than one battery on board, it is convenient to select which battery or bank of batteries is supplying current. In a typical arrangement, one battery bank is reserved for starting the engine, while others are used for the remaining electrical loads. A standard selector switch allows you to choose between bank 1, bank 2, banks 1 and 2 simultaneously, or no current from either bank. If a third battery bank is employed, a standard selector switch and a single on-off battery switch (as shown in Figure 3-6) for the third bank can be used. If single switches are used for all three banks, any combination of batteries is possible.

Another popular configuration uses two battery banks, with each used separately to both start the engine and power appliances. In this arrangement, one battery bank supplies current for electrical loads and receives current from generator sources such as solar panels and wind or water units, while the other bank rests. This allows you to accurately measure the resting battery's state of charge. Using the battery selector switch, battery banks are interchanged every day or so.

Battery selector switches also can be used to determine which battery bank receives current from the generator(s). But if the switch is wired in this manner, an alternator or generator

FIGURE 3-6. **A single on-off battery switch can be wired in parallel with the standard two-battery selector switch on the DC control panel to bring a third battery bank on line. (Courtesy Ample Power Company)**

producing high voltage would be damaged if you were to disconnect it from the battery by throwing off the switch. Some switches now come with a "field-disconnect" feature that temporarily interrupts alternator operation during switching. It is more common now to use battery isolators to keep independent batteries charged as needed. Battery selector switches also provide a convenient method of disconnecting an electrical load from a battery for maintenance.

If one battery is deeply discharged, it will affect the other battery (or batteries) when the main switch is turned to "both." The batteries will then be temporarily connected in parallel and the discharged battery will draw current until the batteries are in equilibrium (same state of charge). Figure 3-7 illustrates this concept with three columns of water separated by valves. With the valves open and the tubes connected, the water seeks the same level in all three. Current acts in the same way, as it attempts to equalize the state of charge under the influence of electrical pressure, or voltage.

DC POWER TRANSFORMERS

A DC power transformer is a simple device that plugs into any 12-volt outlet and can supply a variety of output voltages to flashlights, radios, and other battery-operated appliances. It is also called a universal DC auto adapter (see Figure 3-8), and is available at Radio Shack and other electrical supply stores. This model transforms a 12-volt source into 3-, 4.5-, 6-, 7.5-, or 9-volt output. It can eliminate the need for disposable batteries by powering portable equipment right from your boat's battery bank.

Round dry-cell, disposable batteries are typically rated at 1.5 volts each, regardless of

FIGURE 3-7.   Just as interconnected columns of water seek equilibrium, so do batteries connected in parallel.

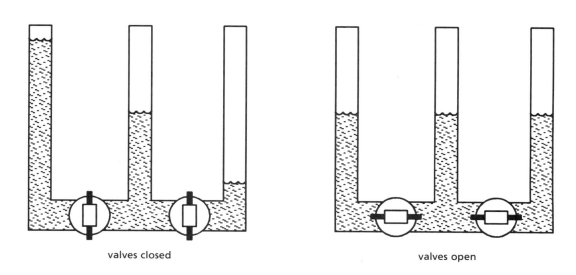

valves closed

valves open

FIGURE 3-8.   Universal DC auto adapter.

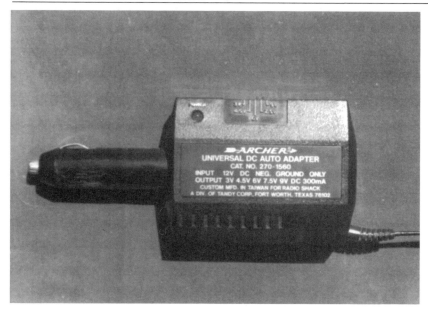

size. If your radio takes two batteries, it operates at 3 volts; four batteries signify 6-volt operation; and so on. Some equipment operates at 9 volts with a rectangular 9-volt dry-cell battery.

DC-TO-AC INVERTERS

Operating household appliances on board can be easy with a properly sized inverter. These devices change 12- or 24-volt DC into usable 110-volt AC electricity. They are rated according to maximum output in watts at 110 volts.

So-called pocket inverters of around 100-watt capacity, such as the PowerStar (140-watt model) or the Statpower (100- and 150-watt models) shown in Figure 3-9, can be plugged into any convenient DC cigarette lighter-type outlet. They weigh about a pound and fit easily in the palm of a hand. These units cost around $150 and are good for computers, stereos, TVs, and other small appliances that draw 150 watts or less.

Larger inverters have capacities up to 2,500 watts. The most popular medium-large inverters for marine use are made by Heart Interface, Trace Engineering, Professional Mariner, and Statpower. Heart Interface offers a 1,800-watt model, shown in Figure 3-10, that retails for around $1,500, together with a 600-watt model and even a 2,800-watt model. Trace Engineering offers 600-watt and 2,000-watt inverters. Professional Mariner has a 2,300-watt model. Statpower has a 600-watt inverter in addition to pocket models. With optional equipment, most larger inverters can be used as battery chargers. Remote-control panels are available so the inverter can be mounted out of the way. Refer to Chapter 11 for more detailed information.

FIGURE 3-9 (left).   **A pocket inverter. (Courtesy Statpower Technologies Corp.)**
FIGURE 3-10 (right).   **Large inverter with a 1,800-watt AC output. See Figure 11-8 for a wiring schematic. (Courtesy Heart Interface)**

You can generate AC power with either a gen-set or a large portable generator. Gen-sets are typically installed permanently and operate at 1,800 RPMs, while large portable generators have handles for moving and usually operate at 3,600 RPMs. These units are either gasoline- or diesel-fueled. AC output ranges from 1,500 up to 15,000 watts (15 kilowatts).

FIGURE 3-11 (left). **Robin diesel-powered portable generator. (Courtesy The Generator Superstore)**

FIGURE 3-12 (right). **Onan gen-set, 6,500-watt output. (Courtesy The Generator Superstore)**

Yanmar offers a line of diesel generators, including a 2,000-watt portable model. Other portable-generator manufacturers include Onan, Robin, Gillette Manufacturing, Honda, Kawasaki, and Yamaha. Manufacturers of marine gen-sets include Onan, Kohler, Yanmar, and Westerbeke. Chapter 12 offers more detailed information.

HIGH-VOLTAGE SPIKE SUPPRESSORS

When the main engine is running and the alternator operating, a sudden break in the circuit can cause the alternator output voltage to rise dramatically. This high-voltage spike can ruin the alternator and regulator, and can damage electronic equipment too, before the voltage regulator has a chance to control it.

The circuit carrying the alternator output can be broken in several ways. As mentioned earlier, switching the battery selector to the off position while the engine is running is one way. The circuit can also be broken by inadvertently disconnecting output wires or by using a battery selector switch that "breaks" contact (or opens the circuit) before it "makes" contact in another position.

A high-voltage spike suppressor like the Zap Stop, shown in Figure 3-13, costs under $15 and can easily be installed on your alternator for worry-free operation. If your battery selector switch is located on the supply to your load, and not in the alternator output wiring (see Chapter 4), the need for this type of device is reduced.

MASTER CONTROL PANEL

A master control panel provides a convenient location for making wiring connections and for mounting fuses or breaker switches for individual circuits. The panel shown in Figure 3-14 has room for eight circuits, each with its own circuit breaker. Also included in the panel is a main battery switch, a battery condition meter, and a testing circuit for two battery banks. There should be one control panel for all DC circuits, and another for permanently wired AC circuits.

SHIP-TO-SHORE SELECTOR SWITCHES

A ship-to-shore selector switch provides a convenient method of switching from utility-generated shore power to your onboard method of producing AC, whether by gen-set, portable generator, or inverter. A typical ship-to-shore switch for onboard diesel-fueled gensets is shown in Figure 3-15.

SWITCHES, OUTLETS, AND PLUGS

Twelve-volt DC components differ from typical household equipment. Outlets are similar to a car's cigarette lighter outlet, with a single round hole. Polarized plugs to fit these outlets are cylindrical, with the positive lead at the point in front and the negative lead along the side.

Extension cords, multiple-outlet boxes, replacement plugs, brass wall-receptacles, and

FIGURE 3-13. **Zap Stop, a high-voltage spike suppressor. (Courtesy Cruising Equipment)**

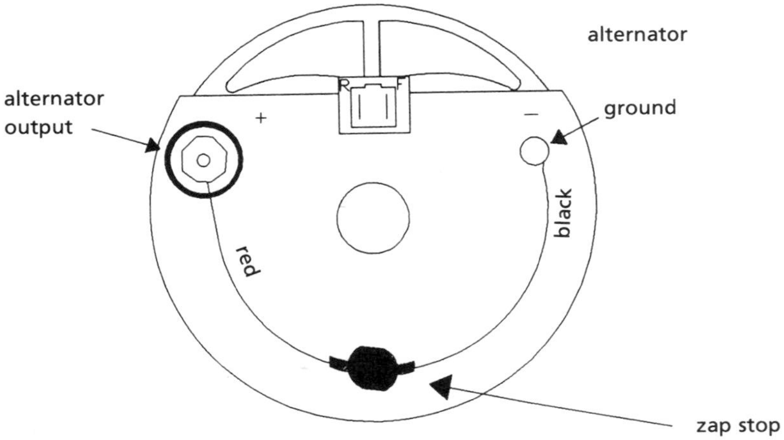

FIGURE 3-14. **DC master control panel. Figure 6-13 shows how the panel is wired into the system. (Courtesy Weems & Plath)**

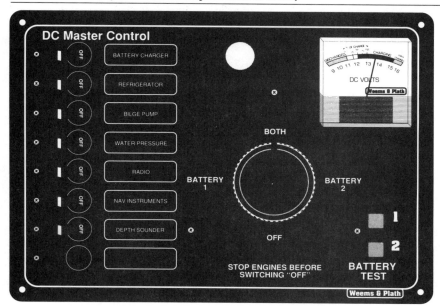

FIGURE 3-15. **Ship-to-shore selector switch to choose between a shore-power AC hookup and on-board AC power from a gen-set. Figure 12-4 shows its system location. (Courtesy Weems & Plath)**

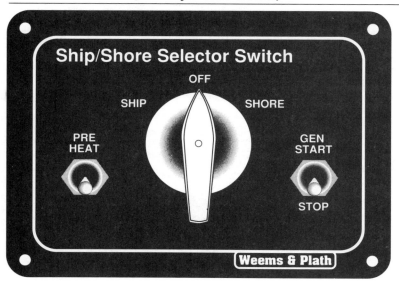

switches are available from Real Goods Trading Company. Twelve-volt components are also available from Radio Shack and other electrical supply stores.

SYSTEM MONITORING DEVICES

Monitors allow you to see what is happening in your energy system, and we strongly recommend them. They range from simple analog meters (with a moving needle) to sophisticated multifunction digital-readout devices.

At the very least it is useful to monitor battery voltage. A simple voltmeter like the one shown in Figure 3-16 is about 3 inches by 3 inches square, can be mounted beside your electrical panel, and can be wired to check one or more banks of batteries. Voltmeters may also be included in prewired master control panels as in Figure 3-14. The voltmeter in Figure 3-16 displays voltage on the bottom scale and has an easy-to-read percent-of-charge scale on top.

An ammeter in a generator's output line will tell you how many amperes are flowing toward your batteries. An ammeter in line with your load will tell you how many amperes you are using. The simple ammeter shown in Figure 3-17 is similar in size and cost to a voltmeter.

More sophisticated, and more expensive, system monitors include the Balmar Products' DCM 2000 (shown in Figure 3-18) and DCM 5000, Cruising Equipment's Quad-Cycle Regulator/Monitor, and Ample Power's Systems Monitor (shown in Figure 3-19). With these units you can monitor a variety of functions, including voltage from multiple-battery banks, amperes from various charging sources, and amperes being consumed by a load. The digital display makes these units highly visible and accurate.

A recent addition to monitoring devices is the ampere-hour meter. This type of monitor can accurately track how many ampere-hours of battery capacity have been consumed or recharged. The Balmar units include ampere-hour monitoring, as do meters from Cruising Equipment and Ample Power.

FIGURE 3-16 (left). **DC Voltmeter. Other models permit the user to monitor his choice of two or more battery banks with the push of a button. (Courtesy Weems & Plath)**

FIGURE 3-17 (right). **Simple ammeter to measure current generation or consumption. (Courtesy Weems & Plath)**

FIGURE 3-18. A multifunction monitor for current and voltage. (Courtesy Balmar)

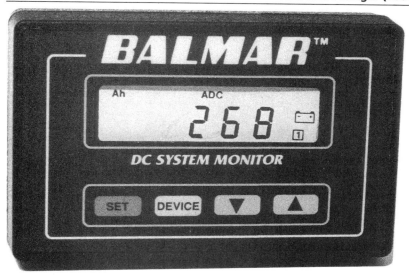

FIGURE 3-19. The Ample Power multifunction monitor.

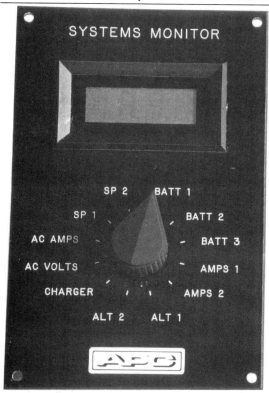

FIGURE 3-20.   **Voltage regulator for a solar panel. (Courtesy Hamilton Ferris Co.)**

VOLTAGE REGULATORS

Almost any generator can potentially overcharge a battery without some form of voltage regulation. Voltage regulators for the marine market come in many forms. Standard marine alternators come with internal or external regulators that operate similarly to automotive units. High-output units come with an external regulator and wiring harness. Several types of fast-charge voltage regulation devices are available. (See the section on fast-charge alternator controls in Chapter 2.)

Most solar, wind, and water generators require voltage regulation if you want the system to operate automatically, although some solar panels can't produce a high enough voltage to overcharge batteries. Voltage regulators for solar, wind, and water systems are usually small devices intended for bulkhead mounting, and may come with voltage and/or amperage monitoring, low-battery alarm or disconnect, charging diode, and fuse. A typical solar voltage regulator that includes current monitoring is shown in Figure 3-20. Voltage regulators cost anywhere from $40 to $200.

4

Basic Electricity For Boaters

REMOVING THE MYSTERY

Chapter 1 mentioned that energy can take several forms: mechanical, electrical, chemical, heat, or radiation. Here we are concerned only with electrical energy and the way it behaves on board a boat, covering the basics of electricity to make it easier and more enjoyable to manage your personal energy system.

For most of us, the difficulty in understanding electrical energy is that we can't see it. We can see the effects of electricity in a light bulb, hear its effect when a radio is turned on, or feel its effect when we operate a fan. We can understand the work being done, but not the electricity itself.

Several approaches can help remove the mystery surrounding electrical energy. First, simple analogies, like the two below, help pave the way for understanding. Second, simple rules and relationships tell us where, when, and how strong (or useful to us) electricity is at a given moment. If we understand these rules and relationships, we know where to look when electrical energy is not present where we think it should be. Finally, simple meters and monitoring devices render electricity almost "visible" to us. As you will see, monitors and meters play an important part in a good marine energy system.

TWO ANALOGIES

Electricity-Sailing Analogy

One simple analogy compares electricity with the mechanics of a sailboat. The energy of the wind is equivalent to the electrical energy present in a battery. When we want to put the wind's energy to work for us we turn on a switch, figuratively speaking, by raising the sails. The boat moves through the water just as electricity moves along a wire. If there were no water resistance on the hull the boat would continue to pick up speed. In reality there is a certain amount of resistance peculiar to each boat—similar to the electrical resistance peculiar to each appliance—that governs the boat's speed through the water. The knotmeter helps us to measure the amount of useful mechanical energy transporting us from one place to another, just as an ammeter in an electrical circuit helps us to measure how much electrical energy we are using.

Electricity-Water Analogy

A common analogy is to liken the flow of electricity to the flow of water. It goes like this:

Visualize a bathtub full of water. That water represents potential energy about equivalent to the energy it took to lift it from your main water pipe to the tub. It is analogous to the potential energy in a battery. When you pull the stopper in the tub, water begins to flow in the same way that electricity flows when you turn a switch. The amount of water that flows depends on two things: the height of water in the tub and the size of the drain hole. The higher the water level and the bigger the hole, the more flowing water. In like fashion, the amount of electricity that flows from a battery depends on the battery voltage and the resistance of the appliance drawing electricity. The higher the voltage and the lower the resistance, the more flowing electricity.

We can refine this analogy a little by replacing the bathtub with a dam and a reservoir of water behind it, as shown in Figure 4-1. The reservoir stores mechanical potential energy in the form of water pressure. The water pressure is determined by the height of water, and the capacity of the reservoir to do useful work is determined by its overall size. When we want to use the water pressure, say to turn a paddle wheel to grind grain, we open a valve and water begins to flow down a pipe. The water pressure and the size of the nozzle at the end of the pipe determine how much water flows. The higher the water pressure and the bigger the nozzle (up to the pipe's diameter), the greater the flow. We can see exactly how much water is flowing by placing a water meter anywhere along the pipe.

On a boat, a battery bank behaves much the way the reservoir does, storing energy until

FIGURE 4-1.   **Electricity-water analogy.**

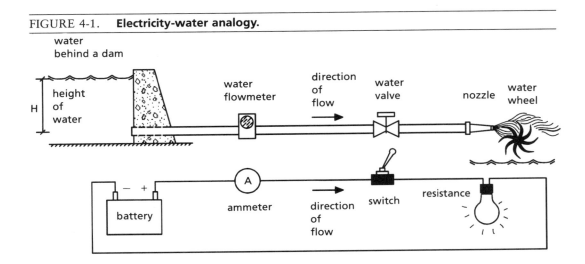

we need it. The voltage of the battery is equivalent to the reservoir's water pressure, and the capacity of the battery bank depends on its size. When we need energy, we turn a switch to start the flow of electricity. The switch acts the same as our water valve. The amount of electricity flowing depends on the battery voltage and the electrical resistance of the appliance we are using. The higher the voltage and the less the resistance, the greater the electrical flow. For example, the boat's weather radio has a large electrical resistance (small flow), whereas the 12-volt refrigerator has a small electrical resistance (large flow). We can monitor exactly how much electricity is flowing by placing an ammeter anywhere in the wire.

TYPES OF ELECTRICITY

We use two distinct types of electricity in everyday life. On a boat, an automobile, or any remote site away from the main electrical grid, we typically use direct current (DC). In our homes or at the dock, alternating current (AC) is available. Each type is appropriate for the task it performs.

Direct Current

In a DC circuit, the electrons—very small charged particles—always move in the same direction. Benjamin Franklin gave us the names *positive* and *negative* for the terminals of a battery, and he assumed that the electrons moved from positive pole to negative pole. We still stick with this conventional view when labeling an electric circuit, even though it has since been found that electrons actually move from negative to positive terminal. The direction of electron movement is less important than remembering the fact that all DC appliances (except incandescent lamps and heating elements) are polarized, or have distinct positive and negative wires that must be hooked up correctly. Accidentally reversing the wires will run an electric motor (like a bilge pump) backwards, or blow the internal fuse (or worse, if no fuse is present) of a piece of electronic gear.

All disposable batteries give direct current at about 1.5 volts per battery, unless otherwise specified. Boat and automobile batteries are typically set up for 12 volts, although 6- and 24-volt systems are also possible. It is essential to remember that only direct current can be used to charge a battery, which is why alternators must rectify their output from alternating to direct current before it goes to the battery. A so-called 12-volt battery will fluctuate between 11 and 13 volts, depending on its state of charge.

Alternating Current

In an AC system the electrons move first in one direction, then in the opposite direction, "alternating" in this manner many times a second. In a United States metropolitan electrical grid, the frequency of these cycles is about sixty times a second, or 60 hertz. Standard house voltage is designated as 110 volts at a frequency of 60 hertz. In Europe the standard is 220 volts at 50 hertz.

Electric companies prefer alternating current at high voltages, because it can be produced and transmitted more efficiently. Since the electrons move in both directions in an AC circuit, appliance wiring is not polarized for positive and negative. Direct current at 12 or 24 volts from a battery can be changed to 110-volt AC through an inverter, thus permitting the use of household appliances on board.

Electrons, Conductors, and Insulators

When we say that "electricity is flowing," we actually mean that the electrons in a conductor such as a copper wire are moving. An electrical conductor has many available drifting electrons and therefore conducts electricity very well. Most metals, salt water, and even the human body can conduct electricity, with copper being the usual choice for electrical wiring. An electrical insulator is just the opposite. It has few available drifting electrons and will not conduct electricity. Wood, glass, and plastics are all insulators, with plastic commonly being used as the insulation for copper wiring.

CONCEPTS OF ELECTRICITY

With the above analogies fresh in mind, let's examine the five basic electrical concepts.

Voltage

Voltage (abbreviated as V) is the pressure, or electrical potential, that moves electrons along a wire. It can be measured with a voltmeter. Typically, the voltage of your boat's battery is around 12.2 to 12.8. The greater the voltage, the greater the tendency for electricity to flow. It is analogous to household water pressure.

Current

Current is the flow of electrons along a wire. It can be measured, in amperes (or amps, abbreviated as A or I), with an ammeter. A weather radio draws less than 0.5 ampere, while 12-volt refrigeration draws about 5 amperes. The larger the current, the bigger the wire size required to handle it safely. Current is analogous to water flow rate.

Resistance

Resistance is opposition to the flow of electrons. It can be measured, in ohms (usually represented by an upper-case omega or a capital R), with an ohmmeter. Twelve-volt refrigeration has an internal resistance of just over 2 ohms, while a weather radio has an internal resistance of more than 24 ohms. The higher the resistance, the lower the current draw of an appliance.

Power

Power is the amount of energy per unit of time that is generated or consumed. Electrical power is rated in watts (abbreviated as W). A small solar panel might produce 10 watts of power, a large wind generator 200 watts, and a high-output alternator over 1,200 watts. One thousand watts = 1 kilowatt (1 kW). Our weather radio consumes about 6 watts, while the 12-volt refrigeration system consumes about 60 watts when running. Power ratings in watts are useful in comparing generators and for calculating your boat's electrical power requirements.

Energy

Electrical energy, measured in watt-hours by a watt-hour meter (the electric meter outside your house or at the dock), represents the amount of power generated or consumed over a measured period of time. If our 6-watt weather radio is left on for one hour, it will consume 6 watt-hours of energy. For comparison, consider that the typical American family uses 750,000 watt-hours of electricity each month!

CONCEPT OF RELATIONSHIPS

Calculating Voltage, Current, and Resistance

The concepts of voltage, current, and resistance are related by a formula called Ohm's law, conceived by the German scientist Georg Ohm in 1827. Ohm's law allows you to find a value for voltage (V), current (I), or resistance (R) if you know the other two. It can be written in several different forms, as shown below:

$$V = I \times R$$

or

$$I = V/R$$

or

$$R = V/I$$

An easy way to remember this relationship is to arrange the symbols in a triangle like this:

$$\begin{array}{cc} & V & \\ I & & R \end{array}$$

Cover the symbol you want to solve for and perform the math indicated. For instance, if you cover V it leaves I and R next to each other, so multiply I by R. If you cover up I it leaves V over R, so divide V by R. If you cover up R, it leaves V over I, so divide V by I.

EXAMPLES:

- A 12-ohm resistance in a 12-volt circuit would draw 1 ampere of current.

- If the resistance in a circuit is 2 ohms and a 7-ampere current is being drawn, then the voltage is 14 volts.

- If the battery voltage is 12.5 volts, and the current being drawn is 2.5 amperes, then the circuit resistance is 5 ohms.

Calculating Power

Our next concept is power (P), an understanding of which helps define the charging rate (power) of a generator and the consumption rate of on-board appliances. The governing formulas for power can be presented as follows:

and

$$P = V \times I$$

$$I = P/V$$

and

$$V = P/I$$

If we substitute $I \times R$ for V from the previous formulas, we get

$$P = (I \times R) \times I$$

EXAMPLES:

- A generator producing 10 amperes at 12 volts has a power output of 120 watts.

- A 12-watt lamp operating from a 12-volt battery would consume 1 ampere of current.

- An AC generator producing 10 amperes at 120 volts has a power output of 1,200 watts.

- A 12-watt lamp operating at 120 volts would draw 0.1 ampere of current.

Calculating Energy

Our final electrical calculation is that for energy. Energy is simply the power being produced or consumed multiplied by the time of operation. It is represented by the formula

$$E = P \times t$$

where t is time in hours.

EXAMPLES:

- A 12-watt lamp operating for 1 hour will consume 12 watt-hours of energy.

- A 600-watt power tool operated for 1 minute consumes 10 watt-hours of energy.

- A 35-watt solar panel faced into the sun for 6 hours will produce 210 watt-hours of energy.

- A 100-watt water generator towed behind a boat for 24 hours will produce 2,400 watt-hours of energy.

- A 1,200-watt high-output alternator operated for 2 hours also produces 2,400 watt-hours of energy.

A circuit is a path that, if followed completely, leads back to the starting place. In electrical terms a circuit refers to a path that can be followed by an electrical current. An electrical circuit is formed by connecting a voltage source (such as a boat's battery) to a load (an appliance) by means of a conductor (typically copper wire). In this example the battery pushes the available electrons in the wire through the appliance. We have used some of the energy in the battery to perform useful work.

An electrical circuit can also be formed by connecting a generator (a producer of electricity and also a voltage source) to a battery by means of a conductor. In this case the higher voltage of the generator pushes the electrons through the battery. The movement of electrons forces a chemical reaction inside the battery, storing energy for later use.

Electrical Schematic Diagram

Anytime you wish to examine an electrical circuit for design, installation, or troubleshooting purposes, it is helpful to put the circuit into schematic-diagram form. In an electrical schematic, there are standard symbols for components; the symbols are shown in Figure 4-2.

In schematic-diagram form, the simple electrical circuit of a boat battery connected to one instrument panel function (in this case a compass light) is shown in Figure 4-3. The switch in the diagram allows you to decide when the electricity should flow. The fuse, or circuit breaker, is in effect an automatic switch that opens the circuit and shuts off electrical flow, protecting components from damage, possible fire, or both. It does this when, for any number of reasons, there is too much current in the circuit to operate safely. Remember that for a given battery voltage, the amount of current is normally controlled by the resistance of the load.

The schematic can become more sophisticated, as shown in Figure 4-4, with the addition

FIGURE 4-2.   **A few of the more common schematic symbols used for boat circuits.**

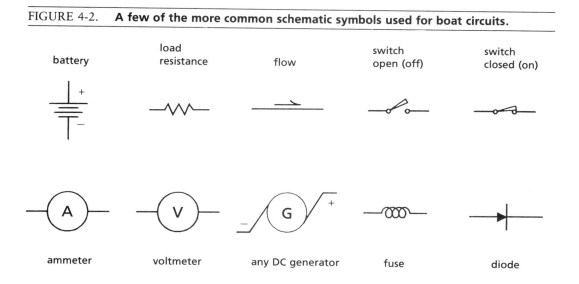

FIGURE 4-3. **Schematic diagram of a simple circuit including battery, a single function on the DC control panel with a switch and fuse, and a single electrical load.**

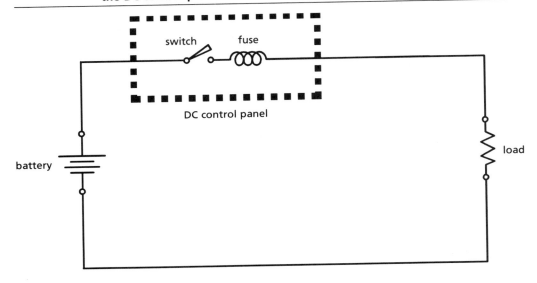

FIGURE 4-4. **A somewhat more complex schematic diagram.**

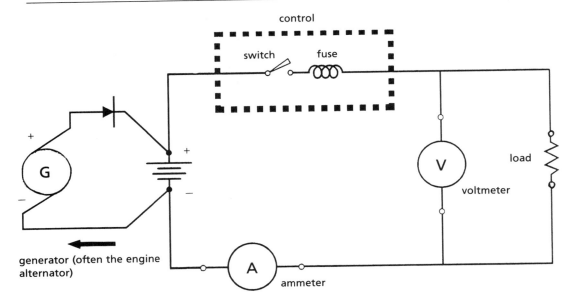

of monitoring instruments, such as an ammeter and a voltmeter, and another circuit with a generator to recharge the battery. Note how the positive wire of the generator is connected to the positive pole of the battery, and the negative wire to the negative battery pole. A diode is shown in the generator circuit; the diode prevents the battery from losing electricity when the generator isn't operating. Note that if an appliance is on and drawing current, some of the output of the generator will go directly to that load and the balance to the battery. If the load is greater than the generator output, all of the generator output will go to the load, and the balance needed will come from the battery. The ammeter in each circuit allows you to tell how much current is being produced or consumed. The voltmeter allows you to monitor the battery state of charge.

Parallel and Series Connections

There are two ways of connecting components in an electrical circuit, either in parallel or in series with each other. If two batteries are connected in parallel, as in Figure 4-5, then the voltage is not increased but the total ampere-hour capacity available will be the sum of the two. If the same batteries are connected in series, as in Figure 4-6, the voltage will double but the total ampere-hour capacity at that voltage will be the same as for one battery.

Solar panels are usually connected in parallel, so the total current is the sum of all the panels, while the voltage remains the same as for one panel. Likewise, in a boat's electrical panel, various loads are wired in parallel so they can have individual switches and circuit breakers. The voltage to each load stays the same, while one ammeter before or after all the loads will read the cumulative ampere draw.

ELECTRICAL METERS AND MONITORS

We said at the beginning of this chapter that certain instruments help to make electricity visible to us. These include voltmeters, which measure voltage; ammeters, which measure current; and ohmmeters, which measure electrical resistance. Also included are the simple test light and new, high-tech ampere-hour meters. Let's take a closer look at how we can put these instruments to use.

FIGURE 4-5 (left).   **Batteries connected in parallel.**
FIGURE 4-6 (right).   **Series connections. (From *Boatowner's Mechanical and Electrical Manual* by Nigel Calder. International Marine, 1990)**

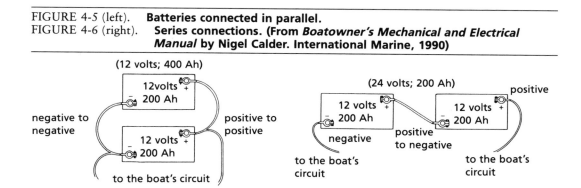

Test Light

A test light, also called a trouble lamp or continuity tester, is the simplest and least expensive tool for testing electrical circuits. You can easily make one from a 12-volt lamp with wires soldered directly to it or in a prewired socket. The two lead wires should be several feet long, with an alligator clip soldered to each end. This allows you to clip them on, leaving your hands free. You can buy a test light at most automotive or electrical stores for under $5.

A test light tells you if there is continuity in the circuit. Most electrical problems come from loose or broken wires or poor contacts that cut off or restrict the flow of electricity. The test light will help you determine the source of the problem.

There are two methods of using a test light. In the first, clip one wire from the test light onto the negative pole of the battery. Take the other wire and, beginning with the positive pole, test the circuit at each new electrical connection, as shown in Figure 4-7. If the light comes on at position A, then the battery has voltage. The brightness of the bulb helps to show

FIGURE 4-7.   **Using a test light. Attach one lead to the battery's negative terminal, and move the other along the circuit to search for faulty wiring or connections.**

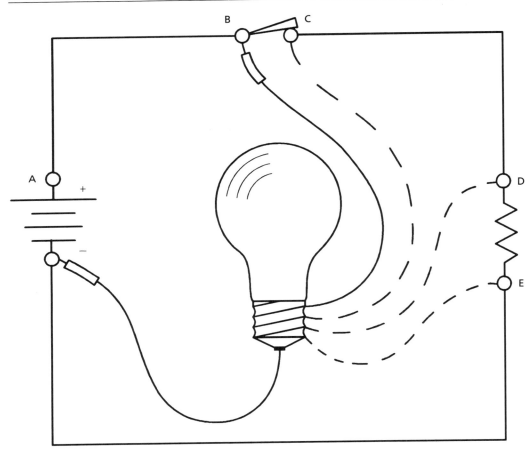

battery state of charge. If the light comes on at position B, then the wire from the battery to the switch is okay. If the light comes on at position C, then the switch is okay, and so on. If you find a spot where the light fails or dims, check the connections at that point.

A second method of using a test light is to attach one lead at the battery's positive terminal and the other at the first connection. The light should not come on if the wire in between is okay, because current will follow the path of least resistance (the wire) rather than flowing through a load (the test light). Do the same for each section of the circuit, moving both leads as you go. The only two places that the light should come on is across a break in the circuit (a broken wire, open switch, etc.) or across a load (any appliance).

It is important to note that there is a voltage drop, equal to the battery voltage, across the electrical load in a circuit. In Figure 4-7, provided there are no faulty connections or wiring and no open swithes, there is system voltage (say, 12.6 volts) on one side of the load (D) and 0 volts on the other (E). A test light will come on only across a voltage difference.

Voltmeter

A voltmeter measures the voltage of a battery (or battery bank) or the output voltage of a generator. Voltmeters come in analog or digital models. Analog voltmeters have a needle indicator and come in various ranges of scale. DC analog voltmeters used to monitor 12-volt batteries typically have a 9-to-16-volt range. Digital voltmeters have a digital readout with precise voltage measurements, and are therefore much more accurate.

Voltmeters come as hand-held instruments or for panel mounting. Many electrical panels on boats come with a voltmeter included. Some voltmeters used for battery measurements have a secondary scale to convey more information on battery state of charge. The Weems and Plath 9-to-16-volt DC meter shown in Figure 3-16 tells when the battery is discharged, when it is between 0 and 100 percent charged, when it is receiving additional charge, or when it is overcharged. The Equus digital voltmeter, sold through the Real Goods catalog, is an inexpensive, panel-mounted device that has user-programmable high- and low-voltage alarms included. The high-voltage alarm signals battery overcharging, and the low-voltage alarm alerts you to a low-battery condition.

To use a voltmeter as a test instrument, connect it as you would a test light. Make sure the red lead goes to the positive side of the circuit and the black lead to the negative side. When installing a voltmeter permanently in a circuit, connect it across, or in parallel with, the load (or generator), as shown in Figure 4-4. Only a very small amount of current goes through the voltmeter.

Voltmeter Variations

Some voltmeters have readouts in units other than volts. One of these is the Weems and Plath Percent Battery Meter, shown in Figure 4-8. It reads in percent of battery state of charge, from 0 to 100. On the lower portion of the unit's face, a normal operating range is indicated, from 40 to 90 percent. This meter, while not quite as accurate, has the advantage of being extremely easy to read.

Another variation is the Altus battery "fuel" gauge. Its top readout is in percent of charge, with a bottom readout from "empty" to "full" just like an auto fuel gauge.

FIGURE 4-8.   **Voltmeter with readout calibrated for state of battery charge as a percentage of full charge. (Courtesy Weems & Plath)**

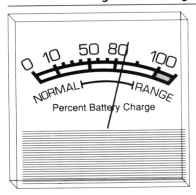

Ammeter

An ammeter displays the current flowing in a circuit. This can be the current produced by a generator or the current consumed by your appliances on board, depending on where the meter is located. Ammeters are either digital or analog, with the digital having a numerical readout and the analog a needle indicator. Ammeters can be hand-held diagnostic instruments, but are most often panel-mounted. They come in a variety of readout scales and should be well-matched to your needs. There is no need for a 0-to-100-ampere ammeter on a boat that consumes only 15 amperes maximum.

Ammeters provide valuable information and are relatively inexpensive. You will probably want two or more on board, one for each electricity producer and one to monitor electrical consumption. Again, select the proper scale for each circuit. Solar panels might need only a 0-to-5-ampere or a 0-to-15-ampere scale, a wind generator a 0-to-25-ampere scale, and a high-output alternator a 0-to-100-ampere or 0-to-150-ampere scale. On the consumption side, you may wish to connect separate ammeters for light and heavy loads to get more accurate readouts. The smaller-draw appliances might get a 0-to-5-ampere scale, while the heavier loads might require a 0-to-25-ampere or 0-to-50-ampere scale. Ammeters are available from most marine energy suppliers. The Weems and Plath DC ammeter shown in Figure 3-17 comes in four scale-ranges and fits the Weems and Plath standard panel layout for multiple-meter displays.

An ammeter is installed in series with the load in a circuit, as shown in Figure 4-4. It can be placed anywhere in the circuit, since the current flowing will be the same at all locations. A separate ammeter could also be used for the generator circuit in Figure 4-4. For smaller amounts of current, ammeters are usually connected directly to the circuit wiring. For larger amounts of current—100 amperes and more—there is typically a separate shunt placed in the circuit. This carries the main circuit current and sends a very small amount to the ammeter. With a shunt arrangement, the ammeter can be at a remote location from the circuit wiring. Correct polarity (circuit plus and minus) must be observed when installing an ammeter.

FIGURE 4-9. **An inexpensive analog multimeter (right) and a more expensive but more useful digital meter (left). The selector switch on the analog meter points to the R × 1 scale, indicating that the operator will be measuring resistance and will not need to multiply his reading in ohms by 10 or 100 to obtain the correct measurement. The following abbreviations are common: ACV (or VAC), volts AC; DCV, volts DC; DCmA, milliamps DC. When measuring voltages of unknown magnitude, start with the selector on a high scale, to be safe, and change to lower scales as necessary for sensitivity. There are two test leads. The red is hot and should be plugged into the + jack; the black is ground and should be plugged into the − jack. When you are testing DC voltages and amperages the red lead must go to the positive side of the circuit; this distinction is not important when you are testing AC voltages. The meter may have different jacks for AC and DC measurements; these will be clearly marked. The needle should point to zero volts when the leads are removed; adjust as necessary with the null adjustment screw. Use the ohms adjustment knob to ''zero out'' the resistance scale before each ohms measurement; to do this, hold the probes together, then turn the knob as necessary. Alligator probes are handy for most tests; needle probes sometimes reach places that alligator probes cannot.**

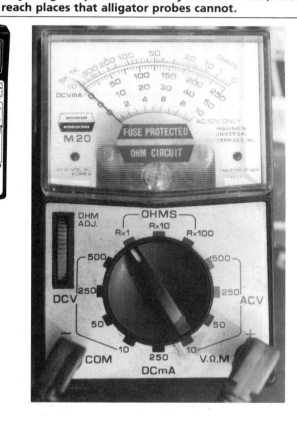

Multimeter

A multimeter is a diagnostic instrument that combines voltmeter, ammeter, and ohm-meter (for measuring resistance) into a small package, usually hand-held, with various scales to choose from. The DC-ampere scales commonly measure up to 250 milliamperes, or at most 1 ampere, and are graduated in milliamps (thousandths of an ampere). This is intended for electronics equipment testing and not suitable for larger amounts of current. Multimeters come with an internal battery for resistance readings. Resistance should always be checked with the circuit voltage source disconnected. Multimeters are great for troubleshooting when no voltage source is available—that is, when your battery is dead or disconnected. A test light will not work in this instance. Multimeters can have either analog or digital readouts, and most come with an audible continuity beeper for testing circuits.

A BOAT'S SIMPLIFIED SCHEMATIC

Two-Battery System

Now we're ready to look at a simplified version of a boat's electrical schematic diagram, including several electricity-producing circuits. As shown in Figure 4-10, let's assume our boat has the following:

FIGURE 4-10.   **Electrical schematic, two-battery system.**

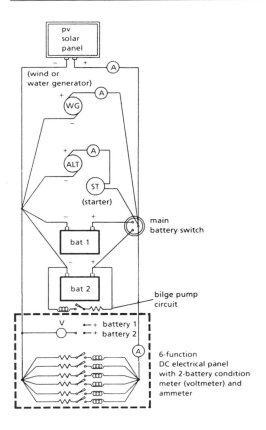

- Two 12-volt battery banks wired in parallel through a battery selector switch. Either or both batteries can supply house loads or be used for engine starting, and the batteries can be charged selectively or simultaneously.

- Three different sources of electricity: solar panels, a wind or water generator, and the main engine alternator. The output terminals of all charging sources are connected to the common terminal on the battery selector switch.

- An electrical panel with six functions on it, including cabin lights, running lights, anchor light, instruments, and two accessories. The bilge pump operates off an independent float switch so it can't be accidentally turned off. The electrical panel contains a voltmeter to display condition of battery bank 1 or 2 and an ammeter to monitor current draw.

- Additional ammeters to monitor the current from each generator.

FIGURE 4-11. **Electrical schematic, three batteries, with selector switch.**

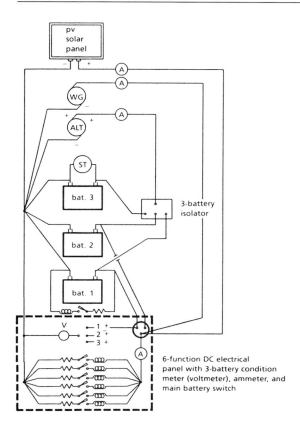

6-function DC electrical
panel with 3-battery condition
meter (voltmeter), ammeter, and
main battery switch

Three-Battery System

We could add a designated starting battery and a battery isolator so that the alternator could charge all three batteries at once while they remain electrically isolated from each other. The battery selector switch, which is shown in Figure 4-11 as part of a DC master control panel, would then be used to determine which battery supplied electrical loads or received solar, wind or water generator charging current. Included on the master panel is a battery condition meter for three batteries.

5

Of Batteries And Charging

STORING ELECTRICAL ENERGY

The method of storing electrical energy for later use is vital, for you can spend large amounts of time dependent on electrical reserves to supply your needs.

How you use those electrical reserves depends on your charging system. If you are using a fossil fuel-burning generator—including the alternator on your main engine—it is best to get the greatest output you reasonably can while it is running, then use your stored electricity until it's time to generate again. If you are using a solar, wind, or water generator, take advantage of the sun and wind while they are available and create enough reserves until the next generating period. Exceptions to this may be using a water generator on a long passage, or using wind generators in reliable tradewind areas. During these times, energy is produced more to serve current needs than to build reserves for the future. Nevertheless, electrical reserves are still important in these situations since, when the passage ends or when you anchor in a protected cove that drastically affects your wind generator's performance, you undoubtedly go back to periodic generating.

Although many other methods have been proposed, the lead-acid battery is still the best way to store electricity in vehicles and on boats. From Chapter 4 we know that electricity is actually moving electrons. It is not these moving electrons that are stored in a lead-acid battery, but the potential to create electricity. Charging a battery with electricity is similar to "charging" a reservoir behind a dam with water to be able to produce water pressure. Charging a battery with a generator causes chemical reactions inside the battery. The exact nature of these reactions depends on the battery, its size and state of discharge, and the charging voltage and current. As a battery is discharged the chemical reactions occur in reverse.

A battery stores chemical energy, and that energy can be used to make electrons flow in an electrical circuit. But where do the electrons come from, and how do they move in and out of a battery? Basic chemistry informs us that the atom—which consists of a dense nucleus of neutrons and protons and a surrounding cloud of electrons—is the smallest part of an element. Atoms remain undivided in chemical reactions, except for the limited transfer of electrons between reactants. This is most important since it is during the chemical reaction inside a battery that free electrons become available. Without free electrons, it would be impossible for a battery to store power. Batteries contain materials with the ability to gain or lose electrons readily, thus acquiring a negative or positive charge. The material in a battery that gives up free electrons is connected to what we call the negative terminal. When you use electricity, electrons flow from here, through the circuit, and back to the positive side of the battery. The electrons then recombine with battery material connected to the positive terminal.

BATTERY CONSTRUCTION AND OPERATION

Battery Components

A standard 12-volt, liquid-electrolyte, lead-acid battery usually has a plastic outer case, part of which may be transparent to display the level of the electrolyte, a solution of sulfuric acid and water. A battery comprises several voltage-producing cells, physically isolated from each other but electrically connected in series, with each cell rated at about 2 volts. Each cell is covered at the battery's top by a fill/vent cap. Since for voltage sources connected in series the total voltage is the sum of the components, a 6-volt battery has three cells and a 12-volt battery has six cells (see Figure 5-1). The voltage of each cell varies with battery state of charge. For greatest accuracy, voltage readings should be taken after the battery has been "at rest"—that is, without charging or discharging current—for a while.

Inside each battery cell are three components:

- Positive plates, or grids, made of lead dioxide, which is represented chemically as PbO_2.

- Negative plates, made of porous sponge lead, which is represented chemically as Pb.

- The electrolyte, made up of a dilute solution of sulfuric acid and water.

Batteries are extremely heavy for their size, since they are mostly lead plates. The relatively thin individual plates are suspended within the battery case, alternating between negative and positive, and held in position with inert separators between them. The electrolyte fills the space around the plates; the level of the electrolyte should be maintained at about $1/4$ to $3/8$ inch above the top of the plates. This arrangement of plates and electrolyte allows for a large exposed surface area where the chemical reaction takes place, and more complete acid diffusion into the plates. The negative plates in each cell are connected together and wired in series to the other cells' negative plates; likewise for the positive plates.

FIGURE 5-1A.   **Typical automobile-type 12-volt battery construction. There are six cells; within each is a series of alternating negative and positive plates, each one isolated from its neighbors by intervening insulators called separators. The plates are immersed in a sulfuric acid solution. On discharge, the lead atoms of the negative plates give up electrons and form lead ions, which combine with the sulfuric acid to form lead sulfate. The lead dioxide in the positive plates consumes electrons, yielding lead ions which again react with the acid to form lead sulfate. The negative plates are connected with each other and with the anode or negative terminal; the positive plates are collectively connected with the cathode or positive terminal. (From *Boatowner's Mechanical and Electrical Manual* by Nigel Calder. International Marine, 1990)**

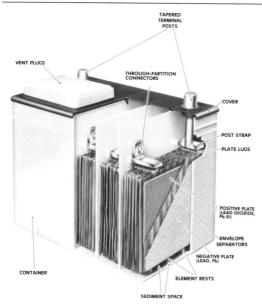

FIGURE 5-1B.   **Deep-cycle battery anatomy. Compare this battery's sturdy construction with the automobile-type battery in Figure 5-1A. (From *Boatowner's Mechanical and Electrical Manual* by Nigel Calder. International Marine, 1990)**

Specific Gravity (SG)

Water, as the most abundant substance on the surface of the Earth, is often used as a reference when classifying materials. By determining the *specific gravity*—a measure of a material's relative heaviness compared with water—we can determine the density of a battery's electrolyte, and thus its state of charge. Water has an SG of 1.000, while pure sulfuric acid has an SG of 1.840. The sulfuric acid-water solution, or electrolyte, in a battery will have an SG somewhere between 1.150 at discharge and 1.265 at full charge. Electrolyte SG varies, since it, like battery voltage, is proportional to the battery state of charge. For greatest accuracy, SG readings should be taken after the battery has been at rest for a while.

Testing Specific Gravity With a Hydrometer

The SG of a liquid-electrolyte battery cell is tested with a hydrometer, a simple instrument that draws a sample of electrolyte into a glass tube. An inner glass tube with a scale on it becomes partially submerged in the electrolyte. The buoyancy of the inner tube depends on the SG of the electrolyte, which can be read directly (see Figure 5-2). SG readings vary slightly with temperature, as does battery voltage, and should be adjusted accordingly. Some hydrometers come with a built-in thermometer, providing greater accuracy. SG readings should be about the same for all battery cells. We can therefore use the SG reading in each cell as an indication of battery state of charge, and to tell us if the individual cells are functioning properly. If there is too much variation in the cell SG readings, the battery probably needs an equalization charge (described below). If an equalization charge doesn't bring all the readings

---

FIGURE 5-2. **A battery-testing hydrometer. The correct method of reading it is shown on the right. Your eye should be level with the liquid surface. Disregard curvature of the liquid against the glass parts. (From *Boatowner's Mechanical and Electrical Manual* by Nigel Calder. International Marine, 1990)**

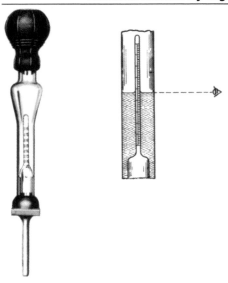

in line, the battery may need to be replaced. The more dilute the electrolyte becomes, or the more it resembles plain water, the closer its specific gravity comes to 1.000. A new battery should come with a chart showing the relationship of its electrolyte SG to state of charge (see Figure 5-3).

A Discharging Battery

The chemical reaction going on inside each cell of a lead-acid battery is shown in Figure 5-4. As the battery is discharging (electricity is being used) the concentration of sulfuric acid decreases, the specific gravity decreases, and the voltage drops. A molecule of sulfuric acid breaks down into two hydrogen ions with a total charge of $+2$, and one sulfate ion with a total charge of -2. On the negative plates an atom of sponge lead gives up two electrons and combines with a sulfate ion to form lead sulfate ($PbSO_4$). On the positive plates oxygen from the lead dioxide combines with hydrogen ions to form water, and the remaining lead combines with sulfate ions and the electrons coming in from the circuit to also form lead sulfate. It is this newly formed water that dilutes the electrolyte and lowers the specific gravity.

A Battery Being Charged

As a battery is charged (electricity is being generated), the concentration of sulfuric acid increases, the specific gravity increases, and the voltage goes up. Sulfuric acid forms from hydrogen and sulfate ions. On the negative plates, sponge lead and sulfate ions are formed from hydrogen ions and the breakdown of lead sulfate, while on the positive plates lead dioxide, hydrogen ions, and sulfate ions are formed.

It should be apparent by now that battery state of charge, specific gravity of the electrolyte, and battery voltage are all interrelated, with each make of battery having slightly different characteristics. Figure 5-3 shows a typical relationship of specific gravity, voltage, and state of charge.

Hydrogen ions produced during vigorous charging can combine to form hydrogen gas, which in the presence of air can be highly explosive. Some of the gas is released through the battery vent caps, which is why proper venting of battery compartments is critical, and why

---

FIGURE 5-3.   **Specific gravity, voltage, and state of charge in a 12-volt battery at 80° F (26.7° C), the benchmark temperature used in the United States, and at 60° F (15.6° C), the benchmark temperature used in the United Kingdom).**

Specific gravity		Voltage	State of charge
at 80 ° F	*at 60 ° F*		
1.265	1.273	12.7	100%
1.225	1.233	12.4	75%
1.190	1.198	12.2	50%
1.155	1.163	12.0	25%
1.120	1.128	11.9	0%

FIGURE 5-4.   **The chemical changes inside a lead-acid battery cell.**

a.) The sulphuric acid (H_2SO_4) in the electrolyte is "ionized" during discharge:

$$H_2SO_4 \quad \overrightarrow{\text{Discharge}} \quad 2H \quad + \quad SO_4$$

H_2SO_4		2H		SO_4
sulphuric acid		hydrogen ions	+	sulphate ion

b.) The chemical reaction at the negative electrode is:

Pb lead	+	SO_4 sulphate ion		$PbSO_4$ lead sulphate	+	2ϵ electrons from hydrogen ion

c.) The chemical reaction at the positive electrode is:

PbO_2 lead dioxide	+	$4H^+$ hydrogen ions	+	SO_4 sulphate ions	+	2ϵ electrons		$PbSO_4$ lead sulphate	+	$2H_2O$ water

the periodic addition of distilled water is necessary. Catalyst battery caps such as those from Hydrocap Corporation, fitted to your batteries, help to recombine excess hydrogen and oxygen back into water. They do not, however, do away with the need for sensible charging techniques that keep battery cell gassing to a minimum.

TYPES OF BATTERIES

There are three general types of batteries appropriate to use on a boat, each designed for a specific task. They are categorized by their ability to deliver current and by how well they hold up to repeated deep discharge. The basic difference between them is in the thickness and number of the positive and negative plates, and the strength of the lead alloy used.

Starting-Lighting-Ignition (SLI) Battery

As the name implies, the starting-lighting-ignition (SLI) battery is used mainly for engine starting and for supplying small electrical loads. It has a greater number of thin positive and negative plates, creating a large total surface area. As a result, an SLI battery can produce high amounts of current for short periods of time, but doesn't have the plate configuration for much reserve capacity or for withstanding repeated deep discharge. All car batteries are relatively inexpensive SLI batteries: They can produce high cranking power for the few seconds it takes to start the engine, as well as operate a few small loads, but they have a relatively high self-discharge rate; when the alternator takes over, it tops off the battery and handles the loads while the car is running. A marine SLI battery-and-alternator combination functions in much the same way. If SLI batteries are used on a boat for engine starting, they should always be isolated from the boat's other batteries through a battery isolator, a switch, or both. Deep discharging will greatly shorten SLI battery life.

True Deep-Cycle Battery

The other extreme from an SLI battery is the true deep-cycle variety. The term *deep-cycle* is used to imply the ability to withstand repeated deep discharge of battery current. Deep-cycle batteries are often referred to as "house batteries" and are used for supplying medium to high electrical loads. The plates in a deep-cycle battery are heavier and thicker, trading surface area for strength and starting power for reserve capacity. True deep-cycle batteries have no real ability for starting engines, but typically have a lower self-discharge rate. They should always be isolated from an SLI battery through a battery isolator, a switch, or both.

Hybrid Deep-Cycle Battery

In between the SLI and true deep-cycle batteries is the hybrid deep-cycle, probably the most common marine battery in use. Labeled as a house battery, it also has some cranking power for occasional engine starting and can handle small to medium electrical loads on board. In addition it can be moderately discharged repeatedly without harm, and has a relatively low self-discharge rate.

BATTERY CAPACITY

The capacity of a battery, or the amount of usable electricity it can provide, is rated in several ways. Battery ratings give valuable information about a battery's construction and allow us to make an intelligent choice concerning which type and how many we should have on board. See Figure 5-5 for a sample battery size and capacity chart.

Cold Cranking Amperes (CCA)

The rating *cold cranking amperes* (CCA) is primarily used for SLI batteries, but also applies to the hybrid deep-cycle variety. Technically, it is the current that a battery at 0 degrees Fahrenheit can deliver for 30 seconds while maintaining a minimum cell voltage of 1.2 volts. Gasoline engines require about 1 CCA per cubic inch of displacement, diesel engines about 2 CCA per cubic inch.

Marine Cranking Amperes (MCA)

Marine cranking amperes (MCA) is a new rating similar to CCA but with a higher temperature requirement during testing of 32 degrees Fahrenheit. A battery rated for 600 CCA will have a much higher MCA.

Reserve Capacity

Another rating, most often used in conjunction with CCA, is the reserve capacity. Reserve capacity refers to the number of minutes that a fully charged battery at 80 degrees Fahrenheit can be discharged at 25 amperes while maintaining a minimum cell voltage of 1.75 volts. Reserve capacity can also be expressed for other rates of discharge, that is, for 5, 10, or 15

FIGURE 5-5. **Dimensions and capacities of Surrette marine batteries. (Courtesy Surrette Storage Battery Co.)**

Type	Assembly	Volts	BCI Group Size	Catalog Number	AMP-Hours @ 20HR Rate	Reserve Capacity (minutes)	Cold Cranking Amps	Length	Width	Height	Wet	Dry	Quarts of Acid
DEEP CYCLING HEAVY DUTY MARINE; DIESEL STARTING; SOLAR/WIND/RV & UPS SYSTEMS SERIES 300-400-500												
HG-1	A	6	1	409	105	160	485	9.1	7.0	8.9	40	30	4.5
XH-2	A	6	2	317	130	215	520	10.1	6.9	9.1	50	40	5.0
XH-3	A	6	3	309	149	270	720	11.8	7.1	9.4	58	48	5.5
HR-4	A	6	4	405	165	310	775	13.0	7.1	9.4	65	52	6.0
HR-5D	B	6	5D	411	182	330	835	13.4	7.1	9.4	70	55	6.5
HR-7D	B	6	7D	407	221	430	920	16.2	7.1	9.4	80	64	7.0
EHG-208	C	6	GC2	415	208	345	727	10.3	7.1	10.3	72	57	5.8
EIG-225	C	6	GC2H	417	225	350	575	10.3	7.1	11.3	77	60	6.5
EIG-262	C	6	SP	419	262	395	785	11.7	7.0	11.3	90	70	7.5
NS-305	B	6	SP	435	305	458	900	12.3	7.0	14.8	115	86	8.8
CH-375	B	6	SP	421	335	460	890	11.7	7.0	16.8	122	98	10.5
6NS-29	DH	6	SP	525	490	780	1580	20.2	9.1	16.4	230	156	20.0
8HR-19	DH	8	SP	455	160	280	695	18.4	7.4	9.5	97	77	8.0
8HHG-175	DH	8	SP	441	175	263	650	21.4	7.5	10.8	110	82	9.0
8HHG-21	DH	8	SP	443	200	310	850	21.4	7.5	10.8	122	94	9.0
8HR-27	DH	8	SP	356	220	350	980	27.5	7.5	10.5	144	107	13.5
8M-23	DH	8	SP	444	225	360	900	27.5	7.5	10.5	146	109	14.0
8HHG-25	DH	8	SP	445	240	384	1032	24.4	7.5	10.8	141	113	11.0
8HHG-29	DH	8	SP	446	290	465	1190	27.5	7.5	10.5	165	130	12.0
8HHG-31	DH	8	SP	447	300	495	1320	26.9	8.4	10.8	183	145	15.0
8HHG-37	DH	8	SP	449	358	598	1575	26.9	10.0	10.8	220	197	17.0
8NS-17	FH	8	SP	501	285	450	910	27.9	6.3	17.9	220	190	13.0
8CH-17	FH	8	SP	502	355	565	1050	27.9	6.3	17.9	240	210	13.0
8NS-23	FH	8	SP	511	385	610	1240	28.3	7.5	17.5	250	213	18.0
8CH-23	FH	8	SP	513	470	750	1460	28.3	7.5	17.5	280	244	16.0
8NS-33	FH	8	SP	521	565	905	1850	28.3	10.5	16.4	359	304	26.0
8CH-33	FH	8	SP	523	681	1090	2090	28.3	10.5	16.4	400	353	23.0
XG-90M	C	12	30H	337	93	135	405	13.5	6.8	9.9	65	52	6.0
12XG-105	B	12	1A	339	105	160	420	18.0	7.6	9.6	89	71	8.0
T-12-120	BH	12	SP	414	120	210	610	13.5	7.0	11.3	84	66	9.0
12XH-130	B	12	1B	314	130	215	520	20.4	7.5	9.6	108	85	10.0
T-12-140	B	12	16TF	425	140	210	535	16.0	7.1	11.1	98	82	9.0
12XH-19	BH	12	4D	303	165	285	775	20.3	8.8	9.8	135	108	12.0
T-12-175	BH	12	SP	426	175	286	510	15.5	7.0	14.5	124	98	11.0
12XH-21	BH	12	6D	305	193	310	825	20.3	9.9	9.8	148	113	13.0
12XH-25	BH	12	8D	307	230	385	900	20.3	11.0	9.8	159	126	14.0
HR-8D	BH	12	8D	427	221	430	920	20.3	11.0	9.8	160	127	14.0
MARINE SMALL CRAFT STARTING; LIGHT CYCLING; ELECTRIC MOTOR SERVICE SERIES 200												
XJ-2SM-70	CH	12	24	289	70	110	380	11.4	6.8	9.5	45	32	5.1
XJ-2SM-85	CH	12	24	284	85	141	410	11.4	6.8	9.5	51	38	5.1
XJ-3SM-100	CH	12	27	283	100	160	480	13.2	6.8	9.8	57	44	5.0

amperes. The higher the rate of discharge, the lower the total reserve capacity rating. Reserve capacity is probably the most universal battery rating.

Ampere-Hour Rating

We most often think of rating a battery for its ampere-hour capacity, which refers to the amperes a battery can supply at 80 degrees Fahrenheit in a specific period of time while maintaining a minimum cell voltage of 1.75 volts. Many U.S. battery manufacturers use a 20-hour rate. In this case a 100-ampere-hour battery could supply 5 amperes for 20 hours. When comparing batteries it is essential to make sure they use the same hour rate. Ampere-hour rating and reserve capacity are essentially the same type of measurement.

Notes on Battery Capacity

- *Ampere-hours and energy*—The ampere-hours rating is really an indicator of the amount of usable electrical energy the battery can provide. Remember that volts × amperes = power, and power × time = energy. This means that ampere-hours × battery voltage = watt-hours, a true measurement of electrical energy.

- *Actual battery capacity*—The rated ampere-hour or reserve capacity of a battery is quite different from the amount of energy you can actually store and retrieve on a daily basis. Deep-cycle or hybrid deep-cycle battery life can be greatly extended if you discharge it to only about half its rated capacity, or 50 percent charged. Frequent deeper discharges will shorten battery life dramatically. In addition, because of the slow rate of charge a battery will accept during the final charging stages (see Charging Characteristics, below), it is likely that you will often charge the battery to only about 90 percent of its rated capacity, or 90 percent charged. In effect you have about 40 percent of the total battery rated capacity at your disposal as usable electrical energy. Solar panels and wind and water generators provide a good method for slowly completing the final stages of charging, making that extra 10 percent of battery capacity available. It is important to bring the battery to a full state of charge periodically.

- *Selecting battery capacity*—Batteries can be purchased in various capacities and voltages, and connected in ways to achieve your desired capacity. You can get individual heavy-duty 2-volt cells and connect them in series to get 6- or 12-volt battery banks. You can connect two 6-volt batteries in series to get a 12-volt battery, or you can buy 12-volt batteries to be used independently or in parallel combinations to get greater capacity. A good battery installation consists of two (or more) battery banks that can be charged and can supply current independently. The combined capacity of the two banks should give you several days' worth of stored energy without discharging below 50 percent of rated capacity. The engine should be able to be started from these two banks, eliminating the need for a separate starting battery.

- *Capacity versus energy to recharge*—Some of the electrical energy generated for charging a battery is lost as heat or wasted on hydrolysis, the breakdown of water into hydrogen and oxygen gas. Hydrolysis in a battery is referred to as battery gassing. It begins when the charge rate exceeds what the battery can naturally absorb. Gassing can be limited by using good charging techniques, but you still lose about 15 to 20 percent of the charging energy. It typically takes 115 to 120 ampere-hours to recharge a 100-ampere-hour battery.

- *Capacity and discharge rate*—The rate of discharge greatly affects the amount of usable electricity you can get from a battery. Even though we can draw an electricity-water analogy, this is one time electricity behaves quite differently. If you adjust the flow rate of water coming from a reservoir, the water comes out faster or slower, but the total amount of water you get is always the same. This is not so for a battery. As a rule, the higher the discharge rate, the lower the total amount of usable energy. Each battery has its own discharge-rate characteristics, and should come from the manufacturer with a chart similar to the one shown in Figure 5-6. This has definite implications when choosing high-draw appliances for your boat.

FIGURE 5-6. **Battery capacity as a function of rate of discharge, using a battery rated to supply 100 ampere-hours at 5 amperes per hour (i.e., a 100-ampere-hour battery). Higher rates of discharge reduce capacity drastically. (From *Boatowner's Mechanical and Electrical Manual* by Nigel Calder. International Marine, 1990)**

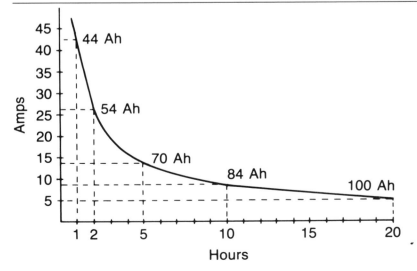

■ *Capacity versus temperature* — Battery temperature will also affect capacity, as it does specific gravity and voltage readings. Since chemical reactions are accelerated at higher temperatures, this is when battery performance will be at its best. While cold severely lessens battery performance, heat most definitely shortens battery life. This is why it is best to keep batteries in a cool, dry location on board.

Capacity depends to some extent on a battery's age and how it has been used. Batteries eventually lose their capacity to store energy, but proper charging methods and routine care will extend the service life. If a battery has been abused, its useful life will be shorter.

SEALED (IMMOBILIZED-ELECTROLYTE) BATTERIES

Up to this point we have been discussing the standard lead-acid batteries most commonly found on boats, ones with the electrolyte in liquid form. Over the past few years a quiet revolution in battery technology has been taking place, one destined to greatly affect the marine market. Batteries that are permanently sealed, with the electrolyte immobilized, are increasing in popularity — and for good reason, as we shall see.

Sealed-Battery Construction

Instead of relying on plate thickness and lead alloys to provide the mechanical strength necessary for deep cycling, sealed batteries utilize the high density of the plate-electrolyte configuration. As a result they can have a greater number of thinner plates of pure lead or lead-calcium. This greatly increases charge acceptance and reduces standby losses. It also makes them a good hybrid deep-cycle battery by providing the large plate surface area required for engine starting and other high-rate discharges. Note: High-quality marine deep-cycle sealed batteries should not be confused with automotive "maintenance free" batteries. There is a great difference in construction, performance, and cost.

Sealed batteries operate at a slight positive pressure. The pressure actually helps to reduce the amount of hydrogen gas produced. If excessive charging rates are used, the pressure is vented through safety relief valves. These valves must not be blocked during installation. Sealed batteries require strong outer cases to handle the internal pressure. As a result they are very rugged and are well equipped to take the rough conditions often encountered on a boat.

There are two basic types of sealed batteries to choose from: absorbed electrolyte and gelled electrolyte.

Absorbed electrolyte.

The GNB Stowaway battery shown in Figure 5-7 is a good example of an absorbed-electrolyte battery. Instead of the electrolyte filling the voids between positive and negative plates, it is absorbed into thick, feltlike glass-fiber mats that are compressed between the plates. During construction, some of the electrolyte is also absorbed by the plates themselves. The mats serve as receptacles for the electrolyte as well as plate separators. Compressing the plates and mats together lowers the internal resistance of the battery and allows for higher discharge rates. The Stowaway 800 is rated as follows: capacity of 100 ampere-hours at the 20-hour rate; a reserve capacity of 160 minutes at a 25-ampere discharge

FIGURE 5-7. **The ProMarine Stowaway absorbed-electrolyte battery. (Courtesy GNB Inc.)**

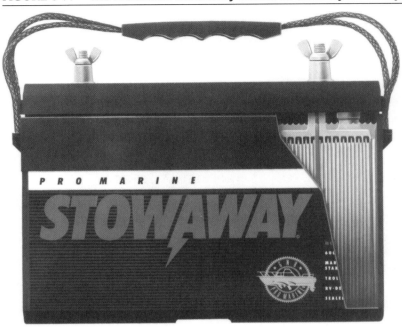

rate; CCA of 600; MCA 800. The capacity is fairly small, making it more suitable for boats with small to medium electrical loads.

Gelled electrolyte. The electrolyte can also be a gel, as in the Sonnenschein Prevailer battery illustrated in Figure 3-1. Due to their construction, these batteries have a low internal resistance for higher charging and discharging rates. Prevailer batteries are exceptional in that they accept higher-than-normal charging current, permitting a very rapid recharge time. They come in a variety of 2- and 12-volt sizes for marine and RV use.

Immobilized-Electrolyte Advantages

Batteries that are completely sealed offer a host of advantages for mariners. They cost a bit more initially, but their use and performance characteristics listed below are probably well worth the investment.

- A sealed battery can be mounted in any position, since there is no liquid to spill, making for more flexible installations. (Pressure release valves must not be blocked by mounting straps.)

- Sealed batteries can be mounted in relatively inaccessible, otherwise wasted spaces, since there is no need for service or for taking hydrometer readings. State of charge is measured with an accurate voltmeter, preferably mounted on your electrical panel.

- There is no contact with acidic electrolyte or fumes. Little or no gassing occurs during normal charging cycles. Hydrometer readings are no longer necessary or possible. Battery acid on hands, clothing, and boat surfaces becomes a thing of the past.

- Sealed batteries have tough outer cases, usually polypropylene, resulting in a reduced risk of cracks and leaks. Their construction also makes them less susceptible to plate damage from vibration.

- There is no terminal corrosion from the acidic mists that escape from nonsealed batteries. Corrosion at the battery terminal can provide pathways for electricity to escape, reducing battery capacity. The amount of hydrogen gas that escapes is greatly reduced. Battery compartments should still be well vented for safety, however.

- Because of the low internal resistance and the high-quality plate materials, higher rates of charge and discharge are possible. The Prevailer battery seems to be exceptional in this regard. Faster charge rates mean potentially less engine running time and fuel consumed.

- The tendency for individual battery cells to lose charge with respect to the others is greatly reduced in a sealed battery, and this means that a periodic equalizing charge (see Charging Characteristics, below) is not necessary.

Are there any disadvantages to sealed batteries? Yes, a few. An accurate voltmeter must be used for state-of-charge readings. This is more important for boats with manually adjusted, fast-charge controllers for the alternator. The initial battery cost is higher, but if you use catalyst battery caps on good-quality liquid-electrolyte batteries, the long-term difference in cost is small. The difference becomes even less when you consider that the total charging time required will undoubtedly be less. Without hydrometer readings for each cell, you can't tell if there is a bad one. This has to be weighed, however, against the fact that bad or weak cells are less likely to occur.

Indications are that more battery manufacturers will switch to sealed construction for the marine market. In the meantime, there are many good deep-cycle liquid-electrolyte batteries to choose from, and they will continue to serve boaters well.

CHARGING CHARACTERISTICS

We have discussed how the electricity-water analogy loses its accuracy for a discharging battery. This is also true when considering a battery being recharged. Compared with a water reservoir filling up, the ability of a battery to accept and store charging current is complex.

Battery charging becomes much more efficient and battery life is extended through knowledge of battery charging characteristics. When we speak of battery capacity in this section, we are referring to capacity in ampere-hours at the 20-hour rate.

Initial Charging

Simply put, deep-cycle lead-acid batteries in a discharged state can initially accept a large charging current. For efficient charging, current should be limited to approximately 40 percent of a battery's rated ampere-hour capacity. With a 100-ampere-hour battery, begin charging with around 40 amperes. This holds true until the battery reaches a 50 percent state of charge. At this point the current should be dropped to about 25 percent of rated capacity (25 amperes) to avoid excessive gassing. Gassing represents wasted energy, and should be avoided during the initial charging cycles. When a battery approaches 85 to 90 percent of full charge, current should be reduced even further, to about 5 to 10 percent of rated capacity (5 to 10 amperes). To get the final 10 percent of full charge, current must be limited even further, to 4 to 5 percent of rated capacity. Since this can take a long time, we try to avoid (when possible) running the engine to achieve the last 10 percent of battery capacity. For regular charging, it is better just to use the 40 percent of battery capacity between 50 percent and 90 percent charged, or to utilize solar, wind, and water generators to provide extended low-current charging.

Float Charging

A marine battery that has reached full charge can be floated at a constant voltage of around 13.2 volts. During this period, the battery is accepting minimal current, hopefully just enough to replace self-discharge losses. This resembles what happens to your car battery after the initial starting current has been replaced, only then the constant voltage is about 13.8 volts, high enough for some gassing to take place. Immobilized-electrolyte batteries generally have a lower self-discharge rate and can have a lower float voltage. Anytime an appliance is turned on, it lowers battery voltage, temporarily increasing the amount of current the battery will accept.

Equalization Charging

Liquid-electrolyte batteries require a periodic overcharge to equalize the specific gravity of the individual cells. During equalization charging, the current should be held constant at about 3 to 4 percent of battery rated capacity, and the battery voltage should be allowed to rise. All cells should begin gassing freely. Check specific gravity readings, and monitor battery temperature every half hour or so. Electrolyte temperature should not go over 100 degrees Fahrenheit, and equalization charging should not go longer than 3 or 4 hours. Solar panels, with the voltage regulator disconnected, provide an easy, safe means of equalization charging.

Charge Controllers

Since long battery life is a primary goal, we don't really want our deep-cycle batteries to be discharged by more than 50 percent on a regular basis. Normally, therefore, we begin charging with about 25 percent of the battery's rated capacity. For a 400 ampere-hour battery bank, this would be around 100 amperes. It becomes clear that we probably should use an alternator with an actual output of around 25 percent of battery-bank capacity. The total battery capacity selected is determined by an estimate of the amount of electricity you expect to consume and how long you want to go before recharging. It should be noted that a larger-capacity battery bank gives you more time before recharge is necessary, and will initially accept a higher charging current for a faster recharge time.

While proper charging techniques are good to know, it is the charge controllers (or voltage regulators) that ultimately determine the way in which you charge your batteries. It is important that you select not only the right generator and battery combination, but also the best type of charge controller for your needs.

Charging cycles vary depending on the type of generator in use. Solar panels operate at a constant voltage, with relatively low current levels, for long periods during the day. It is the difference between solar-panel voltage and battery voltage that provides the push necessary to create current flow. As battery voltage rises, current levels start to fall off, but not by much, since solar panel operating voltage is typically 16 to 17 volts. Simple charge controllers for solar systems disconnect the solar-panel output at a preset battery voltage, then reconnect it when the voltage falls below another preset level. More sophisticated controllers taper the charge as the battery approaches a full charge, then float the battery to maintain maximum state of charge. Wind and water generators operate at variable voltage with small to medium current levels, depending on their size and the battery state of charge, and can operate 24 hours a day. Wind and water charge controllers vary from simple to sophisticated, as with solar controllers. If solar-, wind-, and/or water-generator output matches daily electrical consumption, your battery will rarely be deeply discharged.

On the other hand, a standard automobile voltage regulator installed with the main engine alternator applies what is called constant voltage charging. That is, it limits the charging voltage to around 13.8 volts, a safe limit for long charging periods. The amount of current that flows is dependent on the difference between battery voltage and charging voltage. If the battery is 50 percent discharged, then initial battery voltage will be about 12.2 volts, and initial charging current will be relatively high. During charging, battery voltage rises. (Battery voltage measured during charging is higher than actual voltage measured when the battery has been "rested.") The difference between the battery voltage and charging voltage lessens, making the charging current fall off rapidly. This is fine for an automobile but is usually unacceptable for a boat. Some boaters make the mistake of replacing their existing alternator with a high-output alternator equipped with a standard voltage regulator. The output will certainly increase during initial charging, but the voltage regulator still limits the alternator's output well below its potential. Your alternator supplier should be able to recommend the proper type of controller for your system.

This brings us to manual and automatic versions of "performance" charge controllers for alternators. They are intended for systems in which rapid, complete battery charging is needed. Manual controllers like the AutoMAC from Weems and Plath allow you to temporarily bypass the standard voltage regulator and select desired charging-current levels. Automatic charge controllers include the AutoCHARGE and Balmar's ABC control, which simply fool the alternator into producing high charging current for a given time period, or until a preset battery voltage is reached. When the time is up or when the preset voltage is attained, they allow the standard voltage regulator to resume operation. The Quad-Cycle Regulator/Monitor by Cruising Equipment Company and the 3-Step Deep Cycle regulator by Ample Power Company are two examples of fully automatic, high-performance charge controllers that take the place of standard voltage regulators. They allow rapid, complete initial charging to take place, then maintain batteries at proper float levels. For systems with fairly small battery capacity, it might be better to add a performance charge controller before switching to a high-output alternator. Remember that it is advisable to keep actual alternator output to around 25 percent of battery capacity when regularly discharging to the 50 percent level. Performance charge controllers are discussed in detail in Chapter 6.

BATTERY MAINTENANCE AND SAFETY

Batteries represent a large portion of your total energy system cost, and they should be properly utilized and maintained to ensure long life. Battery protection, maintenance, and safety are interrelated. Listed below are some simple guidelines to follow.

- One of the best things you can do for your deep-cycle batteries is to set up a charging routine that keeps them from discharging more than 50 percent. Learn where the 50-percent state-of-charge level appears on your voltmeter, and check it regularly.

- As an added protection you can get a low-battery alarm or load-disconnect switch that has an adjustable voltage set point. By adjusting the voltage set point, you determine the battery state of charge that trips the alarm or disconnect switch. This either alerts you to a low state of charge so you can shut off the loads or begin charging, or automatically disconnects the electrical loads to keep your batteries from going below the voltage set point. Battery voltage drops temporarily when a load is being drawn. Low-voltage alarms must take this into account or they will trip prematurely. Accurate readings with a voltmeter can only be taken on a "rested" battery.

- If you have liquid-electrolyte batteries, you should seriously consider catalyst battery caps. When using proper charging techniques in accordance with the instructions from the cap supplier, battery life will be extended and watering maintenance will be greatly reduced. Self-discharge rates will also be lower, since acid mist from venting that collects on the battery tops—which causes corrosion and a pathway for electricity to escape—is greatly reduced.

- Keep your batteries cool and dry. Don't allow them to overheat from overcharging or being kept in a hot, confined space, as this will greatly reduce battery life.

- Regularly check battery electrolyte level (liquid electrolyte only) and add distilled water if necessary. Keep the tops of liquid-electrolyte batteries clean and free of corrosion.

- Bring your batteries to a complete, full state of charge periodically, but don't overcharge them unnecessarily. This wastes energy and shortens battery life.

- Install batteries in a secure location, where there is no chance for them to knock about. Strap them down tightly without covering the fill/vent caps or safety relief vents.

- Provide good ventilation in a battery locker, even for sealed, immobilized-electrolyte batteries. The venting of hydrogen and oxygen gas can cause a serious explosion if left to accumulate in a confined space.

- Always keep in mind which pole of the battery is positive and which is negative. The positive pole usually has a red wire and "+" or "POS" printed next to it. The negative pole usually has a black wire and "−" or "NEG" next to it.

- Never allow current to flow from the positive terminal to the negative terminal, such as by touching positive and negative wires together or by letting a metal tool come in contact with both terminals at once. Likewise never connect an ammeter across the battery terminals!

- The voltage on a boat (usually 12 volts DC) is much lower than the voltage in a house (110 or 220 volts AC). You may touch one terminal at a time without fear of getting a shock. Your body is not a particularly good conductor but can become one in certain circumstances, such as when your skin is wet. Make sure you are not standing in water when working on a battery. It's also a good idea to insulate your hands with rubber gloves and use tools with rubber-coated handles.

- The main switch should be turned off before attempting service of electrical circuits.

- The electrolyte in batteries is dilute sulfuric acid and should not come in contact with eyes, skin, clothing, cockpit cushions, and so forth. If electrolyte gets on your skin, immediately flush the affected area with water, apply a solution of baking soda mixed with water, and cover with a dry gauze bandage. Do not apply petroleum jelly. For acid contact with the eye, splash the eye with water for 5 minutes (several changes of water in an eye cup is even better), apply two drops of castor oil to the eye, and cover with compresses dipped in a solution of one teaspoon of salt in a glass of fresh water (not seawater!). Get medical help.

6

Engine-driven Alternators

==

The most common method of generating electricity on board a boat is the standard marine alternator. It is a compact, reliable piece of gear that comes as standard equipment on most marine inboard engines and many outboard engines. Producing electricity from a boat's engine with an alternator when motoring is a good example of *cogeneration,* or the secondary use of a single power source. One engine is simultaneously producing boat movement and electricity. Cogeneration usually increases system efficiency. Adding to the efficiency is the fact that alternator output approaches its rated capacity when engine speeds are higher during motoring, provided that the batteries are sufficiently discharged. Since we rarely take full advantage of the available horsepower of the engine, it makes perfect sense to use a small part of that power to charge the batteries when under way.

Running an engine to operate a standard marine alternator for the sole purpose of charging batteries, however, is not very efficient and in the long run can lead to problems. Using an engine with high horsepower to operate a device with a relatively low power output is obviously inefficient. A typical example of this is a sailboat with a 25-horsepower auxiliary engine driving an alternator rated at 50 amperes, or less than 1 horsepower. This inefficiency is compounded by the fact that a standard marine alternator's output at the lower engine speeds available when just charging batteries is usually much less than its rated capacity, and by the fact that the output from a standard marine alternator is controlled by an automotive-type voltage regulator. As batteries are charged, alternator output falls off dramatically. This protects the batteries during extended periods of engine running, but makes it a long, tedious task to achieve a complete charge. Boaters naturally tend to quit charging when the alternator output falls off, keeping the batteries chronically undercharged. As a result, battery life and available battery capacity are greatly reduced. In reality, because of low engine speeds and voltage regulation, a great deal of charging is done by high-horsepower engines to produce less than 10 amperes of current, or less than $1/4$ horsepower! And remember that marine engines are not intended to run at or near idle speeds, with only the small load of the alternator, for long periods. Doing so increases wear and is likely to shorten engine life.

It becomes clear that the key to successful use of a standard marine alternator and its accompanying voltage regulator is to understand its capabilities and limitations. Take full advantage of its output when it is appropriate, then supplement it if necessary with other generators. For those boaters using the auxiliary engine for long-term battery charging, and trying to get maximum electrical energy output with minimal engine running time, purpose-designed alternators and regulators are available and are discussed later in this chapter.

STANDARD MARINE ALTERNATORS

The alternator that is supplied with most marine engines is similar to those found in automobiles. One of the few differences between the two is that alternators on boats are usually marine certified—that is, they have a protective housing that minimizes the risk of sparks that could ignite gasoline fumes. While it is tempting to use less-expensive automotive alternators on boats with diesel engines, replacements should be marine certified nevertheless, since gasoline may be brought on board to use in portable generators, dinghy engines, and other equipment, or propane gas may be in use.

As is the case with automotive alternators, standard marine units are mass-produced and consequently can be included on marine engines for a modest cost (although the replacement value through a marine parts retailer is usually not so modest). The same holds true for the standard voltage regulator that comes with the alternator. These regulators were developed by the automotive industry, and while they do a fine job on cars, they are simply not right to efficiently charge deep-cycle batteries. Only recently have other methods of alternator control for boats and recreational vehicles become available.

FIGURE 6-1.　**Alternator. (From *Boatowner's Mechanical and Electrical Manual* by Nigel Calder. International Marine, 1990)**

Alternator Output Current—AC or DC?

As the name implies, an alternator initially produces alternating current (AC), while its predecessor, the DC generator, produces the direct current (DC) suitable for charging lead-acid batteries. The initial output from an alternator must be converted to direct current before it can be useful in a car or on a boat. While it was known that alternators could supply more power than generators, with less wear on electrical contacts, it wasn't until the advent of small, integrated silicon diodes to internally "rectify" AC into DC that alternators came into widespread use. This was about the same time that silicon was also being put to use to manufacture photovoltaic solar cells and computer chips. For all practical purposes these diodes enable alternators to provide DC output.

Alternator Theory

The workings of an alternator seem rather mysterious at first glance, but alternators are in fact simple pieces of equipment with relatively few components. Alternator and generator operating theory is based on the principle of *electromagnetic induction,* whereby a magnetic field rotating beside a coil of wire, or a coil of wire rotating within a magnetic field, causes current to flow in the wire. The important factor is that in both cases a magnetic field changes rapidly with respect to a conductive wire, inducing an "electromagnetic" current. This same principle is used in many different types of generating equipment and electric motors.

In a permanent-magnet DC generator, such as the type commonly used for wind and water energy systems, the magnetic field is created by curved ceramic "permanent magnets" that are epoxied to the inside of the generator housing. A coil of wire is wrapped around the center shaft, and as the shaft rotates, current flows along the wire. It is simple and effective, but not perfect. A disadvantage of this arrangement is that the potentially high output current must be transferred from the rotating wire to the stationary housing by way of a large "commutator" (a segmented ring comprised of copper bars) and "brushes," both subject to a fair amount of wear during normal operation.

Commutators and brushes are used for several purposes in DC generators and alternators, as well as in pole mounts for wind-seeking generators (see Figure 6-2), where the commutators take the form of slip rings. They make it possible to complete a circuit between two electrical contact points when one contact point is rotating and the other is not. The brushes remain in a fixed position and are made of soft material so as not to score the commutator or slip rings. They are held firmly against the commutator by coiled springs. As long as there is good contact between rings and brushes, full current will flow. If the brushes become worn, or sit unevenly on the commutator, they must be replaced.

Inside an alternator, the operation is the reverse of a DC generator. It is the magnetic field that rotates on the center shaft while the wire windings that carry output current remain stationary around the inside of the alternator casing. This arrangement produces alternating current, hence the need for rectifying diodes. Since the heavy output wire remains fixed, no slip rings and brushes are needed to transfer the output current to the end housing where the wire connections are made. Permanent magnets are not used in alternators for car and boat engines, although they are in a few marine wind and water energy system alternators. This is because controlling the output current is an essential part of alternator operation, and control

FIGURE 6-2. **Schematic section through a permanent-magnet generator. There are many windings of wire on the armature, although only one is shown.**

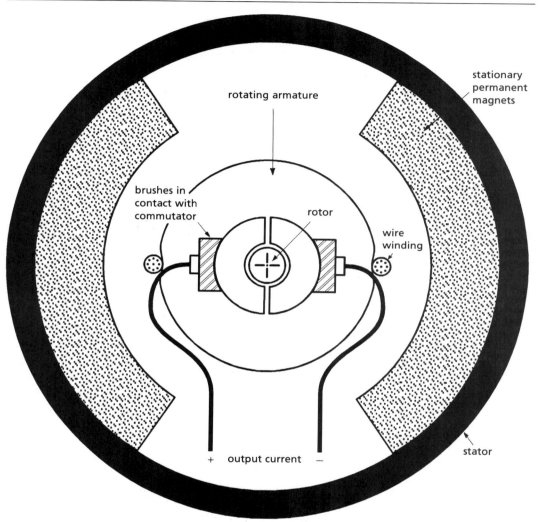

becomes difficult with permanent magnets when current levels are high. There must be an effective method of increasing or decreasing alternator output according to battery state of charge, and this type of control is available when using an "electromagnet."

Electromagnets are temporary magnets created by the flow of a small amount of electrical current. Just as changes in a magnetic field near a wire conductor cause current to flow in the wire, current flowing near a piece of iron can temporarily turn the iron into a magnet. The strength of the magnetic field thus created is proportional to the strength of the current. Alternators take advantage of this phenomenon by providing a small amount of "field cur-

FIGURE 6-3.   **Close-up view of the commutator and brushes on a permanent-magnet generator.**

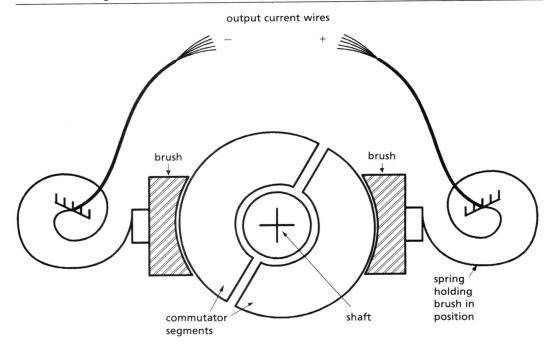

rent" or "control current" to light-gauge wire wound onto the center shaft. Pieces of iron suspended around these wire windings become magnetized (see Figure 6-4). The control windings and the suspended iron are the electromagnet. By varying the control current, and thereby the strength of the magnetic field, the output current is regulated. Small sets of slip rings and brushes are used in alternators, but only for the control current.

Alternator Construction and Operation

With a little theory behind us, we can now take a close look at how an alternator is put together and how it runs.

Construction.   A typical standard marine alternator has the following components:
- *Center shaft*—This is an approximately 5/8-inch-diameter round steel shaft supported by bearings in the housings on either end of the alternator. Attached to the shaft ahead of the front housing are the pulley and fan blades, with the balance of the rotor assembly in the middle.

FIGURE 6-4. **Alternator construction. The labeled parts are: (1) multifingered rotor with field winding inside; (2) slip rings on rotor shaft; (3), (4) rotor shaft bearings; (5), (6) end housings; (7) stator housing; (8) stator windings; (9) stator laminations (serving as core for stator windings); (10) brushes (which contact slip rings when unit is assembled). (From *Boatowner's Mechanical and Electrical Manual* by Nigel Calder. International Marine, 1990)**

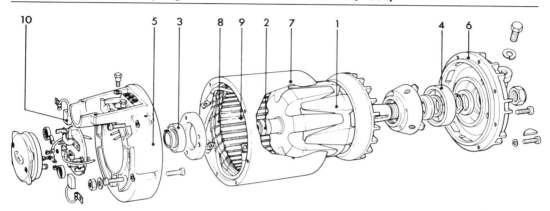

- *Control windings* — These consist of many turns of light-gauge wire around the center shaft. The wire is coated with lacquer, which provides insulation between adjacent windings. Control current (usually around 4 amperes DC maximum for standard marine alternators, depending upon unit output rating) is fed to the spinning control windings via brushes and slip rings. Current levels are controlled by the voltage regulator. Control current is also known as *field control current,* since it controls the magnetic field.

- *Rotor assembly* — The rotor assembly refers to all the internal parts that rotate: the center shaft; the electromagnet, which consists of the control windings and the pieces of iron that become magnetized; and the slip rings.

- *Stator assembly* — This is the stationary series of windings surrounding the rotor, made up of many laminations of sheet iron onto which the output (or generating) wire coils are wound. The output wire is much heavier than that used for the control windings, since it must carry the full current generated.

- *Bearings* — There is one bearing forward and one aft in the alternator end housings, fitted to the center shaft.

- *End housings* — The end housings are usually made of aluminum. They protect the internal parts and provide a place for the bearings to rest, a convenient place to put support brackets for mounting the alternator, and a place to make electrical connections in the rear of the alternator.

■ *Pulley and fan blades*—Forward of the front end housing, fastened to the center shaft, are the pulley(s) and fan blades. The pulley allows use of a standard V-section rubber belt for transferring power from a similar pulley on the main shaft of the engine. Sometimes double pulley and belt setups are used on alternators with higher output to help transfer the load. The fan blades are located just behind the pulley. As the shaft spins they force air through the alternator to keep it from overheating.

■ *Rectifying diodes*—Small diodes that rectify the alternating current into direct current are located inside the rear end housing.

■ *Voltage regulator*—The voltage regulator can be external, either attached to the alternator end housing or a completely separate component, or internal and located inside the alternator end housing.

Power take-off operation.   As soon as the auxiliary engine is started, its main shaft turns, and along with it the alternator take-off pulley. The rubber V-belt transfers power to the pulley on the alternator, which turns the alternator center shaft. The amount of power needed to turn the alternator is a function of how much electricity the unit is producing. The more current being generated, the more power required to turn the alternator. The alternator produces maximum electrical output at high engine RPMs (revolutions per minute) with the batteries discharged, and this is when the most power is taken from the main engine. It produces the least electrical output at low engine RPMs with fully charged batteries, and at this time power required from the engine is also the least. Some amount of power is also lost during energy conversion in the belt(s) and pulley(s), and inside the alternator in the form of heat.

Control current operation.   With the alternator rotor spinning, field control current is transferred to the brushes, from there to the rotating slip rings, then on to the control windings. Some special types of alternators have control windings that do not rotate, thereby eliminating the need for slip rings and brushes. As current reaches the control windings, it begins to set up a magnetic field. The control current can come from the battery through an external relay, or from the output of the alternator itself. In the latter case, since the alternator must be producing power in order for some of it to be used as control current, a small amount of "excitation" current must first come from the battery. Control current is regulated by the voltage regulator.

Voltage regulator operation.   The voltage regulator adjusts the control current according to the battery voltage it senses. It thus indirectly controls alternator output current. Battery voltage drops after the heavy current draw from the starter, so the alternator output directly after starting the engine is high, as the small amount of starting current is replaced. If the battery is only partially discharged, the voltage will soon rise to the regulator set point of 13.8 to 14.0 volts.

This is what is known as *charging voltage,* a higher value than *rested voltage,* or readings taken after the battery has been without charging current for a while. Rested voltage is the actual battery voltage, indicative of state of charge. As more current flows into the battery, the difference between charging voltage and actual battery voltage becomes less. Less voltage difference means less current will flow as the battery becomes charged. At this time the regulator allows only enough control current to maintain the set-point voltage, yielding an output current that is usually a small fraction of alternator capacity. This is why recharging a deep-cycle battery using standard voltage regulation can be such a long process. On the other hand, a full battery has a rested voltage of around 12.8 volts, so prolonged engine running using a standard voltage regulator has the potential to overcharge a battery mildly, making it necessary to add water to the cells frequently, as you must with nonsealed batteries in a car. (This is not a problem with sealed batteries.) In reality, a standard voltage regulator is a compromise between undercharging and overcharging a battery.

Output current operation. When control current is fed to the control windings, an electromagnetic field is created. Two iron disks are attached to the center shaft, each with star-shaped tips bent toward each other and suspended above the control windings (see Figure 6-4). One disk develops north magnetic poles at its outer tips, and the other south magnetic poles, determined by the direction of control current flow. The iron stator also has tips that are matched with, and extend toward, the magnetic poles. Only a small gap separates the two. The stator extensions are shaped so that the output wire windings are held captive.

Since the stator core is made up of iron laminations, the magnetic field extends to it as well. The lacquered output wire, instead of being one individual coil, is actually wound around the stator core extensions as three separate coils. These three output coils are offset from each other in a pattern that produces what is known as *three-phase alternating current.* Three-phase current is produced so that there are three times as many voltage peaks per revolution of the rotor. When this three-phase AC output is rectified into DC, it closely resembles pure DC. Alternator output is shown in Figure 6-5 as the line of highest voltage from the three output coils. Positive DC output current goes to an electrical connection at the rear of the alternator, and from there to the batteries.

Alternator Ratings and Capacity

Energy equipment is generally rated according to the power, in watts, it is capable of producing or consuming. Since batteries are used for energy storage, they deviate slightly from this convention by being rated in ampere-hours of storage capacity. Ampere-hours are a function of current and time, unlike watt-hours, which are a function of power and time, a more accurate designation of energy. Likewise, alternators tend to be rated in amperes, or instantaneous current output, instead of watts, which would be a true indication of instantaneous power.

Output ratings in amperes for standard auto and marine alternators are given by the

FIGURE 6-5.   **Three-phase alternator output.**

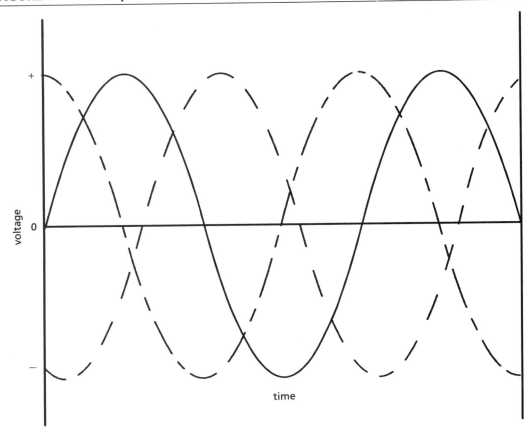

Society of Automotive Engineers (SAE). These SAE ratings are intended for ambient temperature; they do not take into account the fact that alternator temperature climbs rapidly soon after start-up because of the energy lost as heat. Actual output at elevated temperatures is less, this being one of the reasons that your alternator may seldom produce at its rated capacity. Because of the high temperatures generated at high RPMs, and the relatively loose mechanical tolerances of a mass-produced unit, standard marine alternators should not be run for long at more than about two-thirds their rated capacity. A standard voltage regulator usually keeps output low, protecting the alternator but lowering charging efficiency as well. The design and placement of the fan blades play a critical role in keeping the alternator from self-destructing during prolonged operation at high speeds.

SAE ratings also assume appropriately high alternator shaft speed. Alternator output is proportional to the engine RPMs. As the engine speed increases, so does the induction of current, and therefore alternator output, up to its rated capacity. Since most auxiliary engines operate at fairly low RPM ranges, alternators are geared to turn two to three times as fast as the main shaft on the engine. This is accomplished by making the alternator pulley two to three times smaller in diameter than the engine main shaft pulley, the same principle employed on bicycles between front and rear sets of gears. For one revolution of the main shaft, the alternator shaft rotates two to three times. This means that if the main shaft is turning at 2,000 RPM, the alternator is probably turning at 4,000 to 6,000 RPM. The extreme upper limit for most alternators is around 10,000 RPM, and pulley sizes should be selected so as not to exceed this with the engine running at highest speed. The concept of rating the power of equipment according to RPM, up to a theoretical maximum, is also employed when rating engines. You have probably noticed that the power of your main engine is rated in horsepower at a specific engine speed.

It should now be clear that under normal conditions alternator output is governed by a variety of factors, including the following:

1. The rating of the unit, or its upper output limit under normal operating conditions. This depends on the design and construction of the alternator.

2. The actual RPMs of the alternator shaft, which determine the strength of electromagnetic induction between the rotor and stator. The higher the RPMs, the higher the output current up to its rated output.

3. The operating temperature of the unit. Higher temperatures reduce the effectiveness of electromagnetic induction, lessening alternator output.

4. The regulator type and settings. If the regulator limits output strictly on battery voltage readings, then as soon as the set-point voltage is reached, output will be reduced to levels that just maintain that voltage.

5. The battery state of charge affects output, since it determines when the regulator voltage set point is reached. Deeply discharged batteries take longer to reach this voltage, particularly if you are using current from the batteries at the same time you are charging.

6. Battery capacity. A larger battery takes longer to recharge, absorbing greater alternator output for a longer time.

HIGH-OUTPUT MARINE ALTERNATORS

As noted in Chapter 2, high-output alternators are not simply standard alternators with high output ratings. They are a separate breed that can be thought of as custom, handmade units as opposed to mass-produced units. If you are in the market for a replacement alternator for your boat's auxiliary engine, these units are well worth considering. The difference in cost between a high-output alternator and a standard marine type is surprisingly small, and in most cases you will get a good return on your investment.

It is hard to imagine why marine engine manufacturers aren't giving boaters the option of a high-output alternator, so great are the benefits over standard units. Some boatbuilders do incorporate high-output units into their specifications, but the boat owner almost certainly absorbs the cost of the standard alternator that came with the engine in the first place. If you do replace a standard alternator in good condition, keep it as a spare. If you must replace a faulty standard alternator, by all means investigate replacing it with a high-output unit. In both cases the alternator will perform better with a fast-charge control.

This is not to say that all boaters should trade in their standard alternator for the high-output variety. Not everyone needs the extra capacity of a high-output unit. You may choose to supply your energy needs with other equipment, and the cost may not be justified if you use the auxiliary engine for battery charging infrequently. If your battery capacity is small and yet satisfies your needs, a high-output unit is probably overkill. Keep in mind that battery capacity in ampere-hours should be about four times the actual (hot-rated) output of your alternator at typical charging RPMs. A better solution might be to get a fast-charge alternator control for your existing smaller-capacity unit. For more detailed information on sizing and selecting equipment, see Chapter 14.

Differences in Construction

The theory and basic operation of high-output alternators is similar to that for standard units, but the construction is much different. The internal mechanical tolerances of high-output units, including the gap between rotor and stator, are much tighter. Tighter mechanical tolerances mean less electromagnetic radiation and vibration, and less heat produced at high speeds. The output current wire is heavier and is usually hand-wound for a greater degree of accuracy. Often copper brushes replace carbon brushes for better electrical contact and better wear. The internal rectifying diodes are heavier and more reliable. The fan blade and air flow design is improved for better cooling characteristics. A typical high-output alternator is shown in Figure 6-6.

FIGURE 6-6.   **High-output alternator. (Courtesy Cruising Equipment Co.)**

Differences in Operation

As a result of their design and construction improvements, high-output alternators are typically given an additional SAE rating designated as "kkk." This rating means they can meet their specified output with an internal temperature of 200 degrees Fahrenheit, higher than usually achieved under normal operating conditions. Alternators rated kkk are known as "hot-rated" and are specified for use in police and emergency vehicles. They are capable of higher sustained output current without harm, and are potentially more reliable than standard units.

Another advantage of high-output alternators is that they can usually produce more power at lower RPMs. This is especially important when charging batteries at relatively low engine speeds. Not all high-output alternators perform alike, and it is advisable to ask your marine energy system supplier to show you a graph plotting output in amperes versus RPMs for the units they sell.

An additional benefit is that your auxiliary engine will appreciate the added load of a high-output alternator with appropriate charge controller (see Fast-Charge Controls below) when operating solely to charge batteries. It is much more beneficial to run the engine under load for a shorter time than under little or no load for long periods.

High-output alternators typically come with higher voltage-regulator set points for faster and more complete charging. Many units have adjustable set points for an owner-customized charging routine. Figure 6-7 illustrates the relationship of power, efficiency, output current, and rotor RPMs for a typical high-output alternator.

Types of Units Available

A number of marine energy system suppliers have their own brand of high-output alternators, although in many cases they are Lestek or Powerline alternators with a different label. These companies are leaders in manufacturing high-performance, high-output marine alternators.

High-output alternators are available with current ratings from 80 to over 190 (SAE cold-rated) amperes and come with either 24-volt or conventional 12-volt output. Some units have "dual output" capability, which means they have internal isolating diodes that allow you to charge two batteries at once while keeping them electrically isolated from each other. This serves the same function as a battery isolator sold as a separate component.

Most high-output alternators come with an external regulator, making it a simple task to incorporate a fast-charge alternator control. External regulators can be mounted away from the heat of the alternator and engine.

Many high-output alternators have a "small case" size (also called *small frame*), making them relatively easy to use as replacements for standard marine units with much lower ratings. You may need to modify your mounting bracket to ensure that the new alternator pulley or set of pulleys lines up perfectly with the pulley(s) on the engine main shaft. Your equipment supplier will be able to help you determine what is needed to replace existing units, and may even sell a conversion bracket for certain engines. Alternators with especially high ratings will probably have a larger case and weigh a bit more. Make certain you can mount a large unit in the space available on your engine before purchasing one. Again, even if space is available, the mounting brackets may have to be modified so that the pulleys line up perfectly.

FIGURE 6-7.   **Alternator performance curve. (Courtesy Lestek Manufacturing, Inc.)**

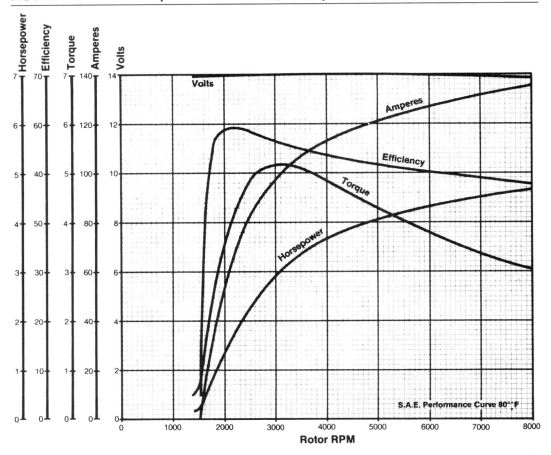

High-output units may also come with a double set of pulleys for use with two V-belts, thus dividing the load and providing built-in security in the event that one belt breaks. In this case you will have to add another main-shaft pulley in line with the existing one.

A sampling of high-output alternators and their characteristics appears in Figure 6-8.

Recommended Control

Even though a high-output alternator is vastly superior to standard marine units, it will still fall short for charging deep-cycle batteries if it is hampered by a standard voltage regulator. The regulator that comes with high-output units is usually adjustable so you can increase charging performance. The fast-charge, or "performance charging," controls described in the next section work well both for standard and high-output alternators.

FIGURE 6-8.   **Comparison chart for high-output alternators.**

Model	Rating*	Voltage	Output	Case size	Regulator	Weight
Ample Power						
105	105 Amps (hot)	12V DC	single	small	external	14 lbs.
130	130 Amps (hot)	12V DC	single	small	external	14 lbs.
160	160 Amps (hot)	12V DC	single	large	external	20 lbs.

Ample Power also offers 24V DC models. These models are also carried by Jack Rabbit Marine and other energy system suppliers.

Model	Rating*	Voltage	Output	Case size	Regulator	Weight
Balmar Marine						
120	120 Amps (cold)	12V DC	single	small	internal	14 lbs.
140	140 Amps (cold)	12V DC	single	small	external	14 lbs.
160	160 Amps (cold)	12V DC	dual	large	external	20 lbs.
190	190 Amps (cold)	12V DC	dual	large	external	20 lbs.

Balmar has other models available, all of them offered by numerous marine energy system suppliers.

Model	Rating*	Voltage	Output	Case size	Regulator	Weight
Cruising Equipment						
105	105 Amps (hot)	12V DC	single	small	external	14 lbs.
130	130 Amps (hot)	12V DC	single	large	external	20 lbs.
165	165 Amps (hot)	12V DC	single	large	external	20 lbs.

Cruising Equipment alternators carry the trade name Silver Bullet. They are carried by Everfair Enterprises and other marine energy system suppliers.

Model	Rating*	Voltage	Output	Case size	Regulator	Weight
Hamilton Ferris						
120	120 Amps (cold)	12V DC	single	small	internal	14 lbs.
140	140 Amps (cold)	12V DC	single	small	external	14 lbs.
160	160 Amps (cold)	12V DC	dual	large	external	20 lbs.
190	190 Amps (cold)	12V DC	dual	large	external	20 lbs.

Hamilton Ferris has other models available, all of them offered by numerous marine energy system suppliers.

*Output from cold-rated alternators will decrease approximately 15% when hot.

FAST-CHARGE ALTERNATOR CONTROLS

Regardless of whether you have a standard marine or high-output alternator, it can reach its full potential only when coupled with a fast-charge, or "performance charging," alternator control. These controls either bypass or completely replace the standard voltage regulator. They are capable of allowing an alternator to supply current according to a battery's natural acceptance characteristics, instead of simply limiting current based on a single voltage set point.

There are four basic types of fast-charge controls for the marine market: the Balmar ABC control, which permits you to manually boost the set point of the voltage regulator temporarily for a more complete charge, then automatically returns regulator operation to normal; the Weems and Plath AutoMAC, a manually operated alternator control that allows you to temporarily bypass the standard voltage regulator and select the amount of charging current; the Weems and Plath AutoCHARGE, a basic automatic control that allows high charging current to be maintained up to a preset battery voltage, then returns output control to the standard voltage regulator; and alternator controls that are completely automatic and closely match alternator output to battery acceptance levels for all stages of charging, such as Ample Power's 3-Step Deep-Cycle Regulator and Cruising Equipment's Quad-Cycle Regulator/Monitor. Each of these is described in detail below.

The intent here is to review the fast-charge alternator controls for the marine market available at the time of publication. In time these controls may be modified, or other similar controls may be introduced, but there will undoubtedly remain two basic fast-charge options, manual and automatic. There are advantages and disadvantages to each. The manual type must be owner-adjusted for each charging cycle, but this also means it can be adjusted for a wide range of charging situations. A simple, automatic control such as the AutoCHARGE doesn't have the flexibility of a manual unit or charge as effectively as other automatic controls, but is simple to hook up and the least expensive to purchase. The 3-Step Regulator doesn't have a conditioning cycle or include monitoring functions, but you can get compatible system monitors from Ample Power and the control is moderately priced. The Quad-Cycle conditions batteries and monitors many electrical functions but is a more expensive unit. You must decide which unit meets your needs. In any event, a good fast-charge control is the first step in improving your alternator's performance.

The ABC Alternator Control

Balmar recently developed the ABC alternator control as a simple fast-charge control for use with any Balmar alternator (see Figure 6-8). It has two inherent control features. The first is an "engine saver" circuit that delays engaging the alternator for approximately 90 seconds after engine start-up. This eliminates that initial load of a high-output alternator on the engine until it has a chance to warm up. The second is a timer circuit that increases the voltage regulator charging set point between 0.8 and 1.0 volt, allowing full alternator output for about 15 minutes. At the end of this time, the voltage regulator resumes normal operation. The boost cycle comes on anytime the engine is started (after the engine-saver circuit is complete), and you can boost the set point anytime for one 15-minute cycle by a remote control.

The ABC (alternator boost control) has two components, the actual control circuitry, which can be located in the engine compartment, and a remote panel with activator switch, which can go in any convenient location. Repeated use of the ABC could conceivably overcharge your batteries, so some monitoring of battery state of charge is recommended.

AutoMAC Alternator Control

This unit was originally manufactured and marketed by Spa Creek Instruments as just the M.A.C., and was truly a *manual* alternator control. It was a simple device that allowed the strength of alternator field current to be owner-varied by means of a rheostat, or variable resistor. The M.A.C. has been in service for many years, yet its simplicity was also a bit of a drawback. Since the operator had total control over charging current levels without any automatic cutoff, a high degree of vigilance was required. Inattentive operators often found themselves with overcharged, or even destroyed, batteries.

The AutoMAC is a refined version of this earlier model, with some built-in safety features and an ammeter (displaying alternator output) included as standard equipment. It has been found that there is no reason to disconnect the existing voltage regulator—as was previously thought—for the AutoMAC to perform correctly. The voltage regulator can remain connected and operate in parallel with, or as a backup to, the AutoMAC. This unit is still only recommended for boaters who aren't bothered by making some periodic manual adjustments during charging, but the new AutoMAC has an automatic cutoff that ensures batteries will not be harmed if left unattended. The worst that can happen is that control reverts to the standard voltage regulator and some efficiency is lost. The attached ammeter allows the operator to know immediately what effect adjustments have on alternator output current.

Control theory.   The AutoMAC is connected to the field windings of the alternator, in parallel with the field wire from the standard voltage regulator. When the voltage regulator would normally begin limiting field current according to sensed charging voltage readings, usually between 13.8 and 14.0 volts, the AutoMAC sends a manually selected amount of field current to keep the alternator output high. The AutoMAC is also capable of monitoring charging voltage, and will automatically cut itself off when the batteries are fully charged or the charging current level is too high for the capacity of the battery at its present state of charge. The smaller the battery capacity in ampere-hours, the sooner the cutoff voltage is reached. The factory preset cutoff voltage is 14.7 volts. Note: If Prevailer batteries are used, this cutoff voltage may need to be reduced to around 14.4 volts. Consult Weems and Plath for recommended set point. This sounds high, and indeed batteries will begin to gas vigorously at this voltage, but if the cutoff voltage is reached the alternator output will immediately fall off and control reverts to the standard voltage regulator. Higher-output current will not resume until the AutoMAC is manually reset with a lower output current level or the charging voltage drops below the standard voltage regulator setting.

Construction and operation.   The AutoMAC conforms to Weems and Plath's standard flush-mounted panel layout of $5^1/_4$ inches wide by 7+ inches high. The front mounting plate is made of $^1/_8$-inch painted aluminum. As seen in Figure 2-3, a standard analog ammeter is located on the upper part of the front face, with a fuse and on-off switch flanking it. Available ranges are 0 to 50, 0 to 100, and 0 to 150 amperes. The 100- and 150-ampere models are supplied with a "shunt" that allows the meter to be wired with 14 AWG wire up to 30 feet from the high-current wire. In the middle of the panel are the manual reset button and cutoff indicator light, and at the bottom is the output current selection knob, attached to a rheostat in the rear of the panel. Behind the panel is the circuit board, an aluminum-finned heat sink/protective cover, and electrical connection terminals.

When the engine is started, output from the alternator will be high as starting current is replaced. If the battery is already charged, alternator output will plummet rapidly. If the battery is partially discharged, the current will remain high for a while, then taper off as charging voltage rises to the standard voltage regulator set point. Remember that this doesn't mean the battery is charged; it simply means that the surface voltage on the battery plates is rising. This can be thought of as the "charging voltage," present under the influence of an external voltage source, as opposed to the true "rested voltage" of the battery. During the brief initial period of high output, the alternator is producing all it can for those RPMs, and the AutoMAC will have no influence over output. Only after the voltage regulator begins limiting current does an external control such as the AutoMAC increase output. At this point, by turning the control knob clockwise, alternator output can be increased back to its maximum for those RPMs. As the battery charges, it is less able to accept high current, and alternator output must be manually lowered to prevent the automatic cutoff from tripping at about 14.7 volts. If it does trip, lower the alternator output by turning the control knob counterclockwise, and push the reset button. The ammeter included with the unit will show alternator output whether or not the AutoMAC is operating, and will function alone or in series with an existing ammeter already mounted on your boat.

Charging routine.   For successful use of the AutoMAC, you should develop a regular charging routine, one that allows you to estimate how many ampere-hours of current you need each charging cycle to restore the battery to full charge. After a while you will know when, and by how much, to adjust the control for your present needs. Other sources of charging, such as solar panels and wind generators, will influence your routine and must be considered. A good charging routine would allow the battery to discharge to the 50 percent level, then recharge with a current of about 25 percent of total battery capacity in ampere-hours. Higher charging currents will only cause the cutoff voltage to be reached sooner.

Other points to note: (1) Prevailer batteries can accept higher levels of current. (2) While with a standard marine alternator you must hold the prolonged charging current to about two-thirds rated capacity, high-output alternators can operate at full capacity. (3) When the cutoff voltage is reached, the battery should be around 75 to 80 percent charged. Lower the current to around 10 percent of battery capacity until the battery is 85 to 90 percent charged, then let the standard voltage regulator take over for the final stage of charging.

Installation.   Installation is covered in the owner's manual available from Weems and Plath for the AutoMAC, but a few things should be touched upon. There are three low-current wires to connect: a plus and minus source of 12 volts DC, and a field wire to the alternator. The only high-current connections are for the ammeter on the output side of the alternator. Some alternators with internal regulators will have to be taken apart to make the field wire connection. If this is beyond your expertise, or you have no access to a local shop for the job, Weems and Plath will be happy to wire it for you. Contact the company for the proper shipping and handling procedure and cost. Weems and Plath also has a 10-ampere booster that is required for most high-output alternators with field currents over 4 amperes.

The Weems and Plath AutoCHARGE is an inexpensive control that provides automatic fast charging for the first phase of battery charging, then allows the voltage regulator to operate normally. It is a simple, low-budget approach to decreasing charging time when using a standard or high-output alternator. Maximum alternator output current is 200 amperes. Since there are no manual adjustments to make, it is well suited to charter boats. This control does not have the flexibility of the AutoMAC, nor will it allow you to continue fast charging past the point when the voltage regulator resumes control.

The AutoCHARGE is not recommended for alternators with internal voltage regulators that have the sense terminal connected internally to the main positive output terminal—such as the Hitachi LR series and Mitsubishi with internal regulators and LF terminals.

Control theory. The AutoCHARGE unit does not control the alternator. Instead of temporarily taking over control from the voltage regulator by supplying additional control current, the AutoCHARGE does nothing more than fool the voltage regulator into sensing that the battery is discharged. With the unit connected, the voltage regulator does not limit control current, thus the alternator operates at maximum output for its RPMs until the charging voltage rises to 14.7 volts. At this time the AutoCHARGE allows the standard voltage regulator to sense the true charging voltage and normal regulator operation resumes.

Construction and operation. The AutoCHARGE has two main components, a plastic terminal base for making electrical connections, and an eight-pin, plug-in plastic module that does the work. The entire unit is only 2+ inches square by just over 4 inches high and weighs about 1 pound.

Once the wire connections are made, everything is automatic, with no adjustments needed. The AutoCHARGE is only effective between the time that the standard voltage regulator would normally begin limiting current and the time that the charging voltage reaches 14.7 volts (a factory preset value, not adjustable). Three factors will influence how much time it will take to reach this voltage setting: the battery state of charge, the battery capacity in ampere-hours, and the RPMs (and therefore output) of your alternator. You can increase the effectiveness of the AutoCHARGE by deep-cycling your battery to a 50 percent discharge level before recharging; by increasing your battery capacity; and by adjusting the RPMs of your alternator. Remember that with the AutoMAC, you adjust control current to lower the alternator output as battery level of charge increases. With the AutoCHARGE, you can adjust the engine speed (thus the speed of the alternator) to accomplish the same thing, prolonging the time before the 14.7-volt setting is reached.

Charging routine. For best efficiency, initial charging should start when the battery is 50 percent discharged, and charging current should be limited to around 25 percent of total battery capacity. Note that standard marine alternators must be limited to two-thirds capacity for prolonged charging. The battery will be about 75 to 80 percent charged when the cutoff voltage is reached. Once the voltage regulator resumes normal operation, the AutoCHARGE will remain disconnected until the engine is turned off and then restarted.

Installation. The AutoCHARGE can be mounted in any position, and just about any-where near the alternator, since only 14 AWG wire is needed for the connections. There are no high-current connections. Three connections are required: 12-volt DC plus and minus, and one wire to the voltage-regulator sensing terminal. The existing wire to 12-volt DC sens-ing source must be disconnected. The 12-volt DC positive wire must be connected so that power is switched off when the engine is turned off.

The 3-Step Deep-Cycle Regulator

The Ample Power Company offers the 3-Step Deep-Cycle Regulator, a completely auto-matic fast-charge control (shown in Figure 6-9) for standard and high-output alternators. It is intended to replace the standard voltage regulator, and provides alternator control during all three stages of deep-cycle-battery current acceptance: bulk charge, absorption charge, and float charge. It can be used on its own or in combination with the Ample Power Systems Monitor. Its automatic operation makes it well suited for charter boats and other situations where manual operation is not feasible or desired.

Control theory and operation. The 3-Step Deep-Cycle Regulator provides an initial bulk-charge cycle until the set point of 14.4 volts is reached (a bit lower for the Prevailer batteries). During bulk charging, the alternator is providing full current for a given level of engine RPMs. When the set point is reached, the voltage is held constant while the current gradually tapers off. This is known as the *absorption charging cycle*. The control then auto-matically switches to a float-charging mode at the constant voltage of 13.8 volts, identical to that of most standard voltage regulators. At this voltage, a battery could become mildly over-

---

FIGURE 6-9.   **The ABC alternator control, together with a manual activator switch to be mounted in a convenient location. (Courtesy Balmar Products, Inc.)**

charged during long periods of motoring. Check the fluid level of liquid-electrolyte batteries on a routine basis and add water as necessary. This is not a concern for sealed batteries.

Installation. Ample Power Company provides complete installation details.

The Quad-Cycle Monitor/Regulator

This automatic alternator control and electrical system monitor from Cruising Equipment is the most complete combined control-monitor available. It not only allows alternator output to match closely the natural battery acceptance characteristics, but lets you know exactly how your total energy system is performing. There is no owner operation needed during normal charging, making this control well suited for charter boats or when manual alternator control is not feasible or desirable. There is, however, an additional "battery conditioning" cycle that is owner-controlled. A separate key switch makes certain the conditioning cycle operates only when you want it to.

Control theory and operation. The Quad-Cycle provides control through the three stages of battery charging: bulk charge, absorption or "acceptance" charge, and float charge. During the first stage of operation, alternator current is allowed to rise to its maximum level for the rated capacity and RPMs. If this level is too high for the battery capacity on board, it can be owner-adjusted on the back of the Quad-Cycle. This adjustment also allows current limiting for standard marine alternators. For these units, output current should not exceed approximately two-thirds of rated capacity during prolonged charging.

FIGURE 6-10 (left).   **Automatic 3-Step Deep-Cycle Regulator. (Courtesy Ample Power Company)**

FIGURE 6-11 (right).   **A completely automatic alternator control and system monitor. (Cruising Equipment Company)**

The first stage lasts until the preset charging-voltage set point of around 14.4 volts is reached. During the second stage of charging, the set-point voltage is held constant and the battery receives current according to its acceptance characteristics. The current will slowly drop during this stage. When the charging current drops to 2 to 2.5 percent of total battery capacity (and if Quad-Cycle is properly adjusted), the control will switch to float charge at a constant 13.2 volts (see Figure 6-11).

Construction. The unit measures 4.5 by 6.0 by 1.5 inches and is intended for flush-mounting on a bulkhead or other interior location. It consists of a painted aluminum mounting plate with a digital display on the front at the top, a function selector knob in the center, and an on-off/light switch and conditioning key switch at the bottom. The control circuits and adjustments are located in the rear of the panel. The Quad-Cycle automatically compensates for variations in battery temperature. The six monitoring functions include voltage for batteries 1 and 2, and any four of the following: voltage for a third battery, battery 1 current draw, battery 2 current draw, alternator current output, AC voltage, AC current, fuel tank level, and water tank level.

Charging routine. Even though the operation is automatic, you can get maximum efficiency and system protection by allowing your deep-cycle batteries to discharge to near 50 percent before recharging. The Quad-Cycle will take the battery through bulk charging, then hold the voltage constant as current levels drop. You should probably stop alternator charging when the current level drops sufficiently for the unit to switch to float voltage, even though the battery will be only 85 to 90 percent charged. Periodic conditioning of the batteries, every month or so during routine use, equalizes cell voltage and extends battery life.

Installation. Detailed information regarding the installation of the Quad-Cycle is available from Cruising Equipment.

SYSTEM EFFICIENCY

How efficient are engine-driven alternators at converting fuel energy into useful electrical energy in our batteries? The overall system efficiency must take into account the energy content of a gallon of gasoline or diesel fuel, the efficiency of the engine, the drive system (pulleys and belts), and the alternator itself. It must also account for energy that is not being produced because of regulation devices. When an auxiliary engine is run just for charging batteries with a standard marine alternator and regulator, and output averages 15 amperes, the overall efficiency is around 5 percent! If you boost the average output using a fast-charge alternator control, then the efficiency can jump to over 10 percent. Systems with high-output alternators can have overall efficiencies of around 15 percent.

OTHER COMPONENTS AND CONSIDERATIONS

The first part of this chapter is devoted to alternators and the various types of charge controllers to go with them. Listed below are a few other components you may want to have to complete your alternator charging system, along with some considerations concerning their use.

Charging Diodes and Isolators

Diodes allow current in a circuit to flow in one direction only, like a check valve in a plumbing system. Earlier in this chapter we reviewed the use of silicon diodes inside an alternator for rectifying AC output current into DC. Diodes can also be used to charge multiple batteries from the same charging source, and to protect your system in the event of a short circuit.

In a typical charging system without isolators, the alternator's output is connected to the common terminal of a two-battery selector switch. The switch allows charging current and load current to come and go from battery 1, battery 2, or both batteries together (when the batteries operate in parallel). The use of charging, or "isolating," diodes allows multiple batteries to be charged simultaneously without electrically connecting them in parallel. This means the batteries can coexist at different states of charge or general condition. The charging current is distributed automatically according to battery need without the deeper-discharged battery bringing down the charge level of the other(s). When charging diodes are used, the battery selector switch is normally used only for distributing load. This eliminates the possibility of opening the charging circuit by switching to the off position when the engine is running. The output from various charging sources is connected directly to the diodes, then on to the batteries.

Charging diodes also serve an important safety function. If a short circuit should occur at the alternator when no charging diode is in place, full battery current could flow in the output wires with a very real risk of fire, especially if multiple batteries are connected in parallel. A properly sized charging diode in the alternator output line would prevent this by not allowing current to flow toward the alternator.

There are two types of charging diodes: silicon diodes and Schottky diodes. Schottky diodes should be used, since they have a much lower voltage drop (about half a volt) across the terminals. A lower voltage drop allows more current to reach the battery during the charging cycle. Charging diodes can be purchased and installed individually, or purchased pre-packaged in a "battery isolator" for two or three batteries (see Figure 3-5). Charging diodes can also come as an integral part of a dual-output alternator, in which two batteries can be charged independently with no external isolator needed.

Because of the voltage drop across a charging diode, the voltage regulator sense line must be able to read true battery charging voltage, not the higher voltage on the alternator side of the diode, in order for the battery to be correctly charged. If a regulator is set at 13.8 volts and senses the alternator side of the diode, the battery charging voltage will be half a volt less, or around 13.3 volts, much too low for a regulator cutoff voltage.

There are several ways to accomplish this:

1. Make certain that the voltage regulator sense line is connected to the battery side of the diode instead of the alternator output side.

2. Connect a secondary diode in the regulator sense line to make an equivalent voltage drop there. This diode should have the exact voltage drop as the charging diode. Note: This approach is not appropriate for internal regulators without sense terminals you can reach.

3. If the regulator senses alternator output only, and your voltage regulator is adjustable, adjust the voltage set point to compensate for the voltage drop across the charging diode. A 14.3-volt set point reading taken on the alternator side will be equivalent to around a 13.8-volt output current to the batteries.

Many regulators are capable of sensing correct battery voltage readings without alterations. Dual-output alternators have built-in charging diodes, and thus the voltage sensing line is always downstream of the diodes. Consult your system supplier regarding which method is best, and how to make the necessary connections.

High-Voltage Spike Suppressors

Despite the use of one or more isolating diodes, open circuits on the alternator side of the diode can still cause high-voltage damage. The solution is to install a high-voltage spike suppressor, such as the Zap-Stop, at the alternator itself. If there is a temporary high-voltage spike, it will be safely conducted to ground (refer to Figure 3-13).

Monitoring Systems

Regardless of the alternator-regulator combination you have, it is most helpful to be aware of how your system is performing. There are a number of good monitoring systems from which to choose. You should at least have a good ammeter with a scale appropriate for your alternator's output, and a good voltmeter/battery-condition indicator that can accurately measure battery state of charge. High-output alternators, because of their high current levels, generally require a shunt-type ammeter. This device uses a current shunt to direct only a small portion of full current to the ammeter. A typical current shunt is shown in Figure 6-12. See Chapter 3 for a complete listing of monitoring equipment.

TIPS ON INSTALLATION, OPERATION, AND MAINTENANCE

This section answers an assortment of the most frequently asked questions concerning the installation, operation, and maintenance of alternator systems. Some of the information here may be a review of material we covered previously, but is important enough to stress again.

Q. *Is alternator output AC or DC?*
A. Alternators initially produce AC, but this output is internally rectified into DC by silicon diodes, making it suitable for directly charging lead-acid batteries.

FIGURE 6-12. **Shunt ammeter. (Courtesy Hamilton Ferris)** **101**

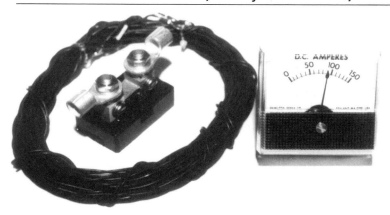

Q. *What things will determine an alternator's output?*

A. Alternator output is determined by the unit's design and rated capacity; the engine speed; alternator temperature; the type of alternator control; and battery capacity and state of charge.

Q. *What is the extra load of an alternator on the auxiliary engine?*

A. The load of the alternator is proportional to the amount of current it is generating. If the alternator is putting out 50 amperes at 14.0 volts, this corresponds to 700 watts or just under 1 horsepower of load (1 horsepower = 760 watts). By the time you account for energy losses in the belts, pulleys, and alternator itself, there might actually be a 1.5- to 2-horsepower load on the engine.

Q. *Is there a risk of overcharging with a manual alternator control?*

A. If it is a simple rheostat that varies the alternator field current without a high-voltage cutoff, the answer is yes. The AutoMAC has a high-voltage cutoff that will protect your batteries, but charging current must be sufficiently lowered manually before resetting or the voltage will rapidly climb back up to the cutoff point. Repeated attempts to charge with too much current could conceivably overcharge the battery.

Q. *How will I know if I can replace the standard alternator on my auxiliary engine with the high-output variety?*

A. If the high-output unit is a small-case type, it will almost certainly fit the space you have available, although some modification of the mounting bracket may be required. A large-case unit may require more extensive modifications. Check with your supplier before purchasing a new unit.

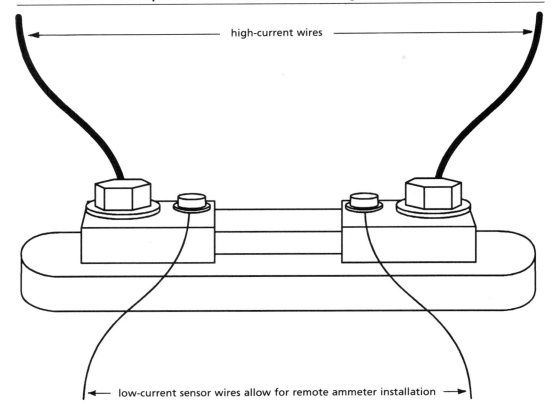

high-current wires

low-current sensor wires allow for remote ammeter installation

Q. *How do I know if I need a high-output alternator?*

A. If improved charging performance is your objective, the first thing you should think about is a fast-charge alternator control. Since this control will allow your existing alternator to perform to its best ability, calculate if this arrangement will meet your needs. If not, then certainly investigate purchasing a high-output alternator with fast-charge control, along with other charging options described in this book.

Q. *What is a good alternator charging routine for deep-cycle batteries?*

A. A good routine is to allow the batteries to cycle to the 50 percent charge point (rested battery voltage at about 12.2 volts), then charge with an alternator output (in amperes) of about 25 percent of total battery capacity until you reach the 75 percent charge point (rested battery voltage at about 12.5 volts), and continue

FIGURE 6-14. **Energy-system schematic with the alternator-based charging and distribution portion highlighted in gray.**

103

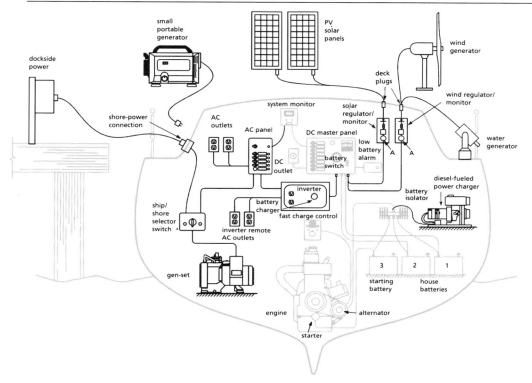

charging with about 10 percent of total battery capacity until you reach the 85 to 90 percent charge point (rested battery voltage of about 12.6 to 12.7 volts). It would be nice to finish charging at a lower current level with solar panels or a wind or water generator. If liquid electrolyte batteries are taken to only the 85 to 90 percent charge level, an occasional equalizing charge will probably be required. It won't take long to establish a comfortable charging routine of your own.

Q. *Is it possible to continue charging if the voltage regulator fails?*
A. You can continue charging under emergency conditions without the voltage regulator by manually switching the field current on and off. Consult your equipment supplier to find out how to do this. You must carefully monitor battery voltage and output current to keep from overcharging the battery. When the field current is on, there is no regulation and alternator output will be maximum. I know of one sailor who uses this arrangement on a perma-

nent basis by manually switching the current on for 10 minutes
and off for 10 minutes while charging. Making a rheostat field
controller would be much easier and safer, and proper fast-charge
controls even better.

Q. *What type of alternator spares should be carried aboard a cruising
boat?*

A. For most cruisers a few spare V-belts, spare pulleys, a set of field
current brushes, a spare voltage regulator or other alternator control, and wire (both output and control-current gauge) and wire
connectors are the only spares you really need. It might be better to
bring along a spare alternator, in which case purchasing a new
high-output unit (so your existing one can be the spare) makes
sense.

Q. *What are the most common things to look for when troubleshooting?*

A. First and foremost is the V-belt tension. The belt must be tight,
and the pulleys must be free of grease or other materials that
would cause the belt to slip. Loose or slipping belts cause erratic or
curtailed alternator output and excessive wear on the belts. Over-
tightening will also shorten belt life. Refer to your engine manual
for correct belt tension, usually given in millimeters of play when
the belt is depressed with your finger with a specified force. The
second thing to check is the electrical contacts, making sure they
are tight and solidly connected. Engine vibration can cause contacts to loosen with time. Next check the condition of the battery.
The problem might be there and not with your alternator system at
all. If you still have a problem, it is either in the wiring supplying
the voltage regulator with current, in the regulator itself, or internally in the alternator. Check with a good alternator service manual or mechanic.

7

Small Portable Generators
And Battery Chargers

═══

SMALL PORTABLE GENERATORS

The emphasis here is on portable generators that are used primarily for charging 12-volt batteries. With this in mind, the term *small portable generator* shall refer to any gasoline- or diesel-fueled engine-driven generator that can be moved about easily, weighs 75 pounds or less, and has at least some DC output. This typically covers units rated up to about 1,500 watts. It does not include larger portables, gen-sets, or units with AC output only. Those are covered in Chapter 12. It should be noted that the industry standard use of the term *portable generator* applies to any unit with handles and integral fuel tank that operates at 3,600 RPMs. For their size and low fuel consumption, the small portable generators described in this chapter can make a significant contribution to your charging system.

Small portable generators offer mariners the option of high-output battery charging without using the boat's main engine. With a portable generator, you are closely matching engine size and power capacity with electrical power output, resulting in a marked increase in energy efficiency. Besides cutting down on main engine wear and tear, most portable generators can also supply 120-volt AC for operating power tools and other intermittent-use AC equipment on board. They provide you with a backup source of power and can be taken off the boat for duty elsewhere if needed.

While portable generators work equally well on land or on almost any size boat, they do have a few potentially adverse characteristics, among which is the fact that they often generate as much noise as electricity. Some units are quieter than others, but they all make substantial noise, as much or more so than the main engine in its soundproofed compartment. Almost all portable generators are air-cooled instead of water-cooled like the main engine. Water-cooling tends to muffle the exhaust. The units that are gasoline-fueled must be run on deck or some other extremely well-ventilated location on the boat because of the gasoline fumes and exhaust gases. This makes the noise level more evident to other boats. Some cruisers have been known to turn on their portable generator, set it on the foredeck in the middle of a quiet anchorage, then row ashore. The other boats that are subjected to the noise inevitably harbor some ill will toward their neighbor, and proposals for throwing the offending generator overboard are often voiced.

In addition to the noise, you might think twice about having a gasoline-fueled portable generator if it is your only reason for bringing gasoline on board. If you already have an engine that runs on gasoline, then an additional gasoline-fueled device presents no cause for concern or need for a separate fuel-storage compartment. Several high-output diesel-fueled units are available if you want to avoid gasoline altogether. Finally, portable generators are really quite reliable, but being mechanical they have the tendency to need repair when you are farthest from a source of parts and service. Knowing how to perform minor repairs, and carrying spare parts on extended cruises, is a good idea.

There are any number of portable generators: the gasoline-fueled AC-DC generators you are probably most familiar with, such as the Honda, the Yamaha, and the Kawasaki units; the Tanaka lightweight gasoline-fueled AC-DC or DC-only generators; and diesel-fueled DC-only high-output generators such as the Balmar PowerCharger. By taking a close look at each, you can determine if you want a portable generator on board, and if so, which one is best suited for your marine energy system.

Standard Gasoline-Fueled AC-DC Units

AC-DC portable generators have been supplying power on construction sites, at remote homes, and on boats for many years. You can choose from units from Kawasaki, Yamaha, Honda, Robin, Nissan, Onan, and Coleman. They are rated according to their AC power output in watts and have a relatively small DC output for charging batteries. A typical example is the Kawasaki model GD-700A (see Figure 2-4), which is capable of producing 120 volts AC with 700 watts of surge power for starter motors, and 600 watts of power during continuous duty. Its 12-volt DC capacity is 8.5 amperes, or only around 120 watts of power. Unlike some other units, the alternating and direct current can be used simultaneously. This is useful for giving the batteries a charge at the same time you are using the 120-volt current for power tools or other AC equipment.

Keep in mind that this type of portable generator is intended primarily for providing remote AC power. If charging batteries is your main concern, a much more efficient method of using a standard portable generator is to run an AC battery charger off one of the 120-volt outlets. Allowing for some energy loss through the charger, a 300-watt generator can run a 15-ampere charger, a 600-watt generator can run a 30-ampere charger, and an 850-watt generator can run a 40-ampere charger. You can use an inexpensive, unregulated automotive battery charger for this task if you carefully monitor battery voltage. Unregulated models that don't taper the charging current have a greater efficiency, a definite consideration when using a portable generator for a limited time. Automatic regulation is less important in this application, since the portable generator is usually operated only for a short time. If you want a fast charge but would prefer an automatic shutoff, a high-performance charger is appropriate (see AC-to-DC Battery Chargers, later in this chapter). Another alternative is to purchase a separate regulator for your unregulated charger. Some DC-to-AC inverters also have a battery-charging option that allows you to use one piece of equipment for both tasks.

Construction. Most models directly couple a small, efficient gasoline engine with an AC generator (see Figure 7-1). The AC generator is basically a simplified alternator without the rectifying diodes that change AC output to DC (see Chapter 6 for alternator theory and construction). As an example, the Kawasaki GD-700A uses a self-excited, double-pole, single-phase alternator with a rotating field. *Self-excited* means that it supplies its own direct current for the field electromagnet mounted on the center shaft; *double-pole* indicates that the electromagnet has two poles, one north and one south; and *single-phase* tells that there is only one set of output-wire windings. As the field electromagnet rotates through one revolution of 360 degrees, a plot of voltage versus time would be in the shape of a sine wave, as in Figure 7-2.

With the AC generator directly coupled to the unit's engine shaft, the generator shaft speed is the same as the engine speed. The Kawasaki GD-700A operates at a constant 3,600 RPMs to yield the standard 60-hertz operating frequency. *Hertz,* abbreviated Hz, is the standard unit of frequency; one hertz is equal to one cycle per second; 3,600 revolutions per minute divided by 60 seconds per minute = 60 revolutions (or cycles) per second. American household AC operates at 60 cycles per second, while European household AC operates at 50 cycles per second.

The DC output in most standard AC-DC portable generators is produced through a separate, smaller wire winding that taps into the output of the main windings. The size of the smaller winding determines the potential output of the DC circuit. The industry standard is a

---

FIGURE 7-1.   **Cutaway view of a Kawasaki Ninja 700 portable generator.**

FIGURE 7-2. **Voltage versus time (here shown as shaft rotation) for a single-phase AC generator.**

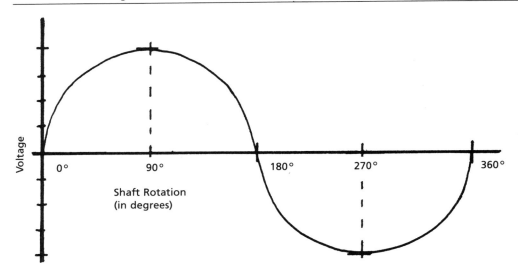

winding that yields 8 to 10 amperes at 12 volts DC. Internal diodes convert the AC output into DC, similar to the rectifying diodes in auto and marine alternators. You can see that AC operation is the primary objective with these units, and the DC circuit is a secondary consideration. Only with the use of an AC-to-DC battery charger can you take full advantage of the generator's power when just charging batteries.

Most of the newer gasoline-fueled AC-DC generators have a four-stroke engine as opposed to a two-stroke type. Two-stroke engines can be found on many outboard engines, chain saws, snowmobiles, and off-road motorbikes. They are much simpler mechanically, but require mixing lubricating oil with the gasoline, typically in a 50:1 ratio. Four-stroke engines are quieter, and since they don't burn the lubrication oil right with the gasoline, they pollute the air less. Many of the new outboard engines are four-stroke, with a separate oil reservoir and cleaner emissions. A generator starts by means of a manual recoil mechanism, like most lawn mower and small outboard engines, although some units, such as the Kawasaki Ninja 700, include electric starting as standard equipment. Electric-start models are somewhat heavier, since they must have an additional starter motor and an internal 12-volt battery.

The alternator-engine assembly is housed in a steel or aluminum casing along with gas tank, muffler, and other internal components. Typically, two AC outlets and one set of DC terminals are mounted through the housing. Cooling air is pulled through the unit by fan blades mounted on the engine shaft. There is a carrying handle either on top or at the ends, and most units have rubber feet at the bottom corners to dampen vibration.

Operation.   To operate, set the unit above decks, preferably on a rubber mat to help dampen vibration and noise and to keep it from sliding. Try to find a location that is out of the way of foot traffic. Start the generator, then plug your AC tools or appliances into one or more of its AC household-type outlets. You should select equipment whose power consumption is less than the continuous-duty output rating of the generator. Most units come with overload protection in the form of fuses or circuit breakers for both AC and DC outlets. If you have a dockside AC power hookup on your boat, you can plug the shore-power cord into the portable generator. Make sure you don't run the AC load above the capacity of the generator, as this will immediately trip the circuit breaker.

For DC operation, simply connect wire of the appropriate gauge from the DC outlets to the battery. Be careful to maintain correct polarity; it's a good idea to color code the positive and negative wires to the battery. If you are running a battery charger, you should monitor battery charging voltage and DC output in amperes (an ammeter is usually included with a battery charger). Risk of overcharging your battery is very real with unregulated automotive-type chargers, so either carefully monitor battery condition, invest in a regulating device such as the Hamilton Ferris Safe-T-Charge (up to 20-ampere charging capacity) or Professional Mariner's Auto Box, or get a battery charger that is made for rapidly charging deep-cycle batteries and has appropriate regulation.

Tanaka Lightweight Generators

The Tanaka portable generators deserve a place of their own. They are truly portable, with both models weighing in at only 19 pounds. As generators go, they are fairly quiet, and are miserly fuel consumers. Tanaka generators have a tiny two-stroke gasoline engine directly coupled to an AC generator. Gasoline is mixed with oil in a 50:1 ratio. You can expect to get 1.5 hours of operation from the 1 pint fuel tank. Tanaka generators have a convenient carrying handle and rubber feet.

The Tanaka QEG-300 operates like other standard AC-DC generators in that it has a 300-watt AC outlet as well as a 10-ampere DC outlet that can be used simultaneously. Although 300 watts of AC is enough to run radios, TVs, personal computers and printers, blenders, sewing machines, and small power tools, the QEG-300 doesn't operate at 60 hertz. This limits the appliances that are compatible with its AC output. Check with your equipment supplier to make certain it will power your appliances.

The Tanaka QEG-250 has the same physical characteristics as the QEG-300, but produces only DC output at a rate of 20 amperes (see Figure 2-6). This is the preferred choice if you have no AC requirements or have an inverter on board. In this model, the alternator output is rectified to DC as in auto and marine alternators. It can be used to charge batteries or operate DC equipment directly. Its 20-ampere output is high for a small generator and could eliminate your need for a separate battery charger.

Starting is by manual recoil mechanism. Tanaka offers a spare parts kit that includes fuel cap, fuel filter, spark plug, and 1 pint of its recommended mixing oil. At a 50:1 ratio, a pint of oil will last about 75 hours.

Not long after high-output alternators became available, the inspiration of mating one with a small diesel engine led to the Balmar PowerCharger (see Figure 2-5). Instead of producing a combination AC-DC generator, Balmar chose to concentrate on a unit with strictly DC output for charging batteries. While their high-output alternator could just as easily be coupled to a gasoline-fueled engine, the PowerCharger is unique in that it incorporates a small, air-cooled Yanmar diesel engine instead. A diesel-fueled portable generator is well suited to operation on a boat. This type of unit renders belowdecks operation of a high-capacity portable generator feasible.

The difference in approach between the PowerCharger and other AC-DC portable generators and gen-sets is important. The former is concerned with directly operating DC equipment and charging batteries quickly and efficiently. The latter are intended primarily for providing a high-capacity AC power source with only a token DC charging circuit. Either approach permits both AC power and high-capacity battery charging on board by the addition of one other piece of equipment: a DC-to-AC inverter for use with the PowerCharger, or an AC-to-DC battery charger operated from the AC side of portable generators and gen-sets. Here are a few thoughts concerning diesel-fueled portable generators that might influence your choice:

1. If you have a diesel main engine, it would be nice to have a portable generator that used the same fuel. The PowerCharger's fuel line can even be connected to your main diesel fuel tank if desired.

2. The PowerCharger PC-100 qualifies as a small portable generator, weighing 65 pounds (75 pounds with the electric start option). Even the smallest Yanmar diesel-fueled AC-DC generator, rated at 2,000 watts, weighs about twice this amount.

3. With a portable generator capable of charging at close to 100 amperes DC and using only about a pint of fuel per hour to do it, you can save the main engine for moving your boat. This would also eliminate time and money spent on improving the performance of the main engine's alternator and regulator.

4. The PowerChargers are noisy, but not more so than a diesel engine. They can be stowed in soundproofed compartments below decks, or you can purchase Balmar's Soundshield mounting box.

5. The PowerCharger is also much more expensive than other portable generators ($2,500 in 1990), more than twice the price of a gasoline-fueled AC-DC generator with equivalent power capability (about 1,500 watts). It is closer in cost to the heavier, 2,000-watt Yanmar diesel-fueled AC-DC gen-set.

Construction. The Balmar PC-100 employs a Yanmar 4.2-horsepower, air-cooled, diesel-fueled engine. The main shaft of the engine is directly coupled to the center shaft of a 100-ampere high-output alternator. Direct coupling means that the alternator RPMs are the same as those of the engine. The alignment of the two shafts must be precise for a direct coupling to function smoothly at high speeds. (A belt-and-pulley system, on the other hand, can tolerate a small amount of misalignment, since the belt is flexible.) A 2.5-liter fuel tank is mounted adjacent to the top of the engine. There is no "outer casing." The engine-alternator assembly is simply mounted on rubber feet for absorbing sound and vibration. An engine base with vibration mounts is available.

Installation and operation. The PowerCharger can be mounted below decks in a well-vented locker, or in the Soundshield case that comes with exhaust hose and fittings. Make certain that adequate fresh air is available. Exhaust hose and double-wall stainless steel through-hull fittings are available from Balmar. The unit should be secured to prevent movement in all sea conditions. The unit measures 16 inches high by 15 inches wide by 13 inches deep, plus 10 inches long by 6 inches in diameter for the alternator. A belowdecks installation with proper ventilation begins to press the use of the word *portable,* but the PowerCharger's light weight and compact size are enough to keep it in the category.

The electrical hookup is the same as for other high-output alternators. The alternator that comes as standard equipment on the PC-100 has an internal regulator and a single output. A dual-output alternator with an adjustable external regulator is available as an option. This means you can connect it to two separate battery banks and they will both be charged while remaining electrically isolated from each other. The need for a separate isolator is avoided. As with other high-output alternators, a fast-charge control may be desirable (see Chapter 6). The voltage regulator that comes with the unit has a cutoff voltage of 14.2 to 14.4 volts. Also highly desirable is an ammeter to display output current.

The PC-100 comes with manual recoil starting; electric starting is available as an option. Fuel consumption is about 1 pint per hour, so you'll get about 5 hours of operation from one tank. Maintenance is as with any small diesel engine: check fuel and oil levels, change engine oil and filter regularly, make sure fuel is clean and fuel filter clear, and check to make sure all fasteners are tight.

Other Small Generators

A few other small generators should be mentioned here even though they don't quite qualify as "portable." One of them is the Ample Power Genie. It is similar to the PC-100 in that it mates a small diesel-fueled engine with a 120-ampere high-output alternator, but the Genie is saltwater-cooled versus air-cooled. Consequently, the installation is more involved, but operation is a bit quieter and the alternator is kept cooler and thus more efficient. The high-output alternator is belt-driven rather than directly coupled to the engine shaft. With an appropriate pulley ratio, the engine can run at much lower RPMs than the alternator and, as stated above, alignment of the components is not quite as critical. There is, however, some additional power lost in a belt-driven system. The Genie includes as standard equipment a fast-charge alternator control and electric starting, as well as an accessory platform for other equipment that can be run off the small diesel engine. The Genie weighs around 140 pounds, and this, along with the water-cooling, removes it from our "small portable" category. It is substantially larger than the PowerCharger and quite a bit more expensive than the standard PC-100, although the price difference is relatively small when comparing similarly equipped units.

Balmar also offers the PC-200, the next size up from the PC-100, with a 6.0-horsepower Yanmar diesel engine, a 150-ampere high-output alternator, and electric start standard. Fuel consumption is twice as much, at up to 1 quart an hour. The PC-200 weighs about 90 pounds and is a bit bigger than the PC-100. The additional weight and engine size place it just outside the "small portable" category.

Both Balmar and Ample Power offer accessory equipment for use with their generators, including reverse-osmosis water making. The Balmar combination generator and water maker is called the PC-100 Aqua-Pac. It can simultaneously charge your batteries and make up to 20 gallons of fresh water an hour. The Ample Power unit can be interfaced with water-making and refrigeration compressors.

Overall System Efficiency

How efficient are small portable generators at converting energy into stored electricity in your batteries? For comparison with other charging systems, the system efficiency must take into account the initial energy content of a gallon of gasoline or diesel fuel versus the electrical energy available at the batteries during operation. Standard gasoline-fueled AC-DC units have only about a 2 percent system efficiency when charging batteries from the 8-to-10-ampere DC circuit. With the use of a battery charger operated from the AC circuit, system efficiency jumps to 7 or 8 percent. The Tanaka QEG-250 has about a 10 percent system efficiency when used for charging batteries, and the QEG-300 has about a 5 percent system efficiency using the DC circuit only. Balmar's PowerCharger boasts a system efficiency near 20 percent when the output approaches 100 amperes, and a 10 percent system efficiency at 50 amperes.

Tips on Installation, Operation, and Maintenance

This section includes an assortment of the most frequently asked questions concerning the installation, operation, and maintenance of portable generators. Some of the information here may be a review of material discussed earlier that bears additional emphasis.

Q. *What can be done about the noise level of portable generators?*
A. As a rule, the higher the output, the noisier the unit. Gasoline-fueled portable generators must be operated above decks for safety reasons, so try to dampen the vibration and noise with stiff foam cushions or other sound-deadening material underneath the unit. If the noise is excessive, you could build your own version of Balmar's Soundshield box, even including tie-down straps as part of the housing. Be careful to ensure that there is adequate air flow

through the soundproof box without allowing exhaust and fresh air to mix. Since the unit operates above decks, run it when you're going to be below, but please be considerate of your neighbors. Don't run a portable generator while no one is on board the boat. With a diesel-fueled unit installed below decks, much can be done to lessen the noise. Soundproofing its compartment might be an expensive and time-consuming project, but you will be rewarded each time you turn on the generator. Again, make certain the unit has adequate fresh air.

Q. *What are the safety considerations when using a portable generator?*

A. They are threefold. The first concerns the use of gasoline on a boat. Gasoline can be highly explosive and should be treated with a great deal of respect. Operate your unit above decks. Store your fuel above decks in a well-vented locker. The people at Cruising Equipment recommend running your generator until it runs completely out of fuel, so that when the unit is brought below, it will have no gasoline in it. This makes good sense. After use, allow the unit to cool off and air out a bit before stowing it. The second safety consideration concerns the exhaust gases given off by a fossil fuel-burning engine. On a saltwater-cooled marine engine, the exhaust is mixed with the cooling water and exits harmlessly from a through-hull fitting. The exhaust of a gasoline-fueled portable generator just exits the attached muffler and passes into the surrounding air. The exhaust gas must not be allowed to accumulate below decks. Keep all hatches downwind of the unit closed during operation. The third safety consideration concerns only diesel-fueled portable generators installed below decks. In addition to venting the exhaust properly, you must make certain that the unit doesn't use up the supply of fresh air in the cabin area during prolonged operation. Either provide a separate fresh air inlet to the unit or keep the cabin area well vented.

Q. *What is the routine maintenance for a portable generator?*

A. The same as for any small engine. If it's a four-cycle engine, check the oil level and change the oil and oil filter as recommended by the manufacturer. If you have a two-cycle engine such as the one on the Tanaka, make certain to mix the oil and fuel thoroughly. With either kind of engine, check the fuel filter periodically and clean or replace if necessary. Be familiar with the carburetor adjustments. Check the spark plug and its electrode gap, and clean or replace as necessary. Diesel engines have no spark plugs, but you should keep the fuel clean and free of water or sediment. Check all fuses or circuit breakers periodically, and all wiring connections and mechanical fasteners on the unit for tightness.

Q. *What is the best portable generator for supplying both AC and DC output?*

A. An obvious answer is the standard gasoline-fueled AC-DC unit, but this is not necessarily the best for your needs. The first thing to decide is how much of your total on-board energy load you plan on supplying with a portable generator. Is it to be used frequently or just as a backup source of power? A properly sized gasoline-fueled AC-DC unit will give you the AC power you need, but you must use a separate AC-to-DC battery charger run off the AC side of the portable generator if you want efficient battery charging. The unit must be operating, with all its attendant noise, whenever you use AC equipment. This is okay for power tools, but maybe not so good for computers or entertainment equipment when you'd like it to be quiet. The only way around this is to also invest in a properly sized DC-to-AC inverter for "quiet time" loads. The ability to carry the unit off the boat easily for use elsewhere is a definite plus. Strictly DC-output units such as the 20-ampere Tanaka QEG-250 and the 100-ampere Balmar PowerCharger give you efficient battery charging, and the addition of a properly sized inverter will give you the AC output you require.

Q. *How is the DC output produced in an AC-DC portable generator?*

A. Since the electrical power is supplied by an AC generator in these units, the DC output is typically produced by a small wire winding that taps into the output of the main stator windings. The size of the smaller winding determines the potential DC output. Internal rectifying diodes convert AC output to DC.

Q. *On an AC-DC portable generator, can both the AC output, by way of a battery charger, and the DC output be used at the same time to charge batteries even more efficiently?*

A. Some units do allow the AC and DC outputs to be used simultaneously, but if you have a battery charger that is properly matched to the capacity of your generator, it won't help much to also run the DC side. If the battery charger output is much lower than rated capacity, you can give an additional boost by also connecting the DC circuit to the batteries.

Q. *How is the electrical output from portable generators regulated to keep from overcharging batteries?*

A. Many of the smaller portable generators don't have much in the way of proper voltage regulation for the DC output, mainly be-

FIGURE 7-3. **115**

FIGURE 7-3. **Schematic of an on-board electrical system with multiple charging sources. Portions of the system directly pertinent to charging batteries or supplying AC power with small petroleum-fueled generators are highlighted in gray.**

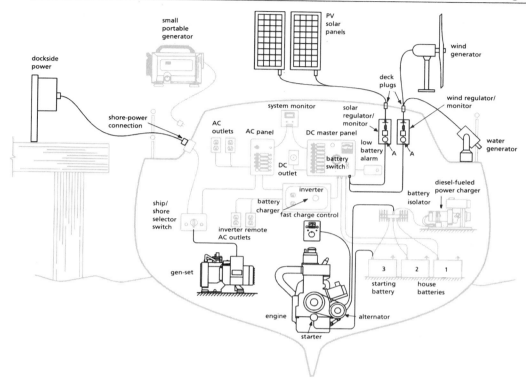

cause the units aren't usually run long enough for overcharge to be a problem. The Balmar PowerCharger and the Ample Power Genie both have built-in voltage regulation.

Q. *Can a portable generator be used for charging batteries at the same time as other charging sources such as solar and wind systems?*

A. Yes, this is usually not a problem. Each charging source should have a properly sized diode internally, or in the positive output wire, so that multiple sources of current won't interfere with each other. Refer to Figure 7-3 for a sample schematic of multiple charging sources.

AC-TO-DC BATTERY CHARGERS

Battery chargers are included in this chapter for several reasons. They are a good complement to a standard AC-DC portable generator when used for charging batteries, and they operate with AC electricity typically generated using fossil fuels—that is, gasoline or diesel fuel for portable generators and gen-sets, and coal, gas, or oil for home and dockside AC from the utility company.

The term *battery charger* refers to a piece of electrical equipment that converts AC (from a house, dock, or electrical generator) into DC power suitable for charging lead-acid batteries. The marine industry recognizes this term even though it is misleading, since many other types of equipment can also "charge" batteries. Battery chargers can't actually produce electricity, as do alternators, portable generators, or solar, wind, and water generators. They can only convert existing AC power into usable DC. Despite this limitation, battery chargers can play a very useful role in your on-board energy system whenever AC is present.

Marine Uses for Battery Chargers

There are several ways to take advantage of a battery charger's capabilities.

Dockside battery charging. The most common marine use of battery chargers is for maintaining battery-bank charge when the boat is at a dock or slip. In this case, the charger input is connected to the dockside source of AC power—through an appropriate isolation transformer—and the charger output is connected to the batteries. Any reputable battery charger has the isolation transformer built into the circuitry for safety and to prevent electrolysis. Charger current replaces electricity consumed by on-board appliances as well as battery self-discharge losses. A charger used in this manner must be truly automatic in its regulation to keep the batteries fully charged without risk of overcharge. These units can be portable for use on or off the boat, or permanently wired as part of the boat's electrical system. With a properly sized battery charger, you can eliminate the need for a separate AC circuit on board for dockside use. Simply use the stored DC electricity from your batteries when dockside to operate your 12-volt appliances as you would at sea, at anchor, or on a mooring. The battery charger should be sized to keep up with current draw. The addition of an inverter allows you to use your batteries to power intermittent use of smaller-draw AC appliances.

Remote-site battery charging. A battery charger is also handy for use away from the boat. If your batteries need a boost, but it isn't feasible to go to a dock where AC power is available, you can take them and the charger to a convenient place. It shouldn't happen with a properly designed and operated energy system, but occasionally you may find yourself with a dead starting battery, no means on board to recharge it, and no access to dockside power. With a small portable battery charger on board you can remove the battery and take it to a location where AC power is available.

Float charging. Battery chargers are often used to float-charge batteries that aren't in use, either on the boat, or at home during the winter months. Proper float charging makes up for normal battery self-discharge losses without overcharging. This can be accomplished with a truly automatic charger that initially charges to a higher voltage, then switches to a lower float voltage. If you have an unregulated or poorly regulated charger, you can safely float-charge your batteries with the Hamilton Ferris Company's Safe-T-Charge (20 amperes maximum current) or Professional Mariner's Auto Box. Battery self-discharge losses are relatively small, so a charger with low output is fine for this application.

Coupled with a portable generator. The effectiveness of DC battery charging with a standard AC-DC portable generator can be greatly increased if a battery charger is operated from one of the AC outlets. The portable generator won't be on long enough for you to need to worry about overcharge, so having a regulated charger is less important. Be sure to size your system so the portable generator can adequately supply the required battery charger input current.

Types of Battery Chargers Available

There are four types of battery chargers from which to choose for the tasks above. They are listed below in order of increasing performance and cost.

Automotive. This simple type of unregulated battery charger, shown in Figure 7-4, typically consists of an isolated voltage transformer and diodes for converting 110-volt AC to DC. An ammeter displaying output current and an internal fuse or breaker are usually included. This charger is unregulated, so battery condition should be closely monitored, although full regulation can be added with the Safe-T-Charge or Auto Box. Automotive chargers are highly efficient, since there is no energy loss due to regulation. These chargers are fine for occasional remote-site battery charging, for float charging when used with a separate regulator, and for use with a portable generator.

Ferroresonant. Many of the marine battery chargers on the market are the ferroresonant variety. They have a moderate means of regulation and are better known for their reliability than for their operating efficiency. Typically, this charger has a finishing voltage of 13.6 to 13.8 volts, similar to an automobile alternator-regulator output. This is too low for good

---

FIGURE 7-4 (left).   **Unregulated battery charger. (Courtesy Ample Power Company)**
FIGURE 7-5 (right).   **The Ample Power Six Shooter, a battery charger offering DC
                       output only.**

performance charging when batteries are discharged, and too high for float charging when the batteries are full. The output falls off as voltage rises, so that by the time the cutoff voltage is reached, the output may be only 5 percent of rated value. As with the automotive-charging system, it is an inexpensive compromise. A few attributes of a ferroresonant charger are worth mentioning, including its inherent ruggedness and ability to cope with heavy DC loads directly. Ferroresonant chargers are best suited to boats that lie dockside much of the time. If high performance is your concern, however, there are more efficient chargers to choose from.

Silicon-controlled rectifier (SCR). This charger (see Figure 2-7) represents the next level of sophistication and performance. SCR chargers often have a means of regulation that allows for a high initial charging voltage (around 14.2 to 14.4 volts), then switches to a lower float voltage (around 13.2 volts), protecting batteries during long charging cycles. The output from these chargers does not taper off as with ferroresonant models, and overall efficiency is higher. One point to note is that SCR chargers are more sensitive to drops in AC input voltages, which occur at many dock facilities. It is also important to make sure that a charger labeled as "automatic" is in fact one that protects your deep-cycle batteries during charging and float operation. This type of charger is best suited for boats that spend moderate amounts of time at a dock and are looking for a higher level of performance.

Pure-DC. A relative newcomer to the battery charger market, pure-DC chargers (see Figure 7-5) offer high performance and efficiency. These chargers have several advantages over others: pure direct current is easier on batteries than the high-current pulses produced by SCR types, and it is more suitable for supplying DC appliance loads concurrently with battery charging during extended stays at a dock. Pure-DC chargers are also less affected by low-voltage dockside AC input you may occasionally find. Pure-DC chargers do have a few drawbacks, including higher cost and the need for fan cooling to protect them from overheating. They are recommended for liveaboards and other boaters looking for a high-performance battery charger.

Battery Charger Selection

You may find that a battery charger is redundant. Small PV solar panels that might already be on board are ideal for float charging idle batteries, even at home during the off season, and solar, wind, and portable generators can provide emergency power to revive dead batteries without the need for being dockside. Battery chargers really come into their own when operated off the AC circuit of a portable generator for short-term battery charging, or for serving as the primary power supply to the batteries when AC electricity is available at a dock.

Battery charging options are also available for many inverters on the market, and if you plan to have an inverter in your system (see Chapter 11), this could eliminate an extra piece of gear.

Listed below in alphabetical order are a few well-known battery-charger manufacturers and a sampling of their products. This is by no means a complete listing.

- 30-ampere automotive charger with isolation transformer.

- 10-ampere Six Shooter charger, pure-DC output, manual or three-step regulation.

- 45-, 75-, and 160-ampere Ample chargers, pure-DC output, three-step regulation.

Dynamote

- 10-, 20-, 40-, and 100-ampere Supercharger, SCR type, fast charge to 14.2 volts, lower float voltage at 13.2 volts.

Professional Mariner (see Figure 7-6)

- 20-, 40-, 60-, 80-, and 150-ampere Pro Mariner ferroresonant chargers, regulated to 13.6 to 13.8 volts.

- 20-, 40-, and 80-ampere Cruising chargers, fast charge to 14.4 volts, complete shutoff until battery reaches 12.5 volts.

- 15-, 30-, 50-, and 100-ampere Ultima chargers, SCR type, fast charge to 14.4 volts, lower float voltage at 13.3 volts.

FIGURE 7-6.　**Cruising Charger. (Courtesy Professional Mariner)**

- 30-, 45-, and 75-ampere, pure DC chargers. Medium-voltage models are rated at 14.8 volts. Fully regulated.

Ray Jefferson (see Figure 7-7)

- 15- and 30-ampere Switcher chargers, SCR type, charges to 100 percent level, then cuts off completely and monitors until the need for recharge.

Overall System Efficiency

Calculating the system efficiency of a battery charger requires taking into account the fuel used to generate the AC input to the charger (coal, oil, gas, or atomic), the efficiency of converting that fuel to electricity and delivering it to the marina or dock, and the efficiency of the battery charger itself. System efficiency can be anywhere from 10 to 20 percent.

FIGURE 7-7.   **A 15-ampere battery charger from Ray Jefferson.**

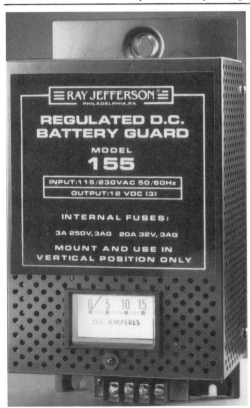

Other Considerations

Ancillary components and considerations for a battery charger are touched on here.

Fuse or circuit-breaker protection. Make sure that your battery charger is fuse or circuit-breaker protected from overload, like any piece of electrical generating equipment.

Ignition protection. A charger with "ignition-protection" rating has a low risk of igniting gasoline or propane fumes, and satisfies U.S. Coast Guard electrical standards for pleasure craft. This is essential for any permanently mounted charger or one that is operated inside the boat.

Isolation of AC from DC. Some effective means of isolating the incoming alternating current from the DC output on the boat is essential for safe operation. An isolation transformer is included in most chargers, and is also sold as a separate component for use between shore-power and boat AC circuits.

Multiple battery charging. Many battery chargers allow you to charge simultaneously two or three electrically isolated battery banks. This feature is especially valuable when charging batteries that are at different levels of charge. The charging voltage should be sensed "downstream" of the isolator circuits, thus eliminating faulty readings due to the half-volt or so of drop across isolating diodes.

Ammeter. Most chargers come with an ammeter built into the outer casing so you can monitor charging current. This is necessary for accurate assessment of charger performance.

Marine-grade construction. Some models have marine-grade stainless steel or aluminum housings to protect the internal components. They are usually more expensive but worth it for long equipment life in a marine environment.

Converters. Battery chargers may also be referred to as converters, since they convert AC electricity to DC. This term usually applies only to units that can supply DC power directly to appliances without a battery bank as intermediary.

8

Photovoltaic (PV) Solar Panels

V oyaging sailors were among the first to use photovoltaic solar panels and other renewable-energy equipment on an everyday basis. Living and traveling at length away from the conventional land-based grid, they were forced to provide their own electrical power. The means of doing so were limited. Although actively seeking other methods, until recently these sailors relied solely on fossil fuels to run their auxiliary engines to generate electricity. Thanks in part to their experimentation and acceptance, we now have quiet, reliable, easy-to-use generating systems powered by renewable, nonpolluting, readily available alternative "fuels." Solar, wind, and water generators, all powered in some way by the sun's energy, offer a viable solution to the problem of supplying offshore electrical power, not only for voyaging sailors but for all boaters. Of these three approaches, photovoltaic solar panels employ the most direct and probably the most benign method of converting sunlight to electricity.

The word *photovoltaic* means "capable of creating a voltage when exposed to radiant energy, especially visible light energy." We've heard it termed "photo-electric," "photo-votechnic," and even "photo-volcanic." If you think of the association of light and voltage, photovoltaic will be the word that comes to mind. Put another way, *photovoltaics* describes solar energy converted directly to electricity. It can thus be easily distinguished from solar energy captured for heating and cooling spaces, for heating domestic water, for producing steam and mechanical power (that can also be used for turning electrical generators), and even for cooking. These other solar-energy systems operate on the principle of converting light energy into useful heat energy. The hot-water "Sun Shower" is a simple version, combining collector and storage medium in one neat package. Heat-producing solar panels can be applied to everyday functions on board a boat, but it is photovoltaic solar panels for making electricity that concerns us here. They can be referred to simply as PV panels.

PV solar energy involves converting sunlight into electricity directly, without first changing it into heat. In fact, any heat produced in a PV solar panel is evidence of inefficiency or lost power. The relationship between light and electricity in the "photovoltaic effect" is not obvious, so a little background may be helpful.

Light

Light is visible radiant electromagnetic energy, most of which comes from the sun. Any light, however, will trigger the photovoltaic effect. A solar calculator, for instance, will operate at night when exposed to a desk lamp. Other forms of radiant electromagnetic energy are radio waves (received by your AM, FM, short-wave, or VHF radio), infrared radiation (given off by any heat source), ultraviolet radiation (which attacks your varnish, sails, and skin), X rays, and gamma rays. When radiation travels from one place to another, its motion has many characteristics of wave motion, hence we refer to wavelengths and frequencies. Each form of radiation has its own range of wavelengths and frequencies.

Heinrich Hertz first discovered what we know as the photovoltaic effect in 1887, but not until Einstein put forth his quantum theory of light was the phenomenon explained. According to this theory, light consists of "quanta" of energy, now known as photons. The energy (E) of each photon is equal to $h \times f$, where f is the frequency of the light and h is Planck's constant (a very small number, 6.6×10^{-27} erg second). Radiation frequency is related to its quanta of energy. The energy of each photon of light is incredibly small, but when you consider that a trillion billion photons of light are emitted each second from a 100-watt light bulb, you begin to appreciate how much power is available from bright sunlight.

PV Solar Cells

The basic component of any PV system is the solar cell, originally developed for use in the space program. There are three types of solar cells in use today: single-crystal cells, polycrystalline cells, and amorphous thin-film cells. Silicon, refined from silica (high-grade sand or quartz rock), has been the main ingredient of all three. It is interesting to note that sand is the second most abundant substance, after water, on the Earth's surface.

Single-crystal PV solar cells. Single-crystal cells were the first to be used commercially. They are made by removing the impurities from molten silicon to create a block of polysilicon. The polysilicon is remelted and doped with a small concentration of boron, then "drawn" into a single long cylindrical crystal. Boron allows the crystal to conduct positive charges, or protons, and crystals with this capability are called P-type silicon crystals. The cylinder is then sliced into very thin wafers and the front surface of each wafer is treated with phosphorus. This produces a thin N-type layer that conducts negative charges. The N-type layer meets the P-type layer at the P-N junction, and it is here that the photovoltaic effect takes place. As you might imagine, growing the crystals and slicing the thin wafers is labor-intensive.

When a single photon of light is absorbed at the P-N junction, it creates one negative charge and one corresponding positive charge. The negative charges tend to congregate in the N-type layer, positive charges in the P-type layer (see Figure 8-1). If metal contacts are placed on each side of the cell, current can be made to flow. The metal contacts must be able to "gather" electrical charges from the entire surface of the cell. This is no problem on the side away from the sun, where the whole surface can be the contact area. On the front side facing the sun, however, the metal contact must be constructed so that it doesn't block too much sunlight from reaching the P-N junction, reducing cell efficiency. Therefore, the front contact configuration usually consists of two parallel metal bars for stiffness, with a superthin metal grid extending perpendicularly from them to gather the electrical current (see Figure 8-2).

Single-crystal PV solar cells in use today are either round like the original wafer, or trimmed to resemble a square with rounded corners. Trimming allows for greater cell density, which means higher PV solar-panel efficiency. Although a fair amount of the expensive crystal material is left over from the process, it can be used in other applications.

Polycrystalline PV solar cells. Rectangular-shaped polycrystalline PV solar cells were developed after single-crystal cells. For these, the drawing process of growing single crystals is replaced by casting a multicrystal, rectangular ingot of silicon that is allowed to cool very slowly. The ingot is sliced into thin wafers, as with the single-crystal cells. The resulting cells are somewhat easier to manufacture, and multiple rectangular cells can be mounted without wasting space or silicon.

The basic operation and metal contact grid is the same as for single-crystal cells. Cell efficiencies (around 11 to 12 percent) are slightly less than single-crystal cells (at around 12 to 14 percent) because of minute electrical shorts that occur along the boundary between crystallites.

FIGURE 8-1.   **Photons of light striking the P-N junction inside a solar cell.**

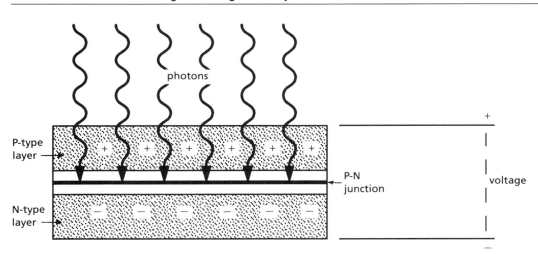

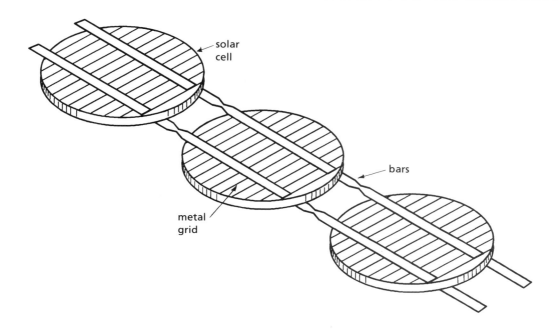

solar cell

bars

metal grid

Amorphous thin-film PV solar cells. Thin-film solar cells are relatively new and are created in a radically different manner, with much less silicon required. Amorphous means that there is no definite crystalline structure. For this cell, a thin film of silicon-based alloys is deposited on a moving roll of substrate material, such as stainless steel, in a process resembling printing. Near total automation reduces labor costs, with solar cells being produced in a high-density, lightweight roll. Since there is no cutting or trimming process, and since the silicon alloy film is much thinner than crystalline wafers, significantly less photovoltaic material is required. Thin-film cell efficiencies are up to 6 percent (after initial output degradation) and promise to be higher in the near future. Presently about twice the cell surface area is needed to match the output of crystalline cells.

Cell Voltage and Amperage Characteristics
PV solar cells exposed to sunlight have a voltage of about 0.5, regardless of size. This is analogous to battery-cell voltage, which, for a given temperature and state of charge, is constant, independent of battery size or capacity. The one exception is the amorphous thin-film cell in the Sovonics PV panel, which is actually a double-layer cell producing 1.2 volts. While voltage remains constant, current increases with cell surface area. In bright sunlight, a typical round crystalline PV solar cell 10 centimeters (4 inches) in diameter produces a current of about 2 amperes at 0.5 volt.

Cell Power and Efficiency

Available power from sunlight is approximately 1 kilowatt (1,000 watts) per square meter at the Earth's surface on a clear day. Today's solar cells are capable of converting 6 to 14 percent of this into electrical power. At first glance this seems a low ratio of potential to usable energy, but it is equal to or greater than energy conversion efficiencies for most other marine generators. For a simple, reliable piece of equipment with no moving parts, using sunshine as a fuel, it's really quite extraordinary. In fact, today's PV solar cells, covering a 100-mile-square piece of land that experiences average sunshine, could produce as much electrical power as the entire generating capacity of the United States. More exotic experimental PV solar cells have reached efficiencies exceeding 30 percent, but their cost at present prohibits commercial use.

Let's see if we can determine the power and the efficiency of the round PV solar cell with a 10-centimeter diameter described above. The total cell power is simply the amperage multiplied by the voltage, or 2 amperes × 0.5 volt = 1 watt. How efficient is this cell? We know the power of bright sunlight is 1,000 watts per square meter, and since 1 square meter = 10,000 square centimeters, this converts to 1 watt per 10 square centimeters. Our round solar cell with a diameter of 10 centimeters has a surface area of 78.5 square centimeters. Its power is then 1 watt per 78.5 square centimeters, just over 12 percent efficient.

PV SOLAR PANELS

PV solar cells become useful to boaters and other "energy managers" when they are grouped in a panel to achieve the desired voltage and amperage for charging 12-volt batteries. A typical PV solar panel has about 36 cells electrically connected in series, with the bottom metal contact of each cell connected to the top metal contact of the next. Series connection means that the amperage of the panel is the same as that for one cell, but the voltage is cumulative and increases with the number of cells. A typical 36-cell PV solar panel has an open-circuit electrical potential of around 18 volts regardless of size, more than sufficient to charge a 12-volt battery. The amperage of the panel depends of the size of the solar cells used, which in turn determines the size of the panel. Smaller solar panels produce less current and therefore have a smaller power rating.

Some PV solar panels have only 30 or so cells in order to limit their voltage potential. These panels, termed "self-regulating," theoretically cannot produce a high enough voltage to overcharge a lead-acid battery, thus eliminating the need for a separate voltage controller. In reality you still must match panel output to battery capacity, and the lower voltage potential makes these panels less effective when light levels are low (early or late in the day and in overcast conditions) and when ambient temperatures are high. They are not recommended for use in the tropics, and should be considered only for a one- or two-panel system in temperate climates.

Panel Construction

Crystalline solar cells are in the form of thin, fragile wafers and must be mounted in a framework that secures and protects them yet still allows light to reach them. During panel manufacture, the cells are placed on a light-colored reflective backing sheet (typically Tedlar or Mylar) and encapsulated in a material that protects them and holds them in place. EVA (ethylene vinyl acetate) is most commonly used for its ultraviolet resistance and its stability with respect to color fading, humidity, and temperature.

Standard PV panels. "Standard" PV panels are designed and primarily intended to be mounted in arrays for land-based power generation. Since models available today are ruggedly built and have a long life expectancy, they are also marketed for marine use. They have a smooth, tempered glass cover with very high light transmission that is placed over the encapsulated cells. The entire assembly is then fitted into a perimeter framework with a watertight gasket. The framework prevents undue bending stress in the cells, and is usually made of silver or black 1-inch-high anodized aluminum. A watertight electrical junction box with positive and negative leads is located on the back side of the panel (see Figure 8-3).

Marine-grade PV panels. So-called marine PV panels differ in several respects. They address a boater's concerns about mounting flexibility, weight, durability, and appearance. The cells are often encapsulated on a stronger backing sheet of aluminum or stainless steel, and the perimeter framework is either very thin or eliminated completely. On top of the encapsulated cells, instead of glass, is usually a lightweight, virtually indestructible cover of Tedlar or other polymer material. These characteristics allow marine panels to be slightly flexible so they can mount on contoured boat surfaces, and also allow them to withstand limited foot traffic. Sovonics marine solar panels, using amorphous thin-film technology, are completely flexible. They can be rolled up for storage or sewn into biminis and dodgers for out-of-the-way mounting. In the past, several manufacturers of standard PV panels have substituted a teak perimeter framework for the standard aluminum one on several models, and

FIGURE 8-3. **A well-designed electrical junction box on the rear of a solar panel. (Courtesy SPC)**

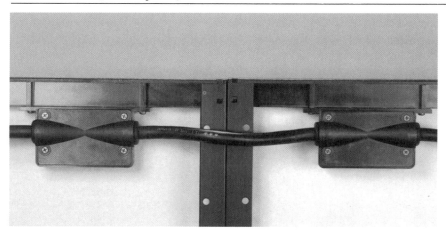

marketed them as marine panels. These are no longer available, but you can add a wood border to any PV panel to enhance its appearance.

Panel Ratings and Reliability

All photovoltaic panels are rated according to "peak power" in watts—that is, power output in optimum conditions. This is the most meaningful rating to size your system. Panels are available with ratings from 5 to 90 watts for a variety of power applications. In addition to the peak power rating, manufacturers also list other electrical characteristics useful for comparing panels. They include the voltage at peak power, the current at peak power, and the guaranteed minimum peak power during the warranty period. A panel with a higher voltage at peak power will operate more efficiently in hot climates and in overcast conditions. Refer to Figure 8-4 for a sample solar panel's current, voltage, and temperature relationship.

How reliable are PV solar panels? Compared with many other pieces of marine electrical generating equipment, they are extremely reliable, with standard panel warranties of 10 years or more. Actual panel life expectancy is in excess of 30 years! Even though the warranty period for marine panels is much shorter, well-cared-for marine panels will last every bit as long as standard ones. PV panels are subjected to rigorous laboratory testing, such as the Jet

---

FIGURE 8-4. **Curves like these, supplied by manufacturers, show how output current and voltage vary with solar-cell temperature.**

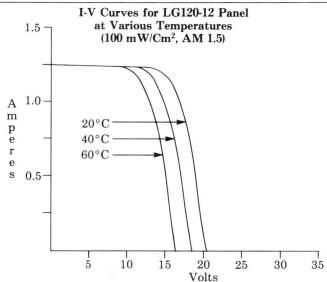

I-V Curves for LG120-12 Panel at Various Temperatures (100 mW/Cm², AM 1.5)

Environmental Operating Conditions

Temperature: −40°C to 90°C
Humidity: 0 to 100%
Altitude: to 25000 ft. (7.620m)

Wind Loading: Modules withstand
sustained winds in excess of 175 mph
(280 kph) or 90 lbs/sq ft

perature cycling, temperature cycling at high humidity levels, wind loading exceeding 125 miles per hour, and surface impact equivalent to 1-inch hail traveling at terminal velocity of 52 miles per hour. Even tempered-glass-covered panels are expected to pass the impact test.

Panel Performance

A PV solar panel's performance depends on several factors, the first being the number of cells used. The greater the number of cells, the higher the voltage, and the higher the output in high temperatures and overcast conditions. The second factor is the cell construction. A panel with amorphous-thin-film cells, exposed to bright sunshine, will have approximately half the output of a crystalline-cell panel of the same size in the same conditions. But cell efficiency is not the only consideration for total panel efficiency. Partial shading from sails or other gear can create the equivalent of an open circuit along the path of series-connected cells, drastically reducing the output of crystalline cell panels. Sovonics panels, with their amorphous thin-film cells, have integrated blocking diodes between the cells to prevent major power loss due to partial shading of the panel. Because of this, the unshaded cells are able to maintain their output. On a boat, this difference can be significant, outweighing the differ-ence in cell efficiency in some instances. It all depends on how and where the panels are mounted, and how diligent you are at keeping them facing into the sun.

PV solar panels are most effective when they are perpendicular to the sun's rays and are unshaded. On land you can mount panels on passive or motorized trackers that automatically follow the sun. On boats this is not practical, and "owner participation" is needed to get maximum output over the course of the day. Panel performance will fall off as it tilts away from the sun or is shaded. Figure 8-5 is a performance chart we compiled for the 35-watt standard solar panel with single-crystal cells used on our first catamaran. When the sun is low in the sky, reflection off the water tends to improve the panel performance just as a blanket of snow does for land-based systems. The effects of shading and the tilt angle from the sun are additive. You can see from the chart that if a solar panel with crystalline cells is tilted 45 degrees to the sun and is shaded by three thin shadows, the output will be $0.85 \times 0.85 = 0.72$, or about three-quarters of a panel's output when unshaded and perpendicular to the sun. Thin shadows from rigging that is well away from the panel will not appreciably affect output.

A PV panel will begin collecting energy as soon as there is enough light in the morning, usually at around 10 percent of noonday-sun levels. Some higher-voltage panels will begin producing at 5 percent of noonday sun. Season, latitude, and battery state of charge all influ-ence the time of day when charging begins, since the panel must develop enough voltage to overcome the battery voltage. Panel output will continue until the light fades in the late after-noon. Output current levels are proportional to the level of light. They will be low at the beginning and end of the day due to refraction of the sun's rays by the Earth's atmosphere, and will diminish during cloudy conditions. The period of solar collection will be longer in the summer than the winter, with the actual length of the solar day depending on latitude.

FIGURE 8-5. **Relative performance chart compiled by authors for a 35-watt solar panel mounted on a catamaran.**

Shading	% of maximum output	Tilt angle	% of maximum output
Full exposure	100%	Panel perpendicular (0°) to sun	100%
One thin shadow across panel (as from stay, sheet or halyard)	95%	Panel tilted 22.5° from sun	95%
Three thin shadows across panel	85–95%	Panel tilted 45° from sun	85%
One thick shadow 3–5″ wide across panel	50%	Panel tilted 77.5° from sun	60%
One-third panel shaded by object at least 2–3′ away from panel	35–40%	Panel tilted 90° from sun	30%
Two-thirds panel shaded by object at least 2–3′ away from panel	25–30%	Panel tilted more than 90° from sun	15–20%
All of panel shaded by object at least 2–3′ away from panel	15–20%	NA	NA

MARINE USES FOR PV SOLAR ENERGY

PV solar panels satisfy such a wide range of generating needs they could be in almost any boat's inventory of equipment. They work as well in trickle-charging applications as they do in multiple-panel systems for medium to large power needs. It's not necessary to make a large PV investment initially. Electrical output is related to the total area of PV cells, making it easy to start with a small system, then gradually increase your capacity. Listed below are the common marine uses for photovoltaic cells and panels.

Direct-Use Appliances

A direct-use appliance is one that can be run directly from PV cells without first storing the energy in the main batteries. After calculators, the most popular direct-use items are PV solar ventilators. They take the place of standard dome vents, which are designed to create a suction only when wind passes over the unit. PV cells increase ventilator efficiency tremendously. Solar vents incorporate a 3- to 4-inch round PV cell (about 1 watt) into the top surface of the vent, with a small 12-volt DC fan wired directly to it underneath. The fans typically can be run in the exhaust or intake mode, with the fan speed and effectiveness proportional to the amount of sunshine present. They work best when the potential for overheating is greatest. In one model the fan is wired to a small rechargeable battery, which in turn is charged by the solar cell. This unit stores excess solar energy during the day so that the fan continues to

FIGURE 8-6. **A solvonics panel mounted on a powerboat.** **131**

function after the sun goes down. PV solar vents are self-contained and require no additional wiring.

PV solar cells are also incorporated directly into flashlights (with built-in rechargeable batteries) and into 12-volt battery chargers. Several models can recharge AA-, C-, and D-size rechargeable batteries, saving money and the waste of disposable batteries. You can even get a solar charger for button batteries used in hearing aids, cameras, watches, and other small appliances. The solar flashlight, the PV battery charger, and the mobile 12-volt charger are all available from Real Goods Trading Company. Note: The same effect can be achieved by having solar panels charge your main boat batteries, and using a mobile 12-volt charger to recharge AA, C, and D batteries from them.

Float Charging

PV solar panels are ideal for float-charging batteries that experience intermittent use or are stored for long periods. They work equally well on powerboats and sailboats, eliminating the typical scenario of finding dead batteries when you return to your boat, or that of seasonal battery replacement. Small PV panels can make up the self-discharge losses of a battery at rest, and keep batteries healthy by maintaining a full charge. A 5- or 10-watt panel is usually sufficient for float-charging applications.

Main-Battery Charging

Larger PV panels are usually required for supplying power to the boat's main batteries. For main-battery charging, you should purchase panels with at least an 18- or 20-watt power rating. Larger panels are more economical than smaller ones. How many you require will depend on your electrical load, how and where you use your boat, and how effectively you keep the panels facing into the sun. Multiple panels can be connected in parallel to supply the required power. They can serve as a supplement to other charging methods or the primary source for on-board charging.

Aids to Navigation

The use of PV panels to power offshore and coastal navigational aids is increasing rapidly. They provide a constant power source for recharging batteries on lighted buoys and remote lighted coastal markers. Their use in these applications is a constant reminder of PV-panel consistency, durability, and low maintenance requirements.

METHODS OF INSTALLATION

Since a solar panel achieves its highest output when perpendicular to the sun, the installation of a photovoltaic system for a house is straightforward. The panels are faced due south and tilted (depending on latitude) to an angle off the horizon that best intercepts the sunlight. The angle of tilt can be seasonally adjusted for better performance. For even more efficient operation, the panels can be placed on a tracking mechanism that follows the sun along the horizon, maintaining the proper attitude. Trackers are either active (electromechanically driven) or passive. The latter accommodate up to eight large panels and contain a refrigerant gas in an iron frame. The frame is constructed in such a way that as the sun hits it, the gas moves to a new location, keeping the panels faced toward the sun. The frame tracks across the horizon, but the angle of tilt must still be adjusted seasonally.

Trackers are impractical for boats, but you can simulate their operation, with close to the same efficiency, by keeping your panels unshaded and orienting them toward the sun several times a day. This is where you decide how much that extra efficiency is worth. You may feel that more PV panels, permanently mounted and receiving a good average amount of sun, is less bother for the same electrical output. Either way, PV solar panels are light and easy to work with, and you can have fun experimenting with different mounting methods.

Unmounted PV Panels

Many boaters simply leave their panels loose so they may be placed in the sun when at anchor or in good sea conditions, as shown in Figure 8-7. This can be one of the most efficient ways to "mount" them, since most of a boat's time is spent at anchor, mooring, or dock. Place the panels on boat cushions or other padded objects that don't allow them to slide around. Panels can be stowed in bad weather or when you leave the boat.

Unmounted panels are easier to steal than mounted ones, and if you stow the panel when you leave, it won't trickle-charge the battery. One solution is a small, permanently mounted PV panel for float-charging the battery, with larger, stowable panels to use when you're on board and incur a larger electrical load. Unmounted panels also have a tendency to "sail away" in sudden squalls. Some method of "quick disconnect" mounting might serve both functions. Wiring should be neat and, to the extent possible, out of the way.

Deck Mount

One of the most popular installations is to mount the panels on a portion of the deck that is away from foot traffic and receives good average sunshine. Standard panels come with a 1– to 1 + -inch-high aluminum frame to which you can attach mounting feet that secure to the deck with stainless steel fasteners. Add a thin layer of rubber or foam under the feet to dampen boat vibrations. You can also mount multiple standard panels on wood runners, as in Figure 8-8. This allows the panels to approximate the crown of a deck without flexing. The wood runners need limberholes to allow water to drain, and they should hold the panels off the deck to allow good air circulation. This keeps the panels cooler and increases efficiency. You might have to mount your panel on a compound curve if the deck slopes in both directions, but unless the curve is pronounced, this should present no problem. Just taper the runners in one direction. PV panels come in various shapes, so look for panels that fit the space on your boat. While larger panels offer a better price per watt, it is sometimes easier to accommodate two smaller panels.

Marine-grade panels are thin and have no perimeter frame, but they usually have mounting eyes in each corner. Wood runners are rarely needed since the panels can assume a slight curve to match a deck. It's best to keep the curve to a minimum to prevent overstressing the solar cells, except in the case of the fully flexible Sovonics panel. Marine panels should also be raised slightly off the deck with plastic or rubber spacers below each mounting eye to allow drainage and air circulation.

FIGURE 8-8.   **Deck-mounted PV Solar panels.**

It is easy to install an electrical connection underneath or next to deck-mounted panels, a clean and neat solution that keeps wiring from entangling other boat equipment.

Quick-Disconnect Mount

A quick-disconnect mounting allows you to secure the PV panels when under way or when you leave the boat, yet allows you to remove the panels quickly to face them into the sun for increased efficiency. Using the wood runner technique described above, set the panels into a deck-mounted framework, then include pivoting fasteners for easy removal. If the panels are sometimes mounted in other locations, wingnuts allow you to disconnect them quickly.

Remember that when panels are removed from a framework, they trail wiring and may entangle other equipment. To keep things neat, you might place deck plugs in several locations. Make certain the plugs are polarized for DC use (they have plus and minus terminals that can't be connected incorrectly).

Rail Mount

Several PV-panel suppliers offer kits for attaching standard panels to boat rails (see Figure 8-9). These kits can also be used for marine panels if you add your own frame. Stern rails are a popular place for mounting, out of the way of sails and rigging. Rail mounts consist of two adjustable sets of clamps that fasten to the rails and provide fasteners for the panel frame. You can adjust the tilt angle of the panel(s) by loosening the clamps and pivoting the assembly. Panel movement is limited to rotating around the rail (varying tilt angle) and does not allow tracking along the horizon. Rail mounts are simple to install and keep the panels well ventilated and tightly secured when under way. Wiring is typically strapped to stanchion posts and led to a nearby deck plug.

Catboats and other boats without jibs usually have a clear bow pulpit, another popular place for rail mounting, although the wiring path to the batteries is likely to be longer. In the bow, the panels are less apt to be shaded by biminis and other equipment.

Gimbal Mount

A variation on rail mounting is the gimbal mount, whereby you create a frame that allows the panel(s) to rotate freely as if they were mounted on a rail. The frame consists of two metal

FIGURE 8-9.   **Rail-mounted panels. (Courtesy Jack Rabbit Marine)**   **135**

arms, similar to small dinghy davits, and is usually cantilevered over the transom. The panel frame is connected to either arm with an adjustable fastener so that the panel(s) can rotate 180 degrees about the gimbal. Movement and wiring considerations are the same as for rail-mounted panels.

Universal Pole Mount

While a rail- or gimbal-mounted panel has only one degree of freedom, panels with a universal mount have two, making it possible for them to tilt and also track along the horizon. A universal pole mount consists of two adjustable clamps, joined but offset 90 degrees from each other, similar to some barbecue mounts for boats. The clamps are connected below to a sturdy pole that is in turn fastened to the deck and/or boat rails, and above to the panel frame. Adjust one clamp to vary tilt angle, and the other to vary angle along the horizon.

The pole and clamps must be sturdy to withstand wind loads. This mount is more complicated to install, but allows the panels to track the sun closely—given some vigilance on the part of the owner. Wiring can be hidden inside the pole, and an ammeter can be placed on the backside of the panels so you can see immediately the effect of panel adjustment.

Rigging Mount

When we first encountered this type of mount, we were intrigued by its potential usefulness on boats with little or cluttered deck space. It is most common on ketches, using the shrouds of the aft mast. This area is generally free from running rigging. The panels are suspended vertically along the stays in such a way that their tilt angle can be adjusted by raising and lowering lines. We've seen fancier setups that also allowed the panels to be rotated along the horizon. Since panels mounted in the rigging are subject to high wind loads at

FIGURE 8-10. **Solar panels on this ketch are suspended from rigging as well as from lifelines.**

times, the mounts should be secure or used only in harbor or calm weather. The wiring can be brought down the rigging to an appropriately placed deck plug.

Bimini/Dodger Mount

It is always possible to place PV panels on top of the bimini or dodger when in harbor for out-of-the-way solar exposure. We often did this with our 35-watt standard panel, but you must be careful not to knock your head against the frame. Safety lines should be rigged in case of sudden squalls. Sovonics has made bimini mounting truly practical with its fully flexible panels, which can be sewn into the bimini permanently. You will need about twice the area of crystalline cell panels for the equivalent electrical output, but there is usually room for this on suncovers and biminis (see Figure 8-11).

Another possibility is an array of standard solar panels mounted over the cockpit, doubling as a bimini. The panels could rest on an aluminum or stainless steel framework, and the cost would probably be little more than for the bimini alone.

PV PANEL SIZING AND SELECTION

The proper approach to panel selection would have you examine your needs and the specifications of the various panels available; but it is also possible just to purchase one or two panels and connect them into your system. Chances are you won't be sorry, and will probably want to add more panels in the future. During our first year in the tropics on our

FIGURE 8-11. **Bimini-mounted panel.** **137**

second catamaran, two 18-watt Solarex MSX-Lite marine panels supplied almost all our electrical needs for cabin and running lights, radio and occasional tape deck use, and powering a small 100-watt inverter for a laptop computer. By the end of the year, we were making provisions for more panels to help with an expected increase in electrical load. For a stepwise approach to estimating and satisfying electrical demands, see Chapters 13 and 14.

Assessing Your Needs

The information in this section will help you estimate your solar-charging needs. The design of an alternative-energy system is determined in part by electrical load, but also by your boat, how and where you use it, and how you mount and operate the system. The output from alternative energy systems is said to be much more "location and owner dependent" than that from fossil-fueled systems.

Electrical load.   This is easy to calculate or to determine empirically by monitoring your daily electrical draw. Make a list of electrical equipment on board, with the number of amperes drawn by each when operating. Then multiply these by the number of hours you operate each one during the course of the day. Use an average for intermittent-use equipment. Total the ampere-hours and you have a good approximation of the electrical energy you consume. Now add an additional 10 to 15 percent for energy storage and retrieval inefficiency. We use ampere-hours as a convention, since batteries are so rated, but it leaves voltage out of the equation. Watt-hours are in fact the correct representation of energy production or consumption.

PV panel output. It would be nice to match your total electrical load with PV-panel output, but this becomes difficult on a boat as energy use rises, especially in cloudy climates. The panels are limited in the output they can deliver, and you begin to run out of mounting space for PV panels and ways to keep them all facing the sun. It is not impossible, however, to meet high energy loads strictly with PV solar panels. We've seen the level of creativity for efficiently mounting solar panels on boats reach truly epic proportions in recent years.

To calculate the electrical energy PV panels can deliver under ideal circumstances, multiply the peak current rating in amperes by the number of hours of peak sunshine. For example, a panel with a 2-ampere rating that faces full sunshine for an average of 8 hours each day can deliver an average of 16 ampere-hours of energy each day. If you use four of these panels, receiving the same levels of sunlight, your total system output would be 64 ampere-hours per day. These are ideal numbers to use as a reference. Actual PV energy output will undoubtedly be lower, and is affected by other factors including mounting, climate, and panel temperature.

Mounting configurations offer the opportunity to get really creative, since the method of PV-panel mounting greatly affects daily electrical output. Some mounting arrangements allow you to adjust the panel tilt angle to the sun as often as you want during the day, while others are less flexible. Some fixed mounting positions leave the panel shaded for a few hours, but get good sunshine the remainder of the day and don't require periodic adjustment. You can be as much of a participant in collecting energy as you wish.

Where you sail plays a large part in determining the average daily output from PV solar panels. Obviously, solar energy devices work best in sunny climates. The ideal 16 ampere-hours per day mentioned above can drop to half that amount in cloudy climates. Most sailing areas, however, have sufficient sunshine to justify a PV system. Figure 8-12 illustrates daily solar radiation for the continental United States. At one end of the spectrum, southern Florida has high sunlight levels throughout the year. At the other end, the coasts of Washington, British Columbia, and southeast Alaska have fair to poor amounts of sunshine. The East Coast from Maine to North Carolina and the Great Lakes (except Lake Ontario) have good sunlight levels from early spring through mid fall, and any place south of latitude 28 north, including the Bahamas, Puerto Rico, the Caribbean and Mexico, is excellent for PV solar energy. The Hawaiian Islands also have very good year-round sunlight levels. In general, there is adequate sunshine in almost any area of the world during the local sailing season to support the use of a PV system. In cloudy climates you will have to increase the number of panels to achieve a given output.

Localized conditions, or microclimates, occur within a regional climate. They are often caused by topographical characteristics or differences in water temperature. For instance, Cape Cod, Massachusetts, experiences frequent fogs and strong onshore winds on its south shore during the summer, while there is little fog and light winds to the north. Maine's coastal islands are often enveloped in fog that burns off quickly along the mainland. Cape Hatteras on the East Coast and Mendocino on the West Coast are notorious for attracting bad weather that often does not affect the surrounding areas.

There is also what we call the mini-microclimate—the immediate climate of your dock, mooring, or anchorage. You may find that in certain harbors hills, buildings, or other boats block a fair portion of available sunlight. On land, there are laws in some states to protect

FIGURE 8-12.   **Mean daily solar radiation in July and February. The legend is as follows:**

0 — < 150	Langleys	6 — 400–450	Langleys
1 — 150–200	Langleys	7 — 450–500	Langleys
2 — 200–250	Langleys	8 — 500–550	Langleys
3 — 250–300	Langleys	9 — 550–600	Langleys
4 — 300–350	Langleys	10 — 600–650	Langleys
5 — 350–400	Langleys	11 — > 650	Langleys

where one Langley = 3.69 Btu/ft2. (Information courtesy Environmental Science Services Administration)

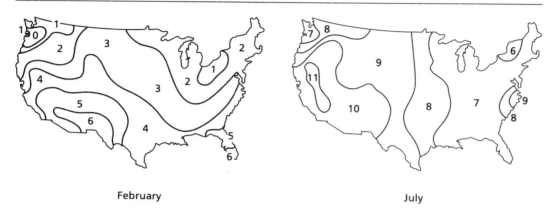

February   July

paths of sunlight from being blocked by new construction. There is no such thing for boaters, and really there is no need, since it is a simple matter to move, but you should nevertheless be aware of the potential power loss in an adverse location.

Even your boat creates a mini-microclimate. If you are anchored or moored, and lying to the prevailing wind or current, one part of your boat may be perpetually shaded and one part always in the sun. We experienced this anchoring in the tradewind belt, where we almost always faced east. In the beginning, our panels were movable, but we eventually secured them to the deck on the side of the boat that always had good exposure to the sun when anchored.

Panel temperature, which is influenced by mounting and climate, also affects output. Panels that are flush mounted on deck can experience power loss due to excessive temperatures if they are not vented from underneath. For correct mounting methods, refer to the section on panel installation. Local ambient temperature also affects panel output. PV panels will have less power potential in hot climates than cold. On the other hand, hot climates also have high levels of sunshine, so things even out. Ambient temperature is not so much a problem on a boat as it is ashore, since water bodies mitigate temperature extremes. Significant power loss due to reduced panel voltage can be experienced in desert areas and other hot inland regions around the globe, which is why higher-voltage panels are recommended for these areas.

Your boat. How much space do you have available for solar panels? Smaller boats have limited deck space, but usually have smaller electrical loads to match. Larger boats can almost always find space for an assortment of solar panels. The wide deck spaces of multihulls lend themselves nicely to vast arrays of PV panels, as do the deckhouses of motorsailers and powerboats.

The appearance of your boat should also be considered. Some boatowners feel that PV solar panels detract from the lines of their vessels, but this need not be the case. Panels can be mounted unobtrusively. Others feel that form is related to function, and the knowledge that these panels are collecting electricity from sunshine somehow enhances their appearance. To these boaters, solar panels should be mounted in places of prominence instead of disguised or hidden. As stated, a wooden frame or border can easily be placed around the perimeter of PV panels to soften their looks.

Incidentally, we learned the hard way that biminis must be taken into account when mounting solar panels. We secured our first 10-watt panel to the center of the aft cabin roof. When we traveled south, our rain tent was converted to a sun cover that effectively blocked sunlight from reaching the panel. In the tropics, boats with biminis that extend the entire length of the cabintop must mount solar panels elsewhere.

How you use your boat. The way in which you use your boat is another consideration when assessing your needs. For the weekend sailor, PV panels are ideal. They are self-tending and could keep the batteries topped up during the week while the boat is idle, then provide enough power for a two- or three-day weekend cruise. The panels can be smaller, since they will have four or five days to make up for the power consumed on the weekend. Boaters who take an occasional extended cruise must decide whether they want solar panels to handle the additional electrical load during this period. You may allow for the occasional extra load when selecting panels, or you may supplement panel output with other methods of generation.

Voyaging and liveaboard boaters favor PV solar panels for their easy, quiet, self-tending operation. Liveaboards impose a higher electrical load, and the selection process often comes down to how many panels can be afforded or will fit on the boat.

PV panels are also the favorite method of generating electricity for ocean racers. Marine-grade panels are necessary for withstanding heavy-footed crewmembers and the pounding of a hard-driven yacht in ocean seas, unless the panels can be mounted out of the way on a secure framework. Solar panels will provide a near constant source of charge without appreciably increasing boat weight or windage. The yacht *Fantasy* demonstrated the reliability of solar panels in the 1982 BOC single-handed around-the-world race. The skipper used a four-panel Solec Solarcharger system to operate his communication system, interior and navigation lights, instrumentation, and autopilot. Even after one panel was bent 90 degrees by a large wave, it continued to function for the remainder of the race. It's now commonplace to see solar panels mounted on ocean racing boats.

If your boat is used in the charter business, it needs an undemanding, fairly foolproof energy system capable of handling a large electrical load. PV panels satisfy the first two conditions, and when used in conjunction with a high-output alternator make a significant contribution toward the total electrical load. The decrease in engine running time makes

Panel Selection

When shopping for panels, use the following criteria:

- *Appearance, durability, and mounting flexibility.* These three characteristics are related to how you intend to install your panels.

- *The ratio of cost to total power output.* As a rule, standard panels and larger, higher-output panels are the least expensive in dollars per watt. Marine-grade panels and small, low-output panels are the most expensive.

- *The ratio of output to size of the panel, in watts per square foot.* Panels with the least-efficient cells will have the smallest ratio, and you will need more of these to achieve a given output.

- *Manufacturer's warranty.* It should be noted that most glass-covered standard panels have a warranty period of 5 to 12 years. Marine-grade PV panels have lower warranty periods of 1 to 5 years, not reflecting an inferior product but only the increased chance of being damaged.

Figure 8-13 offers a comparison of PV panels suitable for boats. Panels with power ratings less than 10 watts have been omitted.

SYSTEM EFFICIENCY

System efficiency when charging batteries with solar panels will be close to individual panel efficiency as long as there is good sunshine and the panels are unshaded and facing into the sun. Efficiencies of around 10 percent are to be expected in good conditions with high-efficiency cells. This means that 10 percent of the solar energy available at the panel is converted to usable electrical energy. Systems with amorphous thin-film panels are around 5 percent efficient in good conditions. Other factors affecting efficiency include battery state of charge and the use of voltage regulators.

OTHER COMPONENTS AND CONSIDERATIONS

The following components may or should be considered in conjunction with PV solar panels.

Batteries

Special lead-calcium, low-self-discharge batteries are available for photovoltaic applications, although 12-volt, deep-cycle marine batteries are fine for these systems. To protect battery life, a low-voltage alarm or load disconnect should be used.

FIGURE 8-13. **PV solar-panel comparison chart.**

Company	Panel	Crystal	Cover	Frame	Peak power (watts)	$/Watt (peak)	Watt/ft² (peak)	Warranty (years)
Kyocera J48	s	pc	g	r	48	7.5	10.0	12
Hoxan	s	sc	g	r	48	7.5	11.0	10
Arco								
M25	s	sc	g	r	22	10.0	10.9	5
M65	s	sc	g	r	42	10.0	10.9	10
M75	s	sc	g	r	47	10.0	10.8	10
M55	s	sc	g	r	53	10.0	11.5	10
Solarex								
MSXL 10	m	pc	p	f	10	17.0	7.0	1
MSXL 18	m	pc	p	f	18	12.0	7.6	1
MSXL 30	m	pc	p	f	30	10.0	8.6	1
MSX 30	s	pc	g	r	30	9.0	9.4	10
MSX 40	s	pc	g	r	41	9.0	8.6	10
MSX 60	s	pc	g	r	60	9.0	9.8	10
Solec								
SC-1	m	sc	p	f	10	17.0	7.0	1
SC-3	m	sc	p	f	20	17.0	8.2	1
SC-2	m	sc	p	f	30	17.0	8.4	1
S4233	s	sc	g	r	70	10.0	8.9	5
S5233	s	sc	g	r	90	9.0	10.6	5
Sovonics								
MA 10	m	aft	p	ff	12	18.0	3.5	1
MA 20	m	aft	p	ff	23	15.0	4.4	1
MA 30	m	aft	p	ff	33	14.0	4.2	1
PL 201	m	aft	p	f	23	10.0	4.4	1
RL 100	m	aft	p	f	32	11.0	4.2	1
P 201	s	aft	p	r	23	10.0	4.4	5
R 100	s	aft	p	r	32	11.0	4.2	5

Key: aft = amorphous thin film; f = flexible; ff = fully flexible; g = glass; m = marine; p = polymer; pc = polycrystalline; r = rigid; s = standard; sc = single crystal

Diode and Fuse

The diode allows current to flow into the battery but stops it from flowing back out at night or during cloudy periods. The use of diodes for one- or two-panel systems is controversial, since the voltage drop across the diode lessens output, offsetting the good it does at night. On larger systems, diodes are a good thing, and they are essential when PV panels interface with other charging equipment. In this case a diode keeps charging current from other sources flowing to the battery and not through the PV panels. A fuse, meanwhile, protects your equipment in the event of a short circuit or current overload. The fuse should be sized slightly higher than maximum panel output. Circuit breakers can be substituted as long as they are properly sized.

Diodes can serve another purpose in multiple-panel systems. If you have panels mounted on both sides of your boat and connected in parallel to the battery, the panel(s) in the shade may rob the ones in the sun of their output. A diode, naturally, will prevent this from happening.

Voltage Regulators and Charge Monitors

Voltage regulators protect batteries from overcharging and come in a wide range of current ratings and features. They often include a diode and fuse. Voltage regulation is essential for systems that are left untended, unless self-regulating panels are used or the ampere-hour capacity of your battery is greater than 50 times the maximum current rating (in amperes) of your solar panels. This rule of thumb is meant for standard batteries with a fairly high self-discharge rate. It does not apply to Prevailer or other low-self-discharge batteries. It is not necessary to install a voltage regulator if you monitor battery condition closely, but a taper-charging regulator can make more efficient use of your PV-panel output and can maintain your system when you are off the boat.

Charge monitors are not a necessity, but great fun, and helpful for instant indication of current being produced by the vessel's panels. Faulty panels can be diagnosed immediately, and you can fine-tune your panel-adjustment angle to the sun. Select an ammeter having an appropriate current scale. For example, if your total PV maximum output is 4 amperes, an ammeter with a 1-to-5-ampere scale would be the best.

There are several solar monitor-regulator units that provide diode and fuse, voltage regulation, and charge monitor in one neat package.

Appliances

With a PV system on board, it is much cheaper and easier to select energy-efficient appliances than it is to add more solar panels. Try to find equipment that does the job with the least power (refer to Chapter 13 for energy-efficient appliances).

Deck Plugs

The most convenient method for taking your PV-panel wiring below is through a watertight 12-volt deck plug. Make certain to get one with a current rating larger than your maximum panel output. Multiple deck plugs make it easy to move your panels to other boat locations.

Electrical Connections

A single PV solar panel typically has a two-wire electrical lead protruding from a water-proof junction box on the rear or top of the panel. The two wires are marked for polarity, one positive and one negative. The diode, fuse, and charge monitor are located in the positive wire. The fuse should be as close to the battery as possible. Voltage regulators come marked with appropriate wiring locations.

Multiple panels are wired in parallel, thus maintaining single-panel voltage levels with cumulative current levels. Diodes can be installed for each array of panels, so if one array becomes shaded it doesn't affect the output of the array in the sun.

The positive wire from PV panels can be connected to the battery positive terminal or to a common positive terminal at the battery switch or other location. The negative wire can be connected to any common negative terminal. When other methods of generation are employed on the boat, including engine alternators, a properly sized diode will prevent their output from flowing through the PV panels.

FIGURE 8-14. **Schematic of an electrical system with multiple charging options. The portion relevant to photovoltaic charging is highlighted in gray.**

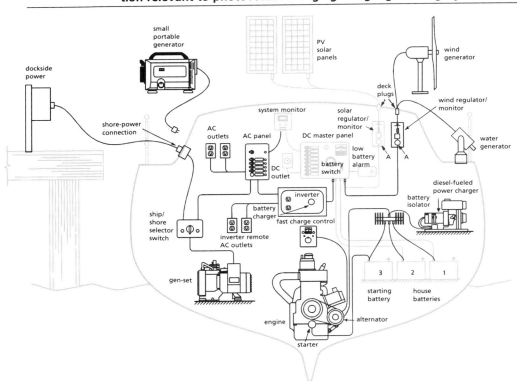

FIGURE 8-15. **Perhaps the largest photovoltaic installation on a pleasure craft (1,060 watts peak power). (Courtesy A.E.G. Telefunken)**

TIPS ON INSTALLATION, OPERATION, AND MAINTENANCE

This section includes an assortment of the most frequently asked questions concerning installation, operation, and maintenance of PV solar panels.

Q. *What are the peak solar collection hours in the day?*
A. For land-based systems the answer is typically 9 a.m. to 3 p.m., but in summer it is longer, and for marine systems, light reflection off the water can greatly lengthen the peak solar day if panels are kept faced into the sun.

Q. *Is there any noise associated with PV systems?*
A. Absolutely none. There are no moving parts in the system.

Q. *What happens if the positive and negative wires of a PV system accidentally come together during setup?*

A. No harm is done to the panel. If it's a larger panel, you might see a tiny spark at the junction of the two wires, indicating voltage is present.

Q. *Do I need to do anything to operate a PV system?*
A. If your panels are permanently mounted and you have a voltage regulator, you need do nothing. If you don't have a regulator, you will need to monitor battery condition, and if your panel is movable, you should try to keep it unshaded and adjust its angle to the sun periodically.

Q. *How many times a day do I need to adjust a movable solar panel for most efficient operation when in harbor?*
A. You would need to adjust it constantly, but three or four times a day should suffice.

Q. *Are there any parts on a PV panel that an owner can service?*
A. All internal solar-cell connections are factory sealed. You may find that the problem is in the external wiring or the junction box, which you can usually get at. One of our solar panels came to us with a slight defect inside the epoxy-filled junction box. We were in the Dominican Republic at the time, with no chance of replacing the panel, and it was necessary to cut away the epoxy coating, resolder the faulty connection, and reseal the junction box with silicon. If you have a problem with a PV panel, it is recommended that you contact your supplier to keep the warranty intact.

Q. *What do I need to do to maintain my PV panels?*
A. Other than an occasional washing with a soft damp cloth (fresh water), nothing.

Q. *Can PV panels be walked on?*
A. All PV panels are made for rough treatment by the elements, but they cannot necessarily stand up to repeated abuse from humans. Marine-panel manufacturers often state that their panels can be walked on, and without glass covers they are capable of tolerating foot traffic, but crystalline cells are still fairly fragile wafers of silicon. It would be prudent to place your panels away from heavily traveled walkways, if for no other reason than to keep the polymer cover from getting scratched. Sovonics panels do not have crystalline cells and can theoretically take more punishment, but even these should be protected from abuse.

Q. *Is a voltage regulator necessary?*
A. No. Many PV-panel owners don't use them for small marine sys-

tems. They are simply a convenience so you won't have to monitor battery condition and shut down output when there is a risk of overcharging the battery. Some boatowners partially cover panels when they are off the boat to keep batteries topped up but prevent overcharging.

9

Wind Generators

S ailors have long known of the energy available in the wind. Indeed, rigging sails to propel boats across the water was likely man's first attempt at harnessing wind energy for his own use. In time, man developed windmills to convert that energy into the energy of rotating shafts, and over the centuries has ground grain, pumped water, and driven simple machinery with wind power. By the early 1900s, windmills that could generate electricity sprouted. In the United States these generators proliferated during the rural electrification effort. A new breed of wind generators—efficient, state-of-the-art models designed to satisfy larger residential electrical loads—was introduced during the energy crisis of the mid 1970s.

This method of generating electrical energy was so successful on small-scale, land-based installations that it was only a matter of time before similar wind generators suitable for small boats became available. In 1977 Hamilton Ferris began supplying wind blades for his water generator, and shortly was joined by many others in the wind-energy market for boaters. Quite a few of these firms stopped production about the time energy tax credits and alternate energy research money were discontinued by the Reagan administration, but a handful of competent manufacturers remain, and their equipment has stood the tests of time and sea. Today's marine wind generators are efficient, durable machines capable of giving years of service. They are reasonably quiet, and the larger units can produce over 15 amperes in good winds.

TYPES OF MARINE WIND GENERATORS

There are two generic types of wind generators available for marine use: the "small prop" units manufactured in Great Britain and Europe, and the "large prop" units made in the United States.

FIGURE 9-1. **The Ampair, a small-prop wind generator. Six blades is a good number: If one breaks, its opposite number can be removed to keep the generator in balance. (Courtesy Jack Rabbit Marine)**

Small-Prop Units

The multiple blades of the small-prop units are reminiscent of farm water-pumping windmills (see Figure 9-1). The diameter of the propeller (the length from blade tip to blade tip measured through the hub) for these units is typically between 36 and 42 inches. The complete units are small, lightweight, and fairly easy to install. They are self-tending in that the blade configuration limits output and prop speed in high winds, eliminating the need for someone to shut them down to protect the unit. They are also quiet, and are safer than large-prop units, since accidentally bumping into an operating unit will probably not cause serious injury (although all wind generators should be mounted well out of reach). Their major drawback is that the multiple-blade design is not particularly efficient compared with large-prop blade configurations, and the smaller prop diameter limits output to 8 to 10 amperes maximum. The manufacturers of the small-prop units feel that the self-tending and safety aspects of their machines outweigh the difference in output.

Large-Prop Units

All American marine wind generators are large-prop units, and are similar to the modern wind generators used on land (see Figure 9-2). They have two or three balanced blades on an airplane-type propeller. Propeller diameter is typically between 4 and 6 feet. The blades are aerodynamically designed for optimum efficiency. Large-prop wind units are a bit heavier, quite a bit more noticeable on a boat, and because of their efficient high-speed propellers, can cause serious injury if accidentally encountered. Most units must be manually shut down in high wind speeds to keep them from self-destructing. Their popularity is based on the single attribute of their potentially high electrical output. Proponents feel that the greatly increased electrical output more than makes up for the negative aspects, and that creative mounting and proper operation can make a large-blade unit a safe, attractive on-board generator.

Some rigging-suspended wind generators of both the small- and large-prop varieties include kits for conversion to water generators when under sail. The alternator or generator is removed from the wind-unit frame and placed in a swiveling mount at the stern. A prop and towline are attached and towed in the water behind the boat.

WIND-GENERATOR CONSTRUCTION

Wind generators for marine use comprise four component parts. The first is a propeller or similar device that transforms the mechanical energy of moving air into the mechanical energy of a rotating shaft. It might more accurately be termed a rotor, since it is not propelling (like an engine or airplane prop) but rather rotating the generator shaft. Present convention in the industry, however, is to use the term *propeller*. The second component, an electrical gen-

---

FIGURE 9-2 (left).   **A pole-mounted large-prop wind generator. (Courtesy Hamilton Ferris)**
FIGURE 9-3 (right).   **A permanent-magnet generator, one component of a wind generator. (Courtesy Everfair Enterprises)**

erator or alternator, transforms the shaft's rotary motion into electrical energy. The third
component is the drive system that transfers energy from the prop to the generator shaft. The
fourth is some means of keeping the unit facing the wind, typically called a tail vane.

Propeller

All units available today use propellers and transfer the wind energy into horizontal rotary motion (shaft mounted horizontally) as opposed to vertical rotary motion (shaft is mounted vertically, like that of a lawn mower). Several early marine wind units no longer in production used a Savonius wind generator, which looks and functions much like an anemometer, to transfer wind energy into rotary motion about a vertical axis. The power potential for these units is low, and consumer enthusiasm was limited. Two-bladed propellers used today are typically machined from a single block of wood—either Sitka spruce or mahogany—for its reasonable cost, strength, and light weight. The blades have a certain pitch, or twist, from the hub to the tip. Changing a blade's pitch changes its performance in different wind speeds. Blade pitch should be well matched to generator RPMs and output. Multi-bladed propellers, for both small- and large-prop machines, are often made of polymer materials, since they can easily be formed with the correct pitch and mass-produced. The blade balance for large-diameter wind-generator propellers, regardless of blade material, is critical, particularly in higher wind speeds. Propellers with unbalanced blades can begin to wobble and fly apart before you have a chance to shut them down. I've even heard of this happening to a small-prop unit after the owners experimentally tried to increase the blade pitch for better performance. Tampering with blade pitch is one of the best ways to damage your propeller. All propellers come balanced from the manufacturer, and it is hard for them to get out of balance during routine use. Damaged or homemade props should be carefully tested before using. Do-it-yourselfers, beware: It is extremely hard to make a well-balanced homemade propeller that comes close to the efficiency of a manufactured one.

Electrical Generator

The generator on large-prop units is usually a permanent-magnet DC generator with a 12-volt output and around a 15-ampere rating, like the one shown in Figure 9-3. These generators have a heavy-duty commutator and brushes that transfer the electrical output to external contacts. One small-prop unit, the Windbat, has a modified car-type alternator with low-current brushes and slip rings for the field current, and none required for the output current (see Chapter 6 for alternator construction and operation). Other small-prop units employ a permanent-magnet alternator with no need for slip rings or brushes at all in the unit itself. Brushes and slip rings, or electrical contacts capable of rotation, are used outside the generator on many pole-mounted wind units. This enables the units to rotate freely through 360 degrees without wires becoming twisted. Generators typically have steel or aluminum housings that are protected from the elements with epoxy paints and finishes. Some manufacturers place the generator inside another housing for added protection. Since heat is produced inside the generator (tangible evidence of energy-conversion losses), any additional housings must have cooling fins or other means of heat dissipation. Sealed, watertight shaft bearings are included on the generator's leading face.

Drive System

All of today's marine wind generators, both large- and small-prop types, are "direct drive" units. This means that the propeller is coupled directly to the shaft of the generator. Propeller speed is the same as generator shaft speed. There have been a few exceptions to this in the past. The first unit we purchased was one of these, a Webcharger made in Provincetown, Massachusetts. It had a 5-foot-diameter propeller rotating in its own journal bearing, and rotary motion was transferred by a small car fan belt and pulleys with a 2:1 ratio. For every rotation of the prop the generator shaft rotated twice. In theory, the concept was sound, for the considerable lateral forces of the large prop were absorbed by the strong journal bearing, leaving the generator bearings nicely isolated. Potentially, the generator speed could be doubled, substantially increasing output. In practice, however, we found that the friction of the belt and extra bearing kept the unit from producing in anything less than 10- to 12-knot winds, and the maximum output was much less than the manufacturer claimed. Another now-defunct operation, Wind Turbine Industries, tried to use a system of gears on their SilentPower unit to transfer power and increase shaft speed, but the company did not enjoy lasting success. Direct-drive systems for small wind generators is now the industry standard.

Wind generators need some means of facing directly into the wind. They lose power rapidly as they turn away from the windstream, just as solar panels lose power when turned away from the sun. The most popular method is to mount the propeller on the front face of the generator shaft and affix a tail vane behind the unit. If the unit starts to deviate from the wind stream, wind pressure on the vane will bring it back again. The other possibility is to set the propeller blades downstream of the generator so the blades track the wind, obviating the need for a tail vane. This method is not often used, since the generator then blocks some of the wind and causes a turbulent airstream. Tail vanes can be built in a variety of shapes and sizes, out of wood, plastic, aluminum, stainless steel, or even canvas. They offer wind-unit manufacturers a chance to create a distinctive flair to their systems. The tail vanes for small-prop wind units are typically tall with a compact width, allowing for very small turning diameters.

WIND-ENERGY THEORY

Below, the theoretical power that can be extracted from the wind is determined, then is tempered with the conditions reality imposes, to yield the usable power we can expect from marine wind units. Wind-generator ratings, performance, and output considerations are also included.

Power Calculations

To describe the energy available in things from motion, including air, consider the formula:

$$E_k = mv^2/2,$$

where

E_k = kinetic energy,

m = mass, and

v = velocity.

For the energy in the wind, we substitute as follows:

E_k = the kinetic energy of the wind,

m = the mass of the air, and

v = the velocity of the airstream.

First, let's determine the mass of air that travels past our generator propeller in a given amount of time. This is mathematically expressed as

$$m = eAvt,$$

where

e = the density, or weight per volume of the air,

A = the circular area defined by the rotating propeller,

v = the velocity of the wind (velocity is similar to speed, but also assumes a direction), and

t = the time elapsed.

We can substitute this expression for the air mass (m) in the energy equation above. Our new equation becomes

$$E_k = [(eAvt)v^2/2 = (eAtv^3)/2.$$

Theoretically, this is the energy available in the wind over a period of time (t). Since power equals energy divided by time, our formula for instantaneous power becomes

$$E_k/t = (eAtv^3)/2t,$$

or

$$P = (eAv^3)/2.$$

This is the theoretical maximum power available from the wind before it comes into contact with the propeller. As the airstream attempts to pass through a wind-generator propeller, however, the air is slowed down from v_1 (initial velocity) to v_2 (downwind velocity). At the same time, the propeller is trying to transform the horizontal kinetic energy of the wind into rotary kinetic energy, the motion necessary to turn an electrical generator. The propeller's ability to transform this energy is called its efficiency.

Figure 9-4 shows what happens as an airstream with velocity v_1 encounters a propeller. Its area is expanded to equal the swept area (A) of the propeller (which must be free to rotate). The airstream velocity is reduced to v_2. Using our knowledge of these events, and the equation for power, we can calculate the efficiency of the propeller.

FIGURE 9-4.   **Characteristics of an airstream meeting a wind generator.**

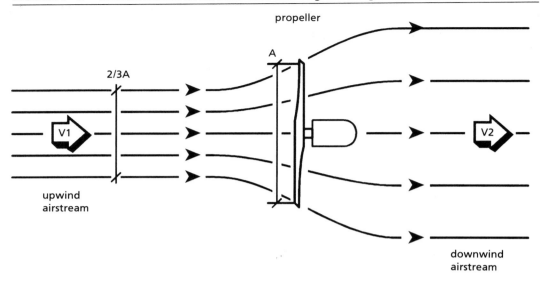

The actual power we extract from the wind is related to the difference between v_1 and v_2, or how much the airstream slows as it passes through the propeller. The power increases as v_2 decreases, until it reaches one-third of v_1. At this point the power is at a maximum. Further reductions in v_2 reduce the power (see Figure 9-5).

Given these considerations, the maximum theoretical power that propeller designers try to achieve is really only 59.3 percent of the power of the wind that would pass through unobstructed. Maximum theoretical power is expressed in the formula

$$P_{MAX} = 0.593 \times (eAv^3)/2.$$

This expression is known as Betz's law. Although certain experimental wind machines have exceeded the maximum power shown here, Betz's law is suitable for our purposes. To make this formula meaningful to us, we need to determine the density of air (at sea level, of course!), and be able to express maximum theoretical power (P_{MAX}, in watts), in terms of the area (A) swept by the propeller with a given diameter (D, in feet) and wind velocity (v, in miles per hour). A good value for air density at sea level is 0.08 pound/per cubic foot, and the circular area swept by a rotating propeller is $\pi D^2/4$. Thanks to the authors of the energy primer *Other Homes and Garbage,* we can substitute these values and make the power formula come out nicely as

$$P_{MAX} = 0.0024 D^2 v^3{}_{THEORETICAL}.$$

It becomes clear that the two variables that affect theoretical power are the diameter of the propeller and the wind speed. Now that the theory is behind us, what happens when we actually hoist our generator into the foretriangle or up on a mast or pole mount? How much

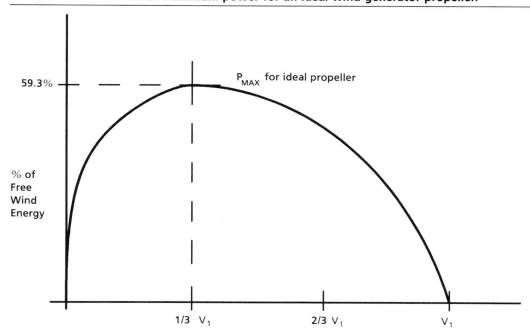

electrical power actually finds its way to our battery? In reality, the theoretical power decreases by the following:

- *Efficiency of the propeller* (Eprop)—Even a well-engineered propeller can take advantage of only about 60 percent of the theoretical power available in a wind stream. Our efficiency factor is therefore 0.60.

- *Efficiency of the generator* (Egen)—Most generators or alternators transform only about 70 percent of the rotary mechanical energy of the shaft into electrical energy at the battery. The efficiency is then 0.70.

- *Efficiency of the drive system* (Edrive)—Energy losses can occur between the propeller and the generator due to gearing system. All current marine wind units are direct drive, however, and have no losses associated with gearing. The efficiency is therefore 1.00.

The total system efficiency is equal to Eprop × Egen × Edrive, or 0.60 × 0.70 × 1.0 = 0.42. This means that with a well-designed and well-constructed system, we can extract up to 42 percent of the theoretical maximum power available in a wind stream, or, in other words, wind machines currently on the market transform between 20 and 30 percent of the energy in the wind to electricity at the battery. Our final expression for usable power is then

$$P = 0.42 \times 0.0024D^2V^3 = 0.001D^2V^3$$

After all this theory, are we even close to being able to predict the output of a marine wind generator? Let's find out. Assuming a large-prop unit with a 5-foot-diameter propeller, operating in a wind of 15 miles per hour (just over 13 knots), the power would be calculated as

$$P = 0.001 \times (5)^2 \times (15)^3 = 84 \text{ watts}$$

Using the electrical power formula $P = VI$, and assuming a charging voltage of 14.0 volts, we can find out the current generated:

$$I = P/V = 84 \text{ watts}/14 \text{ volts} = 6 \text{ amperes}$$

Our Hamilton Ferris rigging-suspended unit with a 5-foot-diameter propeller is rated at 6 amperes of output current in 15-mile-per-hour winds (see Figure 9-6), so the calculations are fairly close. Actual values will vary with system efficiency and battery state of charge.

Rating and Reliability

Wind generators are rated according to their peak power potential in watts. Small-prop units have a maximum of around 120 watts, and large-prop units can have up to 250 watts of peak power. Peak power occurs at a certain wind speed that is particular to each propeller-generator combination. It does not necessarily occur at the highest wind speed.

The reliability of properly designed wind generators is good. Although some parts may need to be replaced periodically (see Tips on Installation, Operation, and Maintenance, below), all units are made of marine-grade materials that can withstand long-term routine use. The reliability of wind to power your unit is another thing (see below).

Performance

The performance of a wind generator depends on the available wind speed, access to the wind stream, propeller size, and unit efficiency.

Wind speed. As seen in the calculations above, the power output is proportional to the cube of the wind speed. Dramatic increases in power can be realized with modest increases in wind speed.

Access to the wind stream. Turbulence, the result of local conditions, causes the propeller to lose efficiency. A wind generator must have access to a steady wind stream for best performance. Moving out of the wind stream is the equivalent of facing a solar panel away from the sun. The output for permanently mounted units also diminishes if the boat is moving downwind. The apparent wind speed is the actual wind speed minus the boat speed, something to consider during long downwind passages.

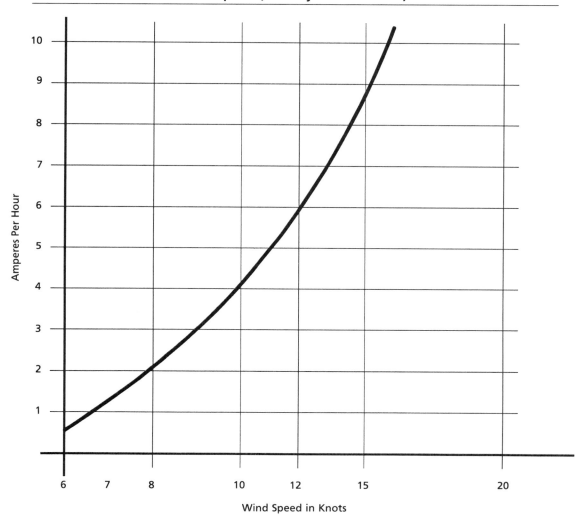

Wind Speed in Knots

Propeller size. The calculations above show that the power output of a wind generator is proportional to the square of the diameter of the propeller. This fact, and that of the difference in blade efficiency, are the reasons that large-prop wind generators have a much higher electrical output.

Unit efficiency. Wind-equipment manufacturers are always trying to find more efficient propeller-generator combinations. The key to increasing efficiency is properly matching the most efficient point on a generator or alternator power curve with the propeller's blade-pitch characteristics. Generators used on wind machines are specially wound to operate at lower RPMs.

METHODS OF INSTALLATION

There are several methods of installing wind generators on a boat, each with its own advantages, aesthetic considerations, and proponents. Some installations are permanent, while others require a periodic setup and lowering procedure.

Rigging-Suspended Mount

Suspending units in the rigging was the original method of mounting wind systems on boats. At the time the consensus was that boaters would prefer to use the wind generator only when in harbor, and not have the unit up when under way. Eventually, though, mariners grew accustomed to the look of a wind generator on a boat, and other mounting methods were pursued. When the jib is furled or stowed on a sloop or cutter-rigged boat, the space between the headstay and the inner stay or mast provides a large unused area that can accommodate a small- or large-prop wind unit.

With these machines there is nothing to install permanently (see Figure 9-7). What goes up comes back down when you're ready to leave the harbor. You do need an exposed stay (or topping lift, if installed in the main triangle) for support, and a halyard to raise and lower the unit. A roller-furling jib makes it a bit more difficult, but not impossible. You will need a smooth sling to go around the jib and back to the top of the wind unit frame, and a spare halyard to hoist the unit in place. The sling must slide without catching the furls of the jib, and be positioned well above the rotating blades.

Most wind generators intended for rigging-suspension have stainless steel swivel fittings on the top and bottom of the frame. The frame is slightly longer than the prop diameter, so the mounting lines won't be hit by the rotating blades. You will need to rig at least two and preferably three lines to the bottom swivel, so you can tie off to port, starboard, and possibly forward as well, using deck cleats, handrails, lifelines, or other convenient locations.

The first time you set up the unit, experiment to get the correct halyard setting and tie-down system. Do this with the prop tied off to prevent it from spinning until your system is perfected. The propeller tie-off strap will come in handy when you want to shut down the system. You'll also need another line to turn the unit out of the wind. It is usually attached to the tail vane, serving double duty as a means for keeping the unit from completing more than one revolution as it tracks the wind. This keeps the wire leads from becoming twisted.

The wiring from the generator must be kept clear of the rotating blades. We run our wiring through a loop in the tie-off line at the bottom of the frame, keeping it tight and out of the way. These units are designed to be set up and taken down frequently, so it is best to install a polarized quick-disconnect plug. A deck plug that takes the wiring below makes for a neat installation. This allows the main wiring leads, diode and controls, and meters to be permanently installed.

FIGURE 9-7 (left).   **Rigging-suspended Aquair. (Courtesy Jack Rabbit Marine)**
FIGURE 9-8 (right).   **The Fourwinds pole mount. (Courtesy Everfair Enterprises)**

Pole Mount

This is becoming the most popular method of installing small- and large-prop wind generators. The unit is permanently installed, usually at the stern, and can operate when under sail (see Figure 9-8).

All wind units can be pole mounted. A socket accepts an aluminum or stainless steel pipe. The customer usually supplies the pole, supporting stays or struts, and deck fittings. Some manufacturers offer a pole-mounting kit for their machines. Most units intended for pole mounting come with a heavy-duty "yaw" thrust bearing in the frame so the unit can swivel easily to track the wind. Some include slip rings for transferring electrical current that also allow the unit to complete unlimited revolutions without twisting the wire leads. Slip rings are convenient, but not absolutely necessary if a tie-off line is employed. Without slip rings, occasional repositioning of the unit may be required.

The mounting pole typically has a 1.5- to 2-inch outside diameter and might be made of T6061-T6 schedule-40 aluminum pipe. The pole must be supported with stays or struts for lateral support, since lateral forces for a large-prop wind system are considerable. Use three wire stays with adjustable turnbuckles, or two aluminum or stainless steel rigid struts. Make certain these supports attach to the pole well below the blade tips.

Once you have a pole, a way for the unit to rotate with the wind, and a neat wiring arrangement, you still need to attach the pole to the boat. Use a deck socket that will accept the outer diameter of the pole, either a metal pipe flange or a custom-made block of wood. Add a rubber pad below this fitting and below each strut or stay support to cut noise and vibration below decks. Poles can also be welded directly to a metal deckplate or other piece of hardware on the boat.

Some boats now use large inverted-U-shaped frames of stainless steel or reinforced fiberglass at the stern to mount radar, antennas, lights, and so on. These supports could accommodate one or two wind generators as well.

It is also possible to mount a wind generator on a pole attached to the top of the mizzenmast. A unit mounted in this way can operate the same as on other freestanding poles, as long as it is mounted well clear of all masthead rigging and fittings.

Mast Mount—Rotating

Another popular location for small-prop wind units is on the leading face of the mast, as shown in Figure 9-9. This can be done on the mainmast above the jib or, more typically, on the mizzenmast above the spreaders. Units mounted on the mizzenmast will have a slightly turbulent airstream from the mainmast. All that's needed is a simple supporting bracket to accept the short pole of the wind unit. The pole is welded or otherwise secured to the mounting bracket. When designing the support, make certain the wind unit can turn without hitting

---

FIGURE 9-9 (left).   **Rotating mast mount for an Ampair generator. (Courtesy Jack Rabbit Marine)**

FIGURE 9-10 (right).   **Fixed mast mount for a large-prop generator. (Courtesy Hamilton Ferris)**

Mast Mount—Fixed

The only way to mount a large-prop wind unit on the mast is to affix it to the leading face, as shown in Figure 9-10. This arrangement is out of the way and has a relatively low profile, but since it can't swivel, it relies on the boat to track the wind. It is not appropriate on boats that spend long periods of time at a dock, and is not very effective when under sail in anything but close-hauled windward work. The mainmast can be used on a catboat, or if there is space above the jib, but more typically this mounting method is used on a mizzen-mast.

Install a bracket capable of supporting the wind generator at or above spreader height, avoiding staysails and other boat gear. Some wiring will be exposed, but most of it can be led inside the mast. It is essential that large-prop units mounted in this manner have some means of shutting down in strong winds. The standard method of turning the unit sideways to the wind cannot be employed unless the entire boat is turned.

Other Mounts

Large-prop wind generators can also be fixed in other locations, including faced forward in the lower shrouds similar to old-fashioned running lights. The shrouds provide adequate support for a mounting bracket, although provision should be made for automatic governing or a means of turning the unit out of the wind to shut it down. The unit cannot be operated when under way with a foresail up, and in any event, it is effective only with the wind well forward of the beam. Make certain that a unit mounted in this fashion is above the reach of any crewmembers and out of the way of other boat gear.

SIZING AND SELECTION

Here we'll discuss the principal considerations, then review the various marine wind generators. For a more detailed analysis of determining electrical load and selecting equipment, refer to Chapters 13 and 14.

Assessing Your Needs

This is in part a personal process. As noted in Chapter 8, the output from alternative-energy systems is much more "location- and owner-dependent" than that from fossil-fuel systems.

Electrical load. Your boat's electrical load is easy to calculate or simple to determine empirically by monitoring daily electrical draw. While watt-hours are the correct representation of energy production or consumption, ampere-hours—even though they leave voltage out of the equation—will give you a good idea of the electrical energy you consume, especially since batteries are rated in ampere-hours. Make a list of your electrical equipment, with the number of amperes drawn by each when operating. Multiply these amperes by the number of hours you operate each during the day; use an average for intermittent-use equipment. Now add an additional 10 to 15 percent to account for the battery's storage and retrieval inefficiency.

Wind-generator output. It would be nice to match your total electrical load with the output from a single wind generator, and you may find that a wind unit will satisfy all your requirements. If not, it's a simple matter to supplement it with other methods of generation.

To calculate the amount of electrical energy a wind generator can deliver, multiply the peak current rating in amperes (associated with a given wind speed) by the number of hours it's used per day. For example, a wind generator that has a 10-ampere maximum rating in 25-knot winds, and experiences that amount of wind for 24 hours, could potentially deliver 240 ampere-hours. These are ideal numbers to use as a reference. Your average wind-energy output will undoubtedly be much lower, and is determined by other factors including battery state of charge, type of mounting, and climate.

Manufacturers' output ratings are usually based on a generator connected to a battery that is about 50 percent discharged. As the battery charges and voltage rises, electrical output drops off.

How you choose to mount your wind generator greatly affects electrical output. If the unit is downwind of an obstruction, the airstream will be turbulent and output will drop. Mounting the unit high on the mast will place it in higher average wind speeds, often less affected by local conditions (see Figure 9-11). Take this into account when examining the output of a small-prop wind unit that can be mounted on the upper part of the mast. Pole mounts or fixed mast mounts are permanent, so the unit operates at all times; others, such as the rigging-suspended mount, are temporary, to be used only in harbor. If the mounting is fixed, the boat itself must track the wind at anchor or mooring, and it will be less responsive than freely rotating units that can track the wind independent of boat motion.

The final factor is climate. Average wind strengths around the world vary considerably. A close look at a book on world sailing routes will give you a good approximation of prevailing wind speeds and directions, as will pilot charts. As a rule of thumb, all coastal areas of the United States experience good average wind speeds, with winter winds being stronger than those in summer. Wind generators work most effectively in northern and southern latitudes with prevailing westerlies, and in the tradewind belts, including the Bahamas and southern Florida. Wind generators are becoming standard equipment for boats traveling to the Bahamas, the Caribbean, or the Pacific islands. They are least effective in areas of variable winds or along the equator.

In addition to regional-scale climates, there are microclimates to consider. Local temperature imbalances and geography modify prevailing winds. Areas of slower winds are typically landlocked and isolated. Long Island Sound, the Chesapeake, and the Intracoastal Waterway are all well-known cruising areas where the adjacent land often blocks the summer winds. Summer sea breezes, occurring very near the coast, often build in intensity during the day and die at night. The position of land and its effect on the wind creates specific microclimates. On Cape Cod, for example, the north shore is blocked from the prevailing southwesterly winds and thus experiences light winds most of the summer. The Cape's south shore, on the other

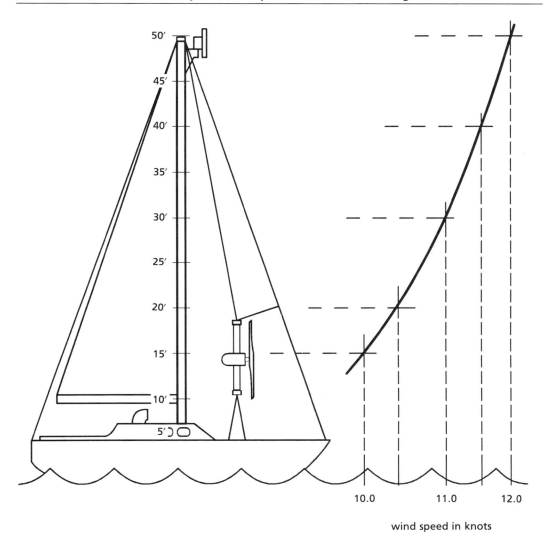

wind speed in knots

hand, is exposed to the strong southwesterlies in summer, making it an ideal place for a wind generator. Another good example is Puerto Rico, where the north and east coasts are exposed to the nearly constant tradewinds, while the west and south coasts experience lower-velocity winds prompted by inland mountains. By knowing the prevailing local winds and their average speeds, and by considering what effect any nearby landmass will have on them, you can determine how effective your wind generator will be.

Mini-microclimates are a particularly important consideration. High land, currents, the position of the shore—even the size and number of nearby trees—all affect the wind that reaches a given spot. While anchored in Vero Beach, Florida, we discovered that a tall group of pines about 300 yards across the harbor created turbulence that affected our wind generator when the wind blew from that direction. A boat less than 100 yards away had a wind unit that completely escaped the turbulence. It was fascinating to see what a powerful effect even a distant stand of trees can have on a wind generator. The situation was reversed when the wind blew from the opposite direction. A nearby island prevented the wind from reaching the other boat, while we continued to generate.

If you prefer only the snuggest of anchorages, it is likely you will get less production from your wind generator. If your load is high, you'll have to choose anchorages where the wind blows freely, or have other means of generating. We spent one winter in Florida anchored close to an island for protection from the winter winds. Our exposure to the wind was not ideal, and our outboard engine had no alternator, but we did have a 35-watt PV solar panel to supplement the output from the wind generator. Otherwise we would have been forced to anchor in a more exposed and uncomfortable spot.

Your boat. Small boats might be better off with a small-prop generator, or a large-prop unit that can be suspended in the rigging, then stowed when under way. Larger boats can have either, and even multiple wind generators if desired. Sloop-rigged boats have a large foretriangle for a rigging-suspended wind unit, and usually ample space on the stern for a pole-mounted unit. If you have a cutter rig with a smaller foretriangle area, you might not have enough swinging room for a rigging suspended large-prop unit. Perhaps a small-prop rigging-suspended unit—or a pole-mounted generator on the stern—would be more appropriate.

Boats with two masts, including ketches and yawls, can use the mizzenmast for permanently mounted wind generators. The mainmast on schooners offers another possibility. They are comparatively free of halyards, whisker-pole tracks, rings or cleats, and have no jib to entangle the propeller (take care with mizzen staysails, however). Pole-mounted units are not often seen on these boats because of overhanging booms. Some sailors get around this with a pole-mounted generator that can be lowered when under sail.

Catboats usually have a clear area ahead of the mast, which is a great place for a pole-mounted unit (see Figure 9-12). The absence of a jib means that a small-prop wind unit can easily be mounted on the forward part of the mast. Without a foretriangle, there is no place for a rigging-suspended unit, although one can be accommodated in the main triangle. The newer breed of catboats with unstayed masts and wishbone or half-wishbone rigs present another set of considerations. Their masts are typically constructed of carbon fiber and should not be tampered with. Much of their strength can be attributed to the lack of winches, cleats, and other fittings that require drilling holes, thus weakening the mast. Experts have advised that only small-prop wind units be secured to freestanding masts, and then only after consulting the mast designer.

Multihulls have ample deck space for one (or more) pole-mounted generators, as well as plenty of storage area for stowing a rigging-suspended unit.

Roller-furled jibs create some turbulence for rigging-suspended wind generators and this is especially true for bulky or loosely rolled jibs. While the effect on performance is probably

minor, as it is when a mainmast disturbs the air stream to a generator mounted on the mizzen, it should be accounted for when estimating expected output.

How you use your boat.   For weekend boaters, a small permanent or pole-mounted wind unit can be left to charge the batteries during the week, and probably supply the necessary electricity for weekend cruising. Voltage regulation is a must for unattended systems. Large-prop wind units are probably overkill for weekenders, but for occasional cruising, a rigging-suspended wind unit might be suitable. Just remember that the wind usually dies down at night when you will be in harbor and ready to use it. If you spend several days in one place, the unit can be hoisted long enough to recharge the batteries.

Boaters who stay on board for long periods often have larger electrical loads, but are also likely to be there to tend a large-prop wind system that requires shutting down in high winds. If the boat is left unattended during the day, it is wise to get a system that can stay up in all but the most severe conditions. A squall coming through the anchorage could cause a large-prop, non-self-tending unit to overspeed and either overheat the generator or cause structural damage. If you frequently stay at dockside, a small-prop unit high on the mast will get more reliable wind. Long-term cruisers tend to favor pole- or mast-mounted units, since they are always up and functioning, and no setup or take-down time is required. On the other hand, rigging-suspended wind units can be removed and don't affect boat appearance or performance while under way.

Wind generators can work equally well for powerboaters who stay aboard for long periods. They can greatly reduce the need for running the main engine just to generate electricity.

Offshore sailors seem to prefer small-prop wind generators over large-prop models for their self-tending character and lower windage in rough weather. Some prefer a combination wind-and-water system, with the water generator used while at sea and the wind system operated in harbor.

Wind systems, especially the large-prop variety, are not particularly appropriate on racing boats. Racers typically employ PV solar panels or water generators. Small-prop wind generators can be accommodated, since they are self-tending, have less windage, and can easily be mounted out of the way. If time is spent aboard between races, a combination wind-and-water system would be appropriate.

If you are boating with friends, children, and pets with a large-prop wind unit on board, it is essential that you use common sense and make sure everyone is aware of the rotating blades. Visitors—young and old—are faced with an additional hazard if they are unused to maneuvering around a wind generator. Make certain it is mounted out of everyone's reach. When operating a wind system, remember that with children even the unexpected can happen. Lines, balls, and other playthings could get caught in the rotating blades. We met one family whose children had accidentally sailed their dinghy mast right into the stern-mounted wind generator, destroying the blades. With proper care, these units pose no great hazard. Our large-prop wind unit was in use from the time our twin sons were two until they were six with no mishaps.

Charter-boat owners can benefit from permanently mounting a small-prop wind generator capable of helping out with the large electrical loads. The small-prop units are undemanding and foolproof, and are able to generate electricity at anchor, mooring, dock, or under way.

Wind-Generator Selection

There are four large-prop and four small-prop marine wind generators from which to choose. The large-prop units are similar in output yet quite different in design and construction. Of the small-prop units, three are manufactured in Britain and one in France, but all are sold in the United States by marine energy suppliers. Figure 9-13 lists specifications for each system. Compare their cost, output, size, mounting possibilities, and appearance.

SYSTEM EFFICIENCY

Earlier in this chapter, it was shown that a well-designed large-prop unit in good conditions could transform 25 to 30 percent of the energy available in a wind stream into usable electrical energy at the batteries. This means that these large-prop wind units have the highest overall energy conversion efficiency of all marine charging sources. Small-prop units have slightly lower efficiencies, due mostly to propeller design. System efficiency will drop as the wind unit is taken out of the direct line of the wind stream, either intentionally or by local conditions.

FIGURE 9-13. **Wind generator comparison chart.**   **167**

Model	Generator	Propeller	Rated output (amps) at 15 knots	Weight (lbs.)	Mounting	Max. operating windspeed	Overspeed protection
Amair 100	PM* alternator	multibladed 36″ dia.	3.0	26.0	pole, radar, mast	unlimited	none needed
Bugger Prod. Windbugger	PM generator	3-bladed 54″ dia.	7–9	35.0	pole, rigging-suspended	25 knots	none available
Everfair Ent. Fourwinds II	PM generator	2-bladed fiberglass 60″/72″ dia.	7–9	20.0	pole, mast, rigging-suspended	25 knots w/o windbrake	optional windbrake
Ham. Ferris Neptune Supreme	PM generator	2-bladed 60″ dia. wood	7.0	23.0	pole, mast, rigging-suspended	25 knots w/o windbrake	optional windbrake
LYM Aerogen 50	PM alternator	multibladed 36″ dia.	3.0	16.5	pole, radar	self-limits in highwinds w/ cutout switches	none required
Perrin Indus. Windbat	Alternator	multibladed 43″ dia.	4–5	?	pole, radar	unlimited	none required
Richard Gaudio Model 7-15	PM generator	2-bladed 60″ dia. wood	6.0	?	pole, mast, rigging-suspended	25 knots	none available
Rutland WG910 'Marine'	PM generator	multibladed 36″ dia.	3.0	30.0	pole, mast	unlimited	none required

*PM = permanent magnet

OTHER COMPONENTS AND CONSIDERATIONS

In addition to the propeller, generator, and tail vane, wind-energy systems may include the following components: mounting hardware, tie-off lines, governors and braking mechanisms, wiring, voltage regulators, diodes and fuses, system monitors, and others. Each of these is discussed below.

Mounting Components

The basic mounting components are usually supplied by the manufacturer. A mounting frame and swivels are included on most rigging-suspended units, while the owner must supply suspension and tie-down lines. Some suppliers offer optional pole-mounting hardware. Owners usually must supply mast mounting brackets to accommodate their needs.

Tie-Off Line

This is a simple piece of line attached to the turning handle or tail vane. The line can be secured to a convenient location, keeping the unit out of the wind stream.

Governors and Braking Mechanisms

Small-prop wind units are self-governed by the blade configuration. There is only one governing mechanism for large-prop units that seems to perform in any wind conditions—a simple device attached to the front face of the propeller, with spring-loaded air brakes that feather as the wind reaches unsafe levels (see Figure 9-2). It looks a bit clunky, but does the job nicely. This type of governor was originally used on Wincharger land units, and a version is now offered as an option for both the Fourwinds and Hamilton Ferris systems. Windbugger units have a clutch braking mechanism as standard equipment for protection in short-lived squalls. The unit should be manually shut down, however, in prolonged winds above 25 knots. There are several land units that govern themselves by having the prop and generator assembly spring-loaded and able to rotate upward as the wind increases. This pushes the unit out of the wind stream until winds abate. The concept works superbly, but unfortunately a prop that starts to assume the likeness of helicopter blades is not safe on a boat.

Some units come with an electrical brake that will work in moderate winds by shorting the generator output with a switch. It is best used during setup and initial starting, and is not recommended for routine use in high winds.

FIGURE 9-14. **Hypothetical schematic of a boat with multiple charging options. The portion of the system relevant to wind charging is highlighted.**

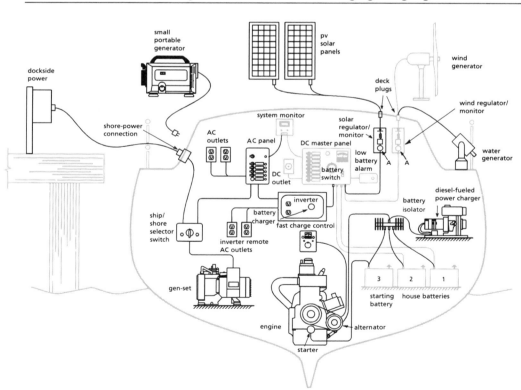

Wiring

A two-wire conductor carries output current to the battery. Additional wiring with a polarized connector (possibly a deck plug) can be added for convenient routing. Refer to the appendices for correct wire sizing. The diode, fuse, voltage regulator, and monitoring devices can be permanently wired below decks.

Voltage Regulator

While not a necessity, voltage regulators are recommended for all large-prop units and on boats left unattended for long periods. Voltage regulation does slightly lessen the performance of a wind unit, and can be avoided if you carefully monitor battery voltage. Just keep in mind that an expensive set of batteries can be ruined by inattention.

Diode and Fuse

A diode is a one-way electronic checkvalve that keeps the generator from becoming an electric motor and consuming battery current when the prop isn't turning. The diode also allows simultaneous operation with other on-board generators. Get one that is mounted on a finned piece of aluminum to dissipate heat. The fuse should be rated slightly above maximum generating current.

System Monitors

It's important to have a meter that displays output current. We used our first wind generator for almost a month before finally taking it apart and discovering it had never put out a single ampere. Meters prove that the system is working properly, and are also handy for measuring the fluctuation in output current prompted by turning the unit partially out of the wind. If you have a wind generator on your boat, it's nice to have an anemometer to measure windspeed as well as output current. Remember that wind strength will vary with height above the water. The windspeed indicator should be at or near the level of the wind generator.

High-Visibility Blade Tips

Guests and other crewmembers are more likely to be aware of a unit that has brightly colored blade tips. The coloring can be painted on or applied with adhesive patches.

Blade Protection

A driving rain or particles in the air will wear down the leading edges of wooden props, reducing blade efficiency. A fine layer of reinforced tape or the equivalent helps to protect the edge. Since the leading edge of the prop is the first to come in contact with the wind stream, make certain anything you put on it is smooth and wrinkle-free.

Conversion Kits

Several manufacturers offer conversion kits that transform a rigging-suspended wind unit into a water generator. In this way the machine can be used in port and under way. Water conversion kits are useful only on sailboats, since they rely on wind-generated boat motion.

Self-Tending Units

By definition, the self-tending small-prop wind units do not require attention during operation. The only thing you might need to do—if there is no voltage regulator—is check the battery condition to prevent overcharge. Large-prop units that are permanently mounted and have a foolproof governing mechanism for overspeed protection are also self-tending. Since they have much higher output potential, voltage regulation is recommended.

Non-Self-Tending Units

Large-prop units suspended in the rigging or mounted on poles require periodic shutdown. You can do this by turning the blade tips into the wind with a line attached to the tail vane or to a short handle on the frame. The prop stops rotating in a surprisingly short time. Shutdown is required in high winds or when the battery is fully charged and no voltage regulation is used. The shutdown line serves another useful function. As the wind increases, the unit (pole or rigging mount) can be rotated incrementally out of the wind to keep the prop rotating at a safe speed. We usually start with about 30 degrees to the wind, then 45 degrees, then a full 90 degrees for complete shutdown. Some units come with an electrical braking mechanism. This should be used only to keep the blades from rotating during setup, or for emergencies. Using the brake routinely will cause premature wear of the brushes and bearings.

Rigging-Suspended Operation

Rigging-suspended units must be set up and lowered. This procedure is described below.

Setting-Up Procedure (see Figure 9-15)

1. Attach generator and tail vane to frame if not already assembled when stowed.
2. Secure hub and prop to generator shaft. Mounting screws should be tight, but take care not to strip the threads.
3. Attach the upper suspension line and lower tie-down lines to the swivels on the frame. (The length of these lines should be determined when the unit is first installed.)
4. Secure the upper part of the suspension line to the shackle at the end of the halyard, then secure this shackle to the stay to keep the pulling force in line with the stay. An alternative arrangement is shown in Figure 9-15.
5. Secure the generator output wires to the frame to keep them clear of the rotating prop.
6. The unit must not be allowed to rotate until hauled up and in place. Someone can hold the prop, or use a tie-off strap that secures the prop to the frame. The electrical brake mentioned above can also be used for this purpose.

FIGURE 9-15. **Installation of a rigging-suspended wind generator.**   **171**

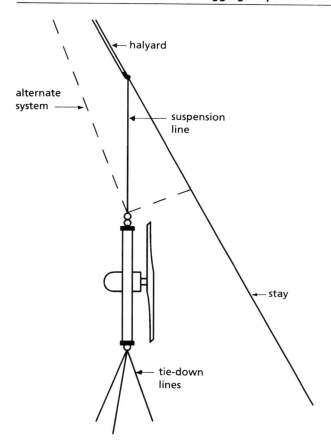

7. Check to make sure the unit is plumb, both fore and aft and side to side. Adjust tie-down lines as necessary. A rigging-suspended mount may jerk back and forth in a chop if lines are not properly adjusted.

Lowering Procedure

1. Stop the unit by turning its blade tips into the wind. Keep the prop from spinning with a tie-off strap, the electrical brake, if it has one, or by hand.
2. Ease the halyard until the unit is resting on the deck. To prevent blade damage, make sure the prop is not the first part to touch down.
3. Disassemble and stow in reverse order to the setting-up procedure.

Following is an assortment of the most frequently asked questions concerning the installation, operation, and maintenance of wind generators.

Q. *Is it necessary to have a mount with yaw brushes and slip rings to allow the unit to rotate 360 degrees without twisting the wire leads?*

A. If you have a small-prop unit mounted where you can't reach it conveniently, the answer is yes. It should be able to track the wind and rotate around as often as needed. The wind usually varies throughout the day, and often changes direction in a sudden squall or during a wind shift at night. If you are under way and changing course frequently, the wind unit should be able to seek the wind without being hampered by the mounting configuration.

If the generator is mounted on a pole, yaw brushes and slip rings are nice but not essential. You can always fasten a line that will allow the unit to rotate a few times but will tighten up before the wire lead does. Periodically untwisting the assembly is no great hardship. Rigging-suspended units are used on boats at anchor or mooring, so they don't require slip rings. A tie-off line to keep them from rotating through 360 degrees is fine, since the boat will track the wind, although a bit slower, on its own.

Q. *Do you recommend using a voltage regulator?*

A. If you have a permanently mounted wind unit, we would say yes, particularly with a large-prop unit. You are more likely to forget to monitor battery voltage with a permanent-mount system. With a small-prop unit, you can store the boat and the generator will continue to maintain the batteries. If the unit is rigging-suspended, a voltage regulator is less of a concern, since you can generate until the batteries are charged, then tie it off. The wind generator gets stowed often, so you are less likely to forget about monitoring battery voltage.

Q. *Can you use the same voltage regulator for a wind and PV solar system if it can handle the total amount of current?*

A. Generally speaking, no. The output characteristics for the two are quite different, and the voltage control circuits are different. Solar panels have a fixed upper-limit voltage they can reach when open-circuited, usually around 18 or 20 volts. Wind and water generators have a much greater voltage potential if the circuit is opened by a voltage regulator. That is why large-prop units must have a reliable governing system, or be tied off, in high winds when a regulator is in use.

Q. *Are wind generators noisy?*

A. Well-balanced small-prop units make almost no noise at all, although if the bearings are in poor condition they can make a racket. Without proper acoustical isolation, however, metal poles can transmit even soft sounds and magnify them down below. The noise produced by large-prop wind units varies with blade configuration. We wouldn't call any of them particularly noisy, although spinning props emit a unique sound that increases with wind speed. Since rigging noise on board a boat also increases with wind speed, the sound of the prop is merely one more contributor to the overall cacophony. Pole-transmitted sounds can be more pronounced on large-prop systems.

Q. *Is it practical to build your own wind system?*

A. It is certainly possible to experiment with your own wind-system design and construction, but be aware that generators are specially made for low-speed operation, and making a propeller that is balanced and efficient is next to impossible. In our experience, it is best to buy the prop and generator from a wind-system supplier and put your creative efforts into the frame, wiring, and mounting system. Hamilton Ferris and Richard Gaudio both sell components in kit form (see Figure 9-16).

Q. *Which is better for a large-prop unit, two or three blades?*

A. Manufacturers have tried and been successful with three-bladed propellers, although the two-bladed variety is more common. The extra blade creates torque, but also creates drag as it spins through the air. The total area of the blades and how well blade design matches a given generator are more important. Tests by Windbugger, which offers a three-bladed version, have shown that as wind speed and direction vary slightly during the day, the third blade helps maintain a more constant output. It is not necessarily a greater instantaneous output, just more constant on the average. Two-bladed props are easier to stow, and are used for all rigging-suspended systems.

Q. *What maintenance is required on a wind unit?*

A. This varies. Generators with brushless alternators and thermoplastic blades require only occasional touching up of the painted surfaces and inspection of the fasteners for tightness. Units with permanent-magnet generators need to have the internal brushes replaced every few years, a simple enough process. Erratic or significantly reduced output can be a sign of worn brushes not making good contact on the rotor. The generator bearings can also wear out, since they are subjected to quite severe lateral loads from

FIGURE 9-16. **Wind-charger components are sold in kit form for customized installations.** (*Left:* courtesy Richard Gaudio; *Right:* courtesy Hamilton Ferris)

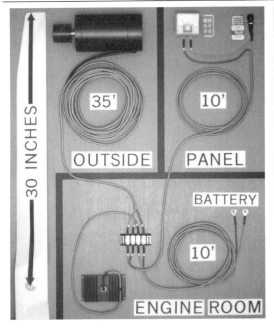

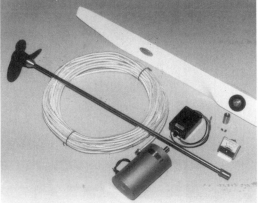

large propellers. Bearings should be checked periodically. Wooden prop blades should be refinished as needed, and their leading edges checked for wear. If a leading edge is damaged, it should be repaired and carefully tested for proper balance before operating in strong winds.

Q. *If a prop is damaged, can one from another wind system be substituted temporarily?*

A. Yes, if it is basically the same type and you are assured of its balance. Don't mix small and large props. I've heard of boaters who have tried to mount large props on small-prop wind units with disastrous results. An advantage of a six-bladed small-prop generator is that if one blade is broken, its opposite number can be removed to keep the propeller in balance.

Q. *What spare parts are recommended for a wind generator?*

A. For units with permanent-magnet generators, an extra set of brushes and shaft bearings are all that is required. Otherwise, a set of bearings, if they are replaceable. For long-distance cruising, a spare prop is recommended if you have one of the two-bladed

wooden variety. If your prop comprises multiple plastic blades,
carrying a few spares would be wise.

Q. *Can a generator overheat in high winds?*
A. Yes, both generators and alternators can overheat from high current levels in high winds. Permanent-magnet generators must be
protected by an overspeed governor or by turning the unit out of
the wind temporarily. Some small-prop wind units have permanent-
magnet alternators with nonferrous stators, and they control current by temperature-activated cutout switches. These units spend
much of the time at higher wind speeds producing no current. This
must be taken into account when examining manufacturer output
curves, which show only on-line current. The Ampair and Aquair
units employ special permanent-magnet alternators with iron-cored
stators. In these units winding inductance causes current to remain
at safe levels.

10

Water Generators

$\blacksquare\blacksquare$

M oving water is another of man's long-standing power sources. Streams and small rivers have for centuries been tapped for the kinetic energy they possess as they race seaward. In the past, the energy that could be extracted was used to turn simple machinery for myriad purposes; now the focus is on producing electricity. Hydroelectric generators are used worldwide to provide renewable electrical power, on both small, local projects and on regional projects of enormous scope.

Hydroelectric power is created when moving water is used to spin an electrical generator. In land-based hydroelectrical systems the generator is fixed in position. The water travels past it in only one direction, as with streams and rivers, or the water flows in two directions, as with the experimental tidal projects in the Bay of Fundy and elsewhere. In both cases, there is relative motion between water and generator. The driving force in a land-based hydroelectric system is gravitational pull, directing water to travel to its lowest energy level, the sea. The greater the vertical drop of the stream or river, the greater the potential electrical output of the system.

On a moving sailboat, relative motion can also exist between a generator that is attached to the boat and the surrounding water. In this case the water is stationary and the generator is in motion, traveling at the speed of the boat. The theory is the same, since the relative motion is similar for both land and boat systems, even though the systems are quite different. The driving force in a water generator system for sailboats is the wind. The more wind there is, the higher the boat speed, and the greater the potential electrical output of the system.

In 1975 Hamilton Ferris began experimenting with water generators for sailboats. Within a year or two he started selling wind propellers for use with his water units, thus the combination wind-and-water marine generator was born. Water generators have much to recommend them. For a start, there is a great deal of power in a small, inconspicuous package.

Water generators are easy to operate and don't affect the appearance of a boat. They generate power any time there is enough wind to move the boat above 3 knots. These units are not appropriate for powerboats, since using a fossil-fuel engine to power the water generator is not as efficient as simply adding this power capacity to the alternator system on board.

TYPES OF MARINE WATER GENERATORS

Several designs evolved from the first trailing-log water generator. They include the short flexible lead, auxiliary propeller shaft through the hull, and generator on existing freewheeling propeller shaft. A brief description of each is given below.

Trailing Log

Trailing-log generators derive their name from the similarity of appearance and operation to taffrail logs used to measure distance run on a boat. With these units, the generator is suspended in a small gimballed bracket on the port side of the stern (refer to Figure 2-13). An 8- to 10-inch-diameter propeller mounted on a short shaft trails behind the boat at the end of a 50- to 75-foot line. As the propeller and shaft are pulled through the water, they spin rapidly, usually "walking" slightly to port. The tightly wound braided line transfers rotary motion to the generator shaft.

A variation on this theme is the Power Log water unit (refer to Figure 2-14), which has the generator attached directly to the propeller, like a wind unit. The entire assembly is trailed behind the boat in taffrail-log fashion or on a short flexible lead (see Short Flexible Lead, below). The generator is waterproof, and propeller motion is transferred directly to the generator shaft without using a connecting line. The unit is attached to the boat with a sturdy cable that does not rotate. The tow cable also houses the electrical output wires.

Short Flexible Lead

Recently, the Power Log system was slightly modified so the prop and generator assembly can be attached to a strong, flexible cable, 12 to 18 inches long, instead of a 50- to 75-foot towline. The cable secures to a strut that extends below the waterline off the stern. The short tow cable still houses the electrical output wires. This system has several advantages: It sidesteps gear trailing off the stern—fishing lines or a towed dinghy, for example—that can interfere with a taffrail log spinner; there is no fear of getting the unit snagged in shallow water; and the generator stays submerged at all speeds.

Perrin Industries of France has also recently developed a version of its Hydrobat Energizer (an outboard-leg water generator) that uses a short flexible lead.

Outboard Leg

Another model can be attached to the stern as you would a small outboard motor. This "outboard leg" unit has a mounting system that allows its prop to be positioned well below the waterline when under way, and to be pulled above the waterline when in port (see Figure 2-15). The generator is at the top of the unit. Through bevel gears, the horizontal motion of the prop is transferred to the vertical motion of a secondary shaft connected to the generator,

FIGURE 10-1. **Hydrobat water generator: view of mounting bracket and lower leg. See also Figure 2-15.**

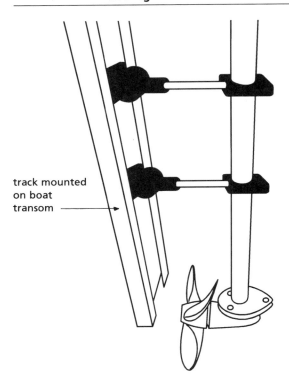

track mounted
on boat
transom

as shown in Figure 10-1. This assembly is easy to operate and simple to remove when not in use. The rigid frame experiences large stress loads at high boat speeds, and is therefore best suited to craft of moderate speed.

Auxiliary Propeller and Shaft

When building a boat, or as an added feature to existing boats, a small, separate propeller and shaft can be mounted through the hull to turn a generator (see Figure 10-2). The generator can be connected to the rotating shaft with pulleys and a drive belt. A little design work is required to match a particular generator to the proper propeller and pulley sizes. Several marine energy suppliers sell permanent-magnet generators for wind and water systems that can be adapted for this purpose. If an 8- to 10-inch outboard-motor propeller mounted in reverse is used, then a 1:1 pulley system is appropriate for most boats. For high-speed sailboats (over 10 knots), consult your marine energy supplier for appropriate component and pulley selection.

A permanently mounted water generator of this nature is always in position to produce electricity. A small propeller causes minimal drag and wear on the support bearings.

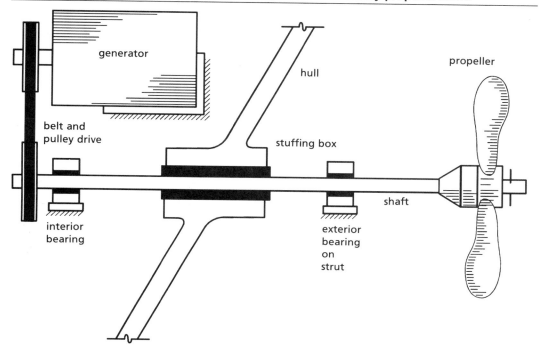

Generator on Freewheeling Propeller

While the boat is under sail, many sailors take advantage of the otherwise unused energy available from a freewheeling propeller. A separate drive pulley mounted at a convenient location provides the power takeoff from the main propeller shaft. The size of a typical auxiliary engine prop allows a larger generator to be used. With the proper selection of pulleys, a high-output alternator could be adapted for use in this application, although drag on the boat will increase with electrical output. A permanent-magnet generator used in a trailing-log water unit will also do nicely. Some means of isolating the generator from the battery is required when the engine is running and shaft speeds are excessive.

The number of amperes the unit can produce while sailing depends on the size and configuration of the propeller, the type of generator used, and the boat speed. Consult your generator supplier for sizing considerations for your boat. This system will not work on a sailboat with a feathering propeller that folds when the engine is not rotating in gear.

CONSTRUCTION

Propeller

Several propeller designs are used on water generators. In this application they should technically be called rotors or spinners, not propellers, since they are being rotated instead of doing the propelling. The industry convention, however, is to use the term *propeller*.

Because water is much denser than air, propeller efficiency is not as critical as with wind units at high speeds. Nevertheless, a well-designed propeller will produce maximum output with the least amount of drag. Most trailing-log units use a three-bladed aluminum outboard-motor prop, painted white and mounted in reverse so that it operates when pulled through the water. Some manufacturers have their props specially made. Low-speed boats should use props with higher-pitched blades than those used on high-speed boats. The propeller is typically mounted on a $5/8$-inch-diameter stainless steel shaft that is about 36 inches long. A shackle at the leading end provides a place to attach the towline. For the Power Log, since the entire unit is towed in the water, the prop is stainless steel and designed to match the generator housing it is attached to (see Figure 2-14).

If you mount a generator on an existing freewheeling propeller shaft, you will be stuck with the engine's propeller, the primary task of which is to propel the boat efficiently. Chances are, though, that a propeller efficient in one task will be efficient in the other. If you plan on installing an auxiliary prop shaft through the hull, take time to research the best prop for your application.

Electrical Generator

Manufacturers that supply wind and water units use the same generator for both applications. Hamilton Ferris and Everfair Enterprises use a 15-ampere permanent-magnet generator; the Aquair 100 employs a special permanent-magnet alternator with iron-cored stator; and the Hydrobat Energizer uses a 20-ampere alternator with an electromagnet supplied by a small field current, similar to car and boat alternators but made to operate at much lower RPMs. Any one of these could be adapted to use on an auxiliary shaft or freewheeling-prop shaft. The Power Log uses cobalt-samarium (samarium is a rare-earth element) magnets in a rotating permanent-magnet field and, as with other permanent-magnet alternators, has eliminated all brushes and slip rings that can potentially corrode or wear out. Some manufacturers place their generators inside an additional protective housing. If the unit is submerged, as with the Power Log, it will be sufficiently cooled at all speeds. If a generator is exposed to the sun, as with a stern mount, it can overheat at high speeds unless it is properly cooled.

Drive System

Trailing-log water generators have a direct-drive system, even though the propeller and generator may be separated by a long towline. Every revolution of the propeller induces a corresponding revolution of the generator shaft. When starting, the line begins to twist well before the generator shaft rotates, but this isn't a problem. In fact the line acts as a shock absorber, isolating the generator from potentially harmful loading. There is a slight energy loss due to the friction of the water on the towline. The Power Log is the only unit that is truly direct drive.

Outboard-leg units use gears to transfer horizontal rotary motion to vertical rotary motion of the generator shaft. While not direct drive, the ratio of prop RPMs to generator-shaft RPMs is usually 1:1. Some energy losses do occur.

With an auxiliary-prop shaft through the hull or a generator on an existing freewheeling-prop shaft, the drive system typically uses pulleys and a drive belt. The speed of the generator

FIGURE 10-3. **The Ampair and Aquair wind-and-water generator. (Courtesy Jack Rabbit Marine)**

181

can be the same as that of the prop shaft with a 1:1 pulley ratio, or twice that of the prop shaft with a 2:1 pulley ratio. Pulley ratio greatly affects how efficiently a particular propeller and generator combination operates; take care in selecting the right size pulleys. There are energy losses associated with a belt and pulley drive system.

WATER-GENERATOR THEORY

Below, the theoretical power that can be extracted from water in relative motion is determined, then tempered with reality to yield the usable power we can expect from water generators. Ratings, performance, and output considerations are also included.

Power Calculations

To find the energy associated with a water-driven generator on a boat, we can use the same equation for energy as that in the wind-theory section:

$$E_k = (mv^2)/2,$$

where

E_k = the kinetic energy of moving water,
m = the mass of the water, and
v = the velocity of the water.

When you trail a propeller through the water, it's actually the propeller that is in motion, not the water. Therefore, in the expression above, v is the speed of the boat. This is the speed registered by your knotmeter, not your speed over the ground, which takes into account any current that is running.

Since water and air are both fluids, we can also use the same expression for mass as that used in the wind-theory section:

$$m = eAvt,$$

where

e = the density of water,
A = the circular area of the water prop,
v = the velocity of the boat, and
t = the time elapsed.

Unlike air density, water density is not appreciably affected by either pressure or temperature. Since the above expressions for energy and mass apply to wind and water generators, the formula for the maximum power available is the same as well:

$$P_{MAX} = 0.593 \times (eAv^3)/2.$$

When you compare the manufacturers' charging curves for wind and water systems, you see that a water generator, with lower velocities than a wind unit (3 to 12 knots for water versus 6 to 25 knots for wind) and a much smaller propeller diameter (0.6 to 1.0 feet for water versus 3 to 5 feet for wind), is able to produce as much power as a wind generator. How is this possible? The answer lies in the relative density of the two fluids. Water, with a density of 62.4 pounds per cubic foot (salt water is slightly higher than this), is about 780 times denser than air. In our search for the usable power output of a water generator, we start by assuming that the expression for the maximum theoretical power a propeller can extract from the water is the same as for our wind propeller (as they are both propellers rotating in fluids). But first we must substitute the water density for air density (0.08 pound per cubic foot). From our section on wind power we have

$$P_{MAX(WIND)} = 0.0024D^2v^3,$$

therefore

$$P_{\text{MAX(WATER)}} = 0.0024D^2v^3 \times (62.4/0.08) = 1.87D^2v^3.$$

This is a water generator's theoretical maximum power. However, as with the wind generator, the usable power output of the water unit is somewhat less. How much less depends on the system efficiency, which is as follows:

- *Efficiency of the generator* (Egen) — We can use the same 70 percent efficiency (0.70 multiplier) as we did for a wind generator, since most manufacturers use the same unit for both wind and water systems, with conversion kits so you can easily change from one to the other.

- *Efficiency of the drive system* (Edrive) — Most water generators have a direct-drive linkage between propeller and generator, and therefore we can use the efficiency multiplier of 1.0. For systems that are not direct drive, such as those that change power-shaft direction from horizontal to vertical before it reaches the generator or those that use pulleys and a drive belt, the drive efficiency will be somewhat lower (a 0.8 or 0.9 multiplier).

- *Efficiency of the propeller* (Eprop) — The propeller used in most water-generator systems is similar to a small outboard propeller mounted on a shaft in reverse. There is very little information available to accurately describe propeller efficiency in this application, so at this point we can take a different approach than with our wind-generator calculations. By consulting the charging curve supplied by a water-generator manufacturer, we can use the actual values for power at various boat speeds. Then working backward, we can solve for the missing propeller efficiency Eprop.

For solving the usable-power calculation, we will use our Hamilton Ferris Neptune Supreme water unit with a propeller diameter of 0.69 feet and a charging curve as shown in Figure 10-4 . Our expression for the usable power available from a water generator to charge a battery looks like this:

$$P_{\text{WATER}} = 0.70 \times 1.0 \times Eprop \times 1.87D^2v^3$$

Plugging in the diameter of the propeller and squaring it, we get

$$P_{\text{WATER}} = 0.70 \times 1.0 \times Eprop \times 1.87 \times 0.48 \times v^3$$

Therefore,

$$P_{\text{WATER}}/(0.63 \times v^3) = Eprop$$

From the information in the charging curve, we can select several boat speeds, calculate the power available (amperes × volts) and solve for the propeller efficiency in each case. The unknown value for the efficiency, which is what we are trying to determine, should be about the same for any speed within the boat's normal cruising range. In fact it is, as shown in the chart in Figure 10-5. In the 4- to 7-knot range, the cruising speed for most boats, the efficiency of the propeller does appear to be fairly constant at around 0.43. As expected, this is much lower than the efficiency of a well-designed wind propeller.

Now we can insert this value and find the system's theoretical efficiency to be 0.70 × 1.0 × 0.43 = 0.30, or a system efficiency of 30 percent. This means that 30 percent of the maximum theoretical power, or about 15 to 20 percent (0.3 × 0.59) of the original energy,

FIGURE 10-4. **Charging output of a Hamilton Ferris Neptune Supreme generator, based on in-use measurements.**

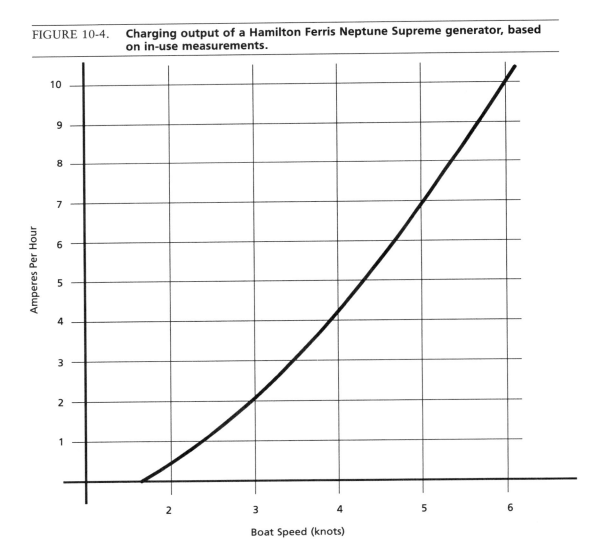

Amperes Per Hour

Boat Speed (knots)

FIGURE 10-5.   **Propeller efficiency of a Neptune Supreme generator, derived from data in Figure 10-4.**

| Boat Speed | | Amps | Power (watts) | Velocity (v^3) | Prop eff. |
Knots	MPH		Amps × 12.5 Volts		
4	4.60	2.0	25.00	97.33	0.40
5	5.76	4.5	56.25	191.10	0.47
6	6.91	7.4	92.50	330.00	0.44
7	8.06	11.0	137.50	524.00	0.42

can be extracted for charging batteries—not a bad figure for such a simple system. Therefore our expression for the usable power output of a water generator operating on a boat is

$$P_{WATTS} = 0.30 \times 1.87D^2v^3 = 0.56D^2v^3,$$

where

D is the diameter of the propeller in feet, and v is the velocity of the boat in miles per hour.

Assuming a generator efficiency of 0.70 does not imply that all units are the same, or that any alternator or generator used in a home-built system will perform in the same way. If you decide to make your own system, the above calculations will be close enough to work with, although the efficiencies of the prop and generator you choose may be quite different. Any commercial marine water generator is accompanied by a charging curve and power scale defining output at various cruising speeds. Remember that generators used on marine water systems are specially made to perform at relatively low RPMs, and are very different from a standard car alternator, which would work with your freewheeling shaft only if you gear up the shaft accordingly. In that case, you must also take into account the efficiency of the drive system, which might be around 0.80, and the extra drag as electrical output increases. You can assume that the propeller efficiency remains constant at normal cruising speeds, but at high speed the prop may lose much of its efficiency if it tends to skip out of the water.

Ratings and Reliability

Water generators are rated according to their peak-power potential in watts. Typical marine units operate in the 100- to 250-watt range, although generators attached to a free-wheeling-prop shaft can be substantially higher.

The reliability of properly designed water generators is generally very good. Although there are some parts that may need to be replaced periodically (see Tips on Installation, Operation, and Maintenance, below), all units are made of marine-grade materials that can withstand long-term routine use. Water generators usually require at least a 3-knot boat speed to operate. The trailing-log spinner assembly can, on occasion during long passages, be attacked by large fish. It is possible, though not probable, that the line might be severed and the assembly lost. The Power Log unit is much less likely to be lost in this manner, since the generator and prop are spinning together and the tow cable has steel reinforcing. On the other hand, if a large fish does take it, you have lost the entire unit. Water generators attached by short leads or on an outboard-leg frame can't be lost in this manner.

Performance

The performance of a water generator depends on boat speed, access to smooth water, propeller size, and unit efficiency.

Boat speed.   As seen in the calculations above, the power output is proportional to the cube of the boat speed. Dramatic increases in power can be realized with modest increases in boat speed.

Access to nonturbulent water.   For best performance a water generator must operate in water free of turbulence, since turbulence hurts a propeller's efficiency. A trailing-log unit operates best in this respect, since the prop is usually 50 feet or more behind the boat. A water generator on the freewheeling-prop shaft is also quite good, since the main engine prop will be running in nonturbulent water. Units on short leads or outboard-leg frames, however, could find themselves in agitated water; take care when selecting a place to mount them. High-speed sailboats, particularly multihulls, create another form of turbulence. If the boat is moving too fast, a trailing-log prop tends to skip out of the water unless a diving plane is used (see Other Components and Considerations, below). In these conditions, props used in the other systems will probably spend a fair amount of time either out of the water or in turbulence.

Propeller size.   The calculations above show that the power output of a water generator is proportional to the square of the diameter of the propeller. Props that are too large or have blades with too great a pitch will cause unwanted drag. A prop must be selected for effective power output without creating too much drag for the boat.

Efficiency.   The search for more efficient propeller-generator combinations continues. The key to increasing efficiency is matching the most efficient point on a generator or alternator power curve with the propeller's blade-pitch characteristics. Generators used on these machines are specially wound to operate at lower RPMs. Remember to take into account the efficiency of the drive system for water generators with an outboard leg, on an auxiliary prop, or on a freewheeling engine-prop shaft.

METHODS OF INSTALLATION

There are basically five methods of installing water generators on a boat, each with its own advantages and proponents. Some units may be installed permanently, while others require periodic setting up and retrieval.

Trailing Log

The installation for a trailing-log unit is relatively easy, since many of the components are in the water and don't require mounting. The only part that needs to be permanently mounted is the gimballed frame that holds the generator in place at the stern. The gimbal can use a quick-connect mounting bracket so it can be readily removed when not in use. The Aquair 100 water generator, a conversion from a wind unit, even eliminates this need because the gimbal-generator assembly is suspended from a line tied to the stern rail, like a taffrail log. The gimbal must provide several degrees of movement, side to side and up and down, so the generator can track the movement of the propeller. This maintains a fair lead on the towline, and allows the rotary motion to be transferred efficiently. Gimbal mounts are supplied with all trailing-log water generators, but you can make your own. Since the propeller is not as critical as it is in a wind system, it is easier to construct a water generator system yourself. You still must have an electrical generator that will produce at low RPMs.

If you are mounting the gimbal to the deck, make sure you seal the fastener holes, or construct a quick-connect bracket that allows the gimbal to be mounted and removed easily. If you like, a polarized electrical deck connector can send the wiring from the mount to the battery without going through or around the cockpit. When selecting a location for the gimbal, remember that the trailing line must always have a fair lead. The entire towline spins rapidly and requires swinging room off the stern. We know of a line that was neatly severed on a self-steering wind vane when the boat had to do some fast maneuvering. The propeller tends to walk slightly to port as it spins, so try to mount it on the port side, away from other trailing lines.

The Power Log requires no gimbal mount on the stern, since the generator is attached to the propeller and the entire unit trails in the water. Consequently, the tow cable does not spin; it needs only to be fastened to the stern, also maintaining a fair lead. The tow cable houses the output wiring, which must be routed to the battery from the point where it exits the cable.

Short Flexible Lead

There are two models that operate on a short flexible lead instead of a long towline. The Power Log can be adapted to this mounting system, and in fact the manufacturer recommends it as the standard mounting method. In this case, you must install a short metal strut off the stern capable of supporting the trailing generator. Greenwich Corporation, which manufactures the Power Log, offers a stainless steel assembly that includes a strut, a sliding tube inside the strut for connecting the flexible lead and allowing the unit to be retrieved from the stern, and a 12- to 18-inch-long hydraulic hose with compression fittings at each end (see Figure 10-6). One end of the hose attaches to the sliding tube and the other to the generator. The output wiring must be routed inside or alongside the strut and to the battery.

The other system suited for this type of mounting is the Hydrobat Energizer. Its manufacturer claims that there is much less stress on the unit with a flexible lead than with an outboard-leg mount, and that the system operates with boat speeds in excess of 20 knots!

Outboard Leg

The only unit that can be mounted like an outboard motor is the Hydrobat Energizer, whose manufacturer furnishes all necessary components. Installation is simple, and is similar

FIGURE 10-6.   **Power Log water generator on a short flexible lead.**

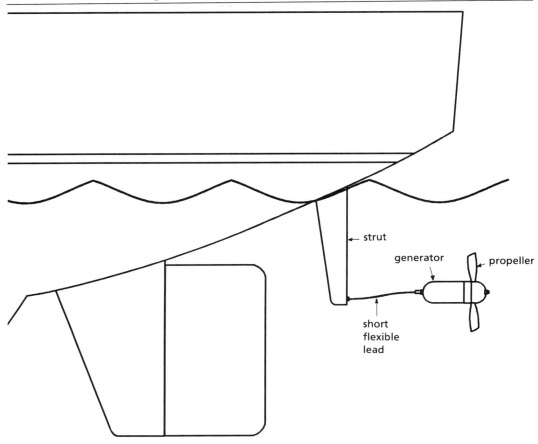

to mounting an outboard-motor bracket on the stern. You must furnish the manufacturer with your boat's stern dimensions. The company provides a track, which should be positioned to allow the unit to slide into the water for operation or up and out of the way when the boat is stationary (refer to Figure 10-1). Lead the output wires to the battery in a neat and orderly fashion.

Auxiliary Propeller and Shaft

Once you have selected your generator-propeller combination, install the propeller shaft through the hull as you would an engine drive shaft. Unless you are familiar with this work, it is best left to a professional: Shaft support and proper alignment are critical. Be sure the shaft is accessible for periodic service. A small stuffing box seals the hull where the shaft passes through. It should take much less abuse than an engine shaft stuffing box, since the shaft speeds are lower and the lateral forces much less. The generator shaft can be joined to the prop shaft by a universal joint or similar arrangement, or with a belt and pulleys as shown in Figure 10-2.

A belt-and-pulley system is preferred, since the generator shaft remains isolated from the forces acting on the prop shaft. It's also much easier to disengage the generator using a simple manual clutch to loosen the pulley belt. The drive-system efficiency depends on the belt, tightness, and pulley ratio, which in turn depends on the RPMs necessary for your generator. The best unit yields a high electrical output at low RPMs, requiring a pulley ratio of 1:1 or 2:1.

Generator on Freewheeling Propeller

For this type of water generator, install a bracket near the transmission shaft to hold the generator securely. Mount the generator so its shaft parallels the transmission shaft. Place a pulley on each shaft in line with the other. Proper alignment is most important. Only by testing your generator on your boat can you determine the correct shaft speed, and thus the most efficient pulley ratio. It is important to have both an electrical and a mechanical means of disengaging the generator from the transmission shaft when the engine is running. An electrical disconnect protects the battery and generator at high engine RPMs, and a mechanical disconnect prevents unnecessary wear on the generator when it is not needed.

SIZING AND SELECTION

This section reviews the relevant considerations and the water generators from which to choose. For a more detailed analysis of determining electrical load and selecting equipment, refer to Chapters 13 and 14.

Assessing Your Needs

The information here will help you evaluate your water-charging needs. As stated in Chapters 8 and 9, the output from alternative-energy systems is much more "location- and owner-dependent" than that from fossil-fuel systems.

Electrical load. Your boat's electrical load is easy to calculate, or to determine empirically by monitoring daily electrical draw. While watt-hours are the correct representation of energy production or consumption, ampere-hours—even though they leave voltage out of the equation—will give you a good idea of the electrical energy you consume, especially since batteries are rated in ampere-hours. Make a list of your electrical equipment, with the number of amperes drawn by each when operating. Multiply these amperes by the number of hours you operate each during the day; use an average for intermittent-use equipment. Now add an additional 10 to 15 percent to account for the battery's storage and retrieval inefficiency.

Water-generator output. It would be nice to match your electrical load with a single water generator, but since the generator charges only when the boat is sailing, this is not practical. A water generator is best used in combination with a wind unit or as a supplement to other charging systems. It serves nicely as the power source while under way, when you will likely need running lights and navigational equipment. And it will usually produce some surplus energy to store for brief periods in port.

To calculate the energy a water generator can deliver, multiply the peak current rating in amperes (associated with a given boat speed) by the hours you sail at that speed. For example, a water generator that has a maximum 8-ampere rating at 6 knots can potentially deliver 192 ampere-hours over 24 hours. These are ideal numbers and your average output will undoubtedly be lower.

Manufacturers' output ratings usually are based on a generator that is connected to a battery about 50 percent discharged. As the battery voltage rises, electrical output drops off.

The installation has much less effect on the output of a water generator than it does with solar or wind-power systems. If the prop can operate in water reasonably free from agitation, the electrical output will be consistent for a given propeller-generator combination. A generator on a freewheeling engine-prop shaft offers a much higher output potential, but only because of the larger prop diameter. The larger the prop diameter and electrical output of the generator, the greater the drag on the boat.

Climate has nothing directly to do with the output of a water generator, but indirectly it plays a large part. Water generators are just as dependent on wind speed as are wind generators, since this is what helps determine boat speed. Areas with consistent winds provide for consistent boat speeds, and thus consistent water-generator output.

In addition, some conditions preclude the use of trailing-log water generators, such as very shallow water, or waters with pots and fishing buoys.

Your boat.   The space available on the stern and the presence of other equipment that might interfere with a water generator are the most important things to consider. If space is limited, it might be hard to find a spot for an outboard-leg unit. Trailing-log systems require a clear path for towing the spinner, and transom-hung rudders, self-steering wind vanes, trailing dinghies, fishing lines, and taffrail log spinners might create congestion. Units attached by a short lead or hung from an auxiliary shaft can be mounted on almost any boat without interference.

Boats with extra-large transoms are ideal. On our catamaran, we have a 12-foot-wide transom with plenty of room for all of the above-mentioned boat gear and a trailing-log water unit. Boats with low average speeds (usually smaller sailboats) should consider a water generator with the least amount of drag—that is, with smaller, more efficient propellers. Consult your marine energy equipment supplier for the best unit for your boat.

How you use your boat.   You'll likely use your water generator with some other marine energy system, whether it is your auxiliary-engine alternator, a portable generator, solar panels, a wind generator, or a combination. A water generator might be a poor choice if you motor frequently. Because of the need for monitoring, even with generators on a freewheeling engine-prop shaft, water units are not appropriate for bareboat charters. They can be effective for crewed charter boats, since they have a large electrical output and are quiet and unob-

FIGURE 10-7.   **Water generator comparison chart.**   **191**

Model	Generator	Propeller	Rated output (amps) at 5 knots	Weight (lbs.)	Mounting type	Max. boat speed
Aquair 100	PM alternator	2-bladed 10″ dia.	3.5	29	trailing log	10 knots
Everfair Ent.	PM generator	3-bladed outboard motor 9″ dia.	5.0	20	trailing log	10 knots
Greenwich Power Log	PM alternator	2-bladed 13″ dia., mounted on alternator	5.5	15	trailing log, short flexible lead	not specified
Ham. Ferris Neptune Supreme	PM generator	3-bladed outboard motor 9″ dia.	4.5	22	trailing log	10 knots w/o diving plane; 16 knots with diving plane
Perrin Ind. Hydrobat	Alternator	3-bladed outboard motor	5–8	?	outboard leg	not specified

trusive. A water generator is probably not appropriate for weekend or occasional sailors. If you take the boat periodically for an extended cruise, however, a water generator can supply the extra power required while you are on board. It might be a nice supplement to a small solar panel that keeps the batteries topped up while you are off the boat.

Water generators, especially trailing logs, come into their own for passagemakers. On longer voyages, with a trailing-log unit, you have only to set out the spinner assembly, then retrieve it at the end of the passage. Sailors who spend a lot of time in port between frequent passages find a wind-water or solar-water combination hard to beat.

Ocean racers favor water generators for their reliability, high output, and low drag. It is often hard to find enough clear space to mount solar panels on racing boats, and if the boat's electrical load is high, water generators are the answer.

Water-Generator Selection

Marine water generators include the Neptune Supreme, the Fourwinds WG-1, the Power Log, the Aquair 100, and the Hydrobat Energizer. The first three are manufactured in the United States. The Aquair is manufactured in England and sold in the United States by Jack Rabbit Marine. The Hydrobat Energizer is manufactured in France. Figure 10-7 lists the specifications for each system.

Earlier we showed that water generators are around 15 to 20 percent efficient at converting the energy in moving water to electrical energy. Since no other devices are used in the conversion process, this is then the system efficiency, which compares favorably with other marine charging sources.

OTHER COMPONENTS AND CONSIDERATIONS

In addition to the propeller, generator, and drive system, water energy systems may include components for mounting, the towline, break links, braking mechanisms, and the like. These components are described below.

Mounting Components

The basic mounting components are usually supplied by the manufacturer. These might be a gimbal mounting frame for a trailing-log generator, or a track and slide for outboard-leg units. Support brackets for other systems are almost always supplied by the owner to fit a particular boat.

Towline or Cable

Most suppliers of trailing-log units include 50 to 75 feet of 7/16-inch tightly wound braided line for the tow cable. It should be tightly wound so rotation of the propeller is transmitted rapidly to the generator shaft. The tow cable for the Power Log is actually high-pressure hydraulic hose. The wire reinforcing mesh provides high tensile strength, and also serves as one of the electrical leads.

Break Link

The break link protects your generator on a trailing-log system. It is a short length of light line that is designed to break before the generator is damaged when the prop is snagged or attacked by a hungry fish. Consult your supplier for proper size and installation procedures.

Braking Mechanisms

As with wind systems, you must have an effective way to stop the propeller in any conditions. The best method is to stop the boat, but this is not always easily done. It is also next to impossible to try to retrieve a rotating spinner assembly. Hamilton Ferris developed and sells a funnel-like piece of gear that can be placed over the spinning line. It is designed to slide down to the prop and block water from the propeller blades, stopping the tow assembly's spinning. Generators on auxiliary shafts or on freewheeling engine-prop shafts use electrical and mechanical disconnects instead of braking mechanisms.

Diving Plane

Hamilton Ferris has developed a diving plane for trailing log units. It is a small aluminum device with winglike extensions that is placed over the propeller shaft to keep the prop submerged at high boat speeds. It has been tested successfully to 16 knots. Hamilton Ferris' funnel braking device metioned above will not work on units with diving planes.

Wiring

All water units come with a two-wire conductor to transfer output current to the battery. Additional wiring with a polarized connector (possibly a deck plug) can be added for convenient routing to the battery. Refer to Appendix B for correct wire sizing. The diode, fuse, voltage regulator, and monitoring devices can be permanently wired below decks between the water unit and the battery. A hypothetical wiring schematic for a water generator is shown in Figure 10-8.

Voltage Regulator

While not a necessity, voltage regulators are recommended for all water generators because of their potentially high daily output. Voltage regulation does slightly lessen the performance of a water unit, and can be avoided if you monitor battery voltage carefully. Just keep in mind that an expensive set of batteries can be ruined by inattention.

FIGURE 10-8.   **Schematic of an electrical system with multiple charging options. Components relevant to water charging are highlighted.**

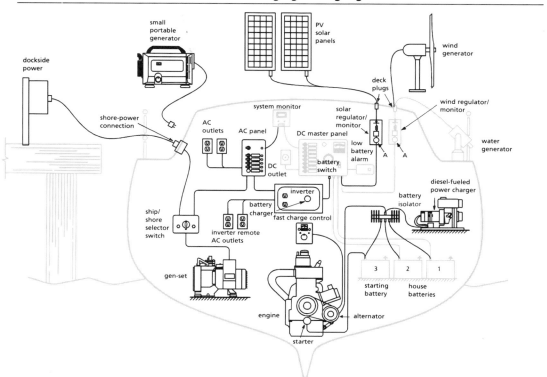

Diode and Fuse

A diode keeps the generator from becoming an electric motor and consuming battery current when the prop isn't turning. It also allows you to use other generators at the same time. The diode, mounted on a finned piece of aluminum for efficient heat dissipation, and the fuse should be rated slightly above the maximum generating current.

System Monitors

Meters to display output current and voltage are vital not only to prove that the system is working properly, but to measure the effect on output current of various boat speeds. If you have a water generator on your boat, it's nice to have an accurate knotmeter to measure boat speed and compare it with output current. With this information you can construct your own system output curve.

Conversion Kits

Several manufacturers offer conversion kits to transform trailing-log units into rigging-suspended wind generators. This way the machine can be used in port and under way. Wind conversion kits include wind propeller and mounting hub, and rigging-suspended mounting frame.

OPERATION

Self-Tending Units

By definition, self-tending units need no operator, although they may require periodic care. Water generators on auxiliary-prop shafts through the hull are self-tending once they are set up, provided that a voltage regulator is used. If not, you'll need to monitor the battery's state of charge regularly. Preventive maintenance includes checking the stuffing box regularly for leaks and wear, and keeping the prop free of barnacles and other marine growth. If a belt-and-pulley drive system is used, check the belt for correct tension and wear, and keep a spare belt on board.

Generators on freewheeling prop shafts are also basically self-tending. Either electrically or mechanically disconnect the generator before starting the engine. High engine RPMs could damage the generator; check with your supplier for proper RPM range. Mechanically disconnect the generator if motoring for long periods to save on bearing and brush wear. (Brush wear is not a factor if an alternator is used.)

Non-Self-Tending Units

Trailing-log units and units on short flexible leads do require some looking after.

Trailing-log operation. If the unit has a spinning towline and the generator is in a gimbal mount at the stern, the starting procedure is as follows:

1. Mount the generator on its gimbal at the stern.

2. Connect the forward end of the towing line to the generator shaft and neatly coil the remainder of the line, including the prop and shaft.

3. Connect the generator wiring to the battery.

4. Make certain there are no obstructions on the boat or in the water and that the trailing line has a fair lead (watch your hands and feet).

5. Lower the prop into the water while the boat is moving forward and rapidly pay out the coiled line. This is easily done if the boat is moving slowly, but is more difficult at higher speeds. With practice this can be done in one quick motion.

The system is so quiet you won't know it's working without looking at the spinning line. On long sails, remember to check your battery state of charge regularly if you don't have a voltage regulator. Once your battery is charged, you can retrieve the unit and stow it until it's needed again, saving wear on the generator and eliminating any slight drag.

Two effective techniques will stop the spinning prop so the unit can be hauled aboard. The first is simply to turn the boat into the wind or let the wind spill from the sails, pull in the unit as the boat stops, then get under way again. Another technique is to use a split-funnel arrangement, as described above in Other Components and Considerations. Coil the towline neatly and tie it off securely for the next generating period.

Note: Operating the Power Log is similar to operating other trailing logs, except that it is much easier to set out and retrieve, since the tow cable does not spin. Make certain the cable is secured to a strong cleat with an extra safety line before tossing the unit overboard.

TIPS ON INSTALLATION, OPERATION, AND MAINTENANCE

This section includes an assortment of the most frequently asked questions about the installation, operation, and maintenance of water generators.

Q. *What type of electrical disconnect switch should be used for water generators? How does this affect the generator if it continues to spin?*

A. Any simple two-position switch rated for the maximum output of the generator and located anywhere in the output wire will be fine. Even though the generator continues to spin, it produces no current when the switch is open (there is an open circuit). Therefore, it doesn't build up excessive heat and remains protected.

Q. *Can excessive boat speeds damage the generator? When should you disconnect the generator?*

A. Excessive boat speeds can harm a generator or alternator by causing it to build up more heat than can be dissipated. Consult your equipment supplier to get a range of operating RPMs. If the unit experiences speeds higher than recommended, the generator should be electrically disconnected. If you also mechanically disconnect, either with a clutch arrangement or by retrieving the unit, it will save on needless wear and tear of the bearing and brushes—if brushes are used.

Q. *What is the best water generator for a high-speed sailboat?*
A. Many will work, but units on a short flexible lead have the best chance of remaining submerged and are the easiest to operate at high speeds.

Q. *What happens to a trailing-log spinner assembly in rough weather?*
A. If a diving plane is used, the prop should stay submerged at up to 15 knots or so. Otherwise the propeller can periodically skip out of the water. This reduces electrical output and subjects the generator mounted on the stern to unnecessary and possibly harmful stress.

Q. *For a wind-water combination unit, how easy is it to convert from one to the other?*
A. It's not something you'd want to do every day, but then you shouldn't have to. The procedure is not difficult. First you must disconnect the wiring and remove the wind propeller from the generator (usually one or two bolts to loosen), then take the generator out of the rigging-suspended mounting frame (another few bolts). The frame and wind prop should be stowed while under way. Place the generator in its gimbal at the stern (the Aquair 100 will already be in its gimbal), and tighten the fastenings. A small safety line can be tied from the generator to a convenient place on deck or railing. The towline usually connects to the generator shaft with a coupling with one or two Allen head screws that need to be tightened securely. Afterward, connect the output wires and you are ready to go.

Q. *What spares should be kept on board for a water generator?*
A. If your unit has a permanent-magnet generator, a spare set of brushes would be advisable. An extra set of generator bearings, if replaceable, would also be a good idea. A spare spinner assembly should be carried for all water generators except the Power Log, which has an integrated prop and alternator. If you have a belt-and-pulley drive system, carry a spare belt.

Q. *What maintenance is required for a water generator?*

A. Not much. Check the painted surface of the generator and prop, and touch up if necessary. Place a little grease on the front bearing of a permanent-magnet generator to help seal it. Check belt tension and tighten as required; replace the belt when you notice obvious signs of wear. Occasionally wash a rope towline in warm water to remove salt and dirt. Check any fasteners for signs of fatigue and for proper tightness.

Q. *Can you operate a water generator at the same time as other marine electrical generators?*

A. Yes, as long as all charging sources have properly sized diodes that prevent current from reversing direction.

11

DC-to-AC Inverters

D irect current (DC) battery power is safe, easy to work with, and satisfies the electrical needs of many boaters. Yet alternating current (AC) is what we have at home, work, and at the dock. AC is so prevalent—all household appliances run off AC power—that it's natural to want it on a boat. While dozens of marine appliances now available operate on 12-volt DC, many still require 110- or 220-volt AC. There are several ways to provide AC power on board, but none other matches the freedom and convenience of DC-to-AC inverters. If your AC loads are moderate and your battery capacity sufficient, inverters can eliminate the need for any other AC source.

INVERTER ADVANTAGES

Inverters allow you to have AC power anywhere—on a mooring, at anchor, or under way in practically any conditions. Unlike gen-sets and portable generators, inverters don't create electricity, they only change it from one form to another. Solid-state inverters draw upon the stored energy of lead-acid boat batteries, raise the voltage and invert the current from DC to AC, then supply this electricity to your AC loads. Inverters can also draw directly off 12-volt charging sources. If the charging current is adequate, the inverter won't deplete your batteries as long as you are charging. Recent advances in inverters have helped to make their use efficient, practical, and affordable.

Inverters are whisper quiet, perfect for those "quiet time" loads. Most marine AC appliances are used at times when the sound of a generator engine is annoying at best. Computers and other work-related appliances, stereos, TVs and VCRs, AC lighting, and even kitchen appliances are best used in a quiet surrounding. Of course, the batteries must eventually be recharged and that operation can be a noisy affair, but you can schedule the charging for more convenient times.

The electricity inverters draw from the batteries might come from renewable sources of energy, such as solar, wind, and water generators. In fact, inverters are prevalent in remote-home power systems supplied solely by PV solar and/or wind generators. Whether renewable energy generators can supply your total load depends on many factors, but at least you have the opportunity to do so with this type of AC system.

A modern inverter uses very little power when on standby—when the unit is on but no load is being drawn—compared with a gen-set or large portable generator. For many boaters, this can be a large portion of the time. It used to be necessary to turn on an inverter for a specific task, then turn it off again to prevent standby losses. Now an efficient inverter may consume only a half watt on standby, whereas a gen-set will crank away, consuming fuel whether you are using the AC power or not. Other advantages of inverters are their compactness, their lower cost, and their reliability. Installation is uncomplicated, and there is no additional engine to maintain, as with gen-sets and portable generators.

WHEN TO USE AN INVERTER

Inverters are most practical for AC loads up to 2,000 or 2,500 watts, particularly when the larger loads are intermittent. Even though the current draw of large intermittent loads may be high, the total energy consumed is usually moderate. Larger-capacity inverters are available, but the battery bank needed to supply them gets to be impractical on boats. (A 600-watt inverter operating at full capacity would draw 50 ampere-hours, enough to bring a fully charged battery of 200 ampere-hours' capacity to 50 percent in less than 2 hours.) Fortunately, most high-draw appliances are indeed used intermittently, and 2,000 to 2,500 watts of AC power is adequate for the majority of boaters.

Loads that are usually not supplied by inverters include external battery chargers, air conditioning, and appliances with large heating elements, such as hot water and space heaters and electric ranges. If the size of your AC load places you on the borderline between an inverter and a gen-set, try staggering the use of AC loads to make it work. In other words, don't run the power tools when dinner is cooking in the microwave or when other high-draw appliances are on. This may be inconvenient, but a little scheduling can save a lot of money otherwise spent on generating equipment.

If your AC requirements exceed the practical limits of an inverter and you invest in a gen-set or portable generator, an inverter is still useful for quiet-time loads and for some intermittent loads when running the gen-set is not efficient. Use the generator for the large AC loads, and possibly for battery charging, when the noise won't disturb you or others. Operate the inverter for smaller AC appliances used when you'd rather enjoy peace and quiet. The inverter's ultralow current drain on standby allows you to leave it on when moderate loads might be used. For instance, if you are running AC constant-cycling refrigeration, powering it with an efficient inverter makes more sense than a gen-set. The refrigeration compressor comes on for only a short time each hour, then turns off, cycling as needed. The inverter remains on standby until power is required, and there is no unnecessary noise to contend with. On the

FIGURE 11-1.   **Square-wave AC output from a DC-to-AC inverter.**

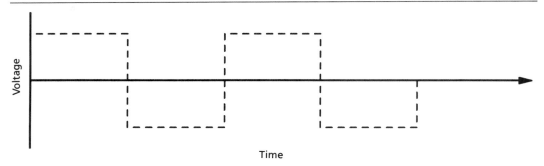

other hand, if the refrigeration system uses holding plates with a high-current-draw compressor unit, turning on the gen-set for a short time each day makes more sense. You can charge the batteries at the same time.

Generators and inverters complement each other for another important reason: many inverters can also double as battery chargers. Use the inverter as a battery charger when the generator is running, then use it in the AC supply mode as needed. The same applies for shore-power connections while at a dock. Use the shore power with the inverter in the battery-charging mode while at the dock, then use the inverter in the AC-supply mode when on the water.

TYPES OF INVERTERS

Inverters vary in size and output, beginning with the 100-watt "pocket-size" models (see Figure 3-9). All inverters fall into one of three categories:

1. The older "rotary inverters" (also called motor-generators)

2. Static square-wave inverters

3. Static sine-wave inverters

Rotary inverters are nothing more than a DC electric motor coupled directly to an AC generator. The motor and generator windings are wound on the same shaft. As the DC motor draws battery power and turns the shaft, sine-wave AC electricity is created by the generator windings. Rotary inverters are rugged and reliable, but are heavy and grossly inefficient compared with solid-state inverters. Up to 25 percent of their rated power is needed just to turn them on, even in standby. They might be useful on a construction site, but they are not suited for an energy-conscious boater.

Static square-wave inverters, such as the Tripp Lite models, have been around for quite a while and are still hard to beat in the cost-per-watt category. These inverters produce alternating current in the form of a square wave, as shown in Figure 11-1. This very roughly approximates the sine wave produced by the utility company, portable generators, and gen-sets.

FIGURE 11-2.   **The modified sine-wave output from a DC-to-AC inverter, shown in comparison with an idealized sine-wave output at left.**

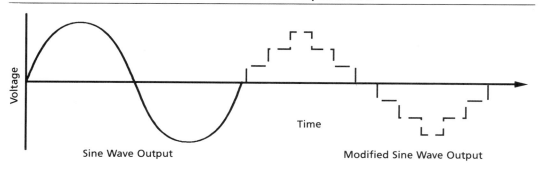

Sine Wave Output   Modified Sine Wave Output

Square-wave inverters can be used for a wide range of appliances, including TVs, stereos, and small hand tools. Some square-wave inverters have frequency control to allow running computers and VCRs.

Square-wave inverters are not suitable for sensitive electronic equipment that requires sine-wave output. They have limited surge capability and are not suitable for induction or capacitor-start motors with high start-up loads. The surge capability for Tripp Lite inverters, for example, is only about 10 percent above rated value. Square-wave inverters are less efficient than modern sine-wave inverters, so they are best used for short-term loads, then turned off. Standby losses can be 100 times that of more efficient types. Less expensive inverters can also cause more radio-frequency interference in TVs and stereos.

Static sine-wave inverters, such as those from Heart Interface (see Figure 3-10) or Trace Engineering (see Figure 11-5) cost a bit more but are remarkably efficient, and are capable of running almost any AC appliance. Standby losses are typically less than 1 watt. The alternating current produced by these inverters is called a modified sine wave (Figure 11-2), which more closely approximates a true sine wave. These inverters are suitable for running electric motors with high start-up loads, since their surge capability is 3 to 6 times their rated power.

INVERTER RATINGS AND SPECIFICATIONS

In addition to the size and weight of the unit and the wave form of the output, other ratings and specifications are useful when shopping for inverters. These tell you how the unit will perform under various conditions.

AC Power Output

Inverters are rated according to their maximum continuous AC output, as well as their initial surge capacity, in watts. The initial surge output can be many times the continuous rated output, and is useful for running appliances with motors that have high start-up loads. Surge capacity is sometimes given in terms of the maximum horsepower of an inductive motor that can be run by the inverter. After the initial surge of power, a higher-than-rated output is available for a short period. As heat builds inside the unit, output decreases until it reaches

FIGURE 11-3. **Representative graph of Statpower ProWatt 600 inverter power vs. running time.**

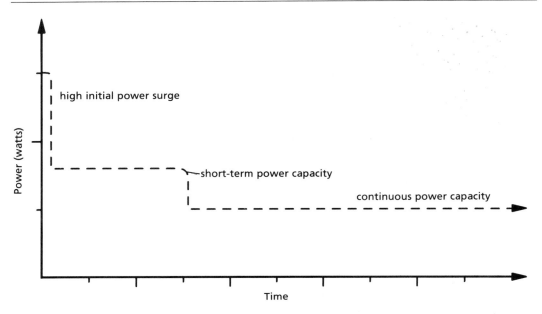

the level of continuous operation. A graph displaying typical output versus time is shown in Figure 11-3.

No-Load Current

No-load current refers to the current drain when the unit is on standby—that is, when it's turned on but no load is being drawn. This is an important specification that is always prominently displayed by the manufacturers of more efficient inverters and quietly ignored by makers of less efficient models. It can make a great difference, especially if you have loads that go on and off regularly. If you turn on the inverter only for a specific task, then turn it off, no-load current rating is less of an issue. Efficient units have no-load current draw on the order of 0.02 to 0.07 ampere.

Efficiency

Efficiency varies with output power. Most modern sine-wave inverters operate above 90 percent efficiency under normal appliance loads. This means that the inverter itself consumes about 10 percent of its output power whenever a load is drawn. A graph depicting power versus efficiency for a Trace Engineering model is given in Figure 11-4. Efficiency is usually listed at its maximum value for a specified power output.

Input Voltage Range

The input voltage rating lets the buyer know the range of battery supply voltages over which other specifications will be valid. Most of the better sine-wave inverters allow input

FIGURE 11-4.   **Performance curve for a Trace Engineering inverter.**

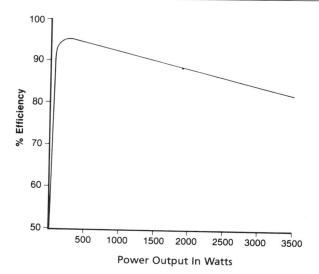

voltages to vary over the battery's entire normal operating range without disrupting output voltage. Some are equipped with low-battery cut-out protection that prevents the inverter from working if battery voltage drops below around 10.5 volts.

Output Voltage Regulation

This describes how constant the output voltage will be over the range of usable DC input voltages. For example, voltage regulation on Trace inverters is given as "117 V AC, ± 2 volts." Other manufacturers may give output voltage regulation in terms of a percentage of voltage variation. More efficient models will have tighter control over output voltage.

FIGURE 11-5.   **Inverters from Trace Engineering.**

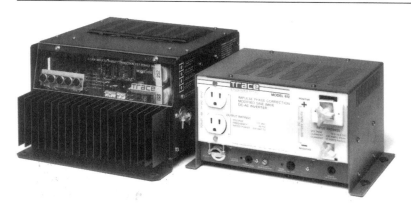

Frequency Regulation

Some sensitive equipment can't tolerate large fluctuations in output frequency, and this important specification lets you know how well a particular unit is regulated. For example, a sales brochure on an efficient inverter may state that it has crystal-controlled frequency regulation of 0.005 percent at 60 hertz. This means that the output frequency is 60 cycles per second, like normal U.S. household AC, and that it won't vary more than 0.005 percent from this value. This is extremely tight regulation. Many companies also offer models with European voltage and frequency output.

SPECIAL FEATURES AND OPTIONS

To survive in this competitive field, manufacturers are constantly improving their units and providing them with special features and options. Some inverter features are geared specifically for the marine environment, although most inverters are also used in recreational vehicles and remote homes. Below are a few features to look for.

Battery-Charging Option

The battery-charging option is one of the most useful features a marine inverter can have—if only all marine energy components could be so versatile. Not all inverters are capable of use as battery chargers. Many inverters use a transfer switch to automatically begin charging the battery when the inverter senses another AC source, such as when shore power or gen-set AC power is plugged in.

Efficient inverters used as battery chargers provide the proper charge to deep-cycle batteries, operating in a constant-current mode up to a preset voltage of around 14.3 volts, then either shutting off until a low battery voltage is sensed or switching to a constant-voltage "float charge" at around 13.3 volts. The charger may also have a timed equalization cycle that allows you to periodically remove the sulfation that reduces the life of a liquid-electrolyte lead-acid battery.

Protection Devices

Modern inverters are packed with features that protect your equipment from harm. Typically, the inverter itself is protected from overcurrent, overheating (thermal overload), and short circuits. The inverter may also be protected from battery voltage that is too high—usually over 15 volts—caused by faulty or inadequate voltage regulation of the charging source. Some models feature protection from accidentally reversing the circuit, and from lightning. Heavy-duty circuit breakers protect other equipment and wiring from overload. The batteries themselves are usually protected from deep discharge by a low-battery alarm or by a load cut-out switch that disconnects all loads when the battery voltage reaches approximately 10.5 volts.

Other Voltages and Frequencies

Some of the higher-end inverters can produce other output voltages and frequencies. Know what output levels you want before ordering your unit. Typical output for domestic

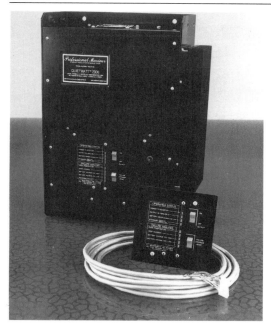

equipment is 120 volts AC at 60 hertz. The output for European equipment usually ranges from 100 to 240 volts AC, at either 50 or 60 hertz. Optional transformers are also available to "step up" output voltage, allowing you to operate 220-volt appliances.

Remote Control

Another option for some high-end inverters is a remote-control panel that allows you to control and monitor inverter operation from anywhere on the boat. This is particularly useful when the inverter is hard to reach. The remote-control panel typically includes on-off and reset controls, along with monitoring displays for the safety features.

Fan Cooling

In an attempt to increase continuous power output, many inverters offer fan cooling, or so-called turbocharging. The internal buildup of heat is one of the limiting factors of a unit's rated output. For example, the fan-cooling option on Trace inverters increases the continuous power output by about 400 watts. The Statpower pocket inverter has a fan-cooling option that raises the output from 100 to 150 watts of continuous power.

Stacking Interface

If you require more AC power than your inverter will produce, you can often purchase a module that allows you to connect multiple inverters in parallel to double the power output at the same voltage. When stacking multiple units, you must make certain your batteries can supply the power required.

INVERTER SIZING AND SELECTION

Sizing

To get the proper inverter for your boat you'll need to know the maximum continuous power and surge capability you need. Then you'll need to know the boat's battery capacity.

Continuous power. Determining needed maximum continuous power is a simple matter of adding up the power requirements of the AC loads you use, or anticipate using, at any one time. By staggering AC loads, you can significantly reduce the inverter size you need. To cut down on instantaneous power consumption, make certain that high-draw appliances don't get used at the same time. For example, you may have the following AC appliances on board:

Appliance	Power required
power tools	1,200 watts
coffee maker (large)	1,200 watts
toaster	1,000 watts
microwave (small)	800 watts
coffee maker (small)	600 watts
blender	400 watts
computer	200 watts
color TV	150 watts
stereo	50 watts

If you want to use all these appliances at the same time, you must get an inverter capable of producing over 5,000 watts. On the other hand, by staggering your loads you can get by with an inverter sized to run your largest appliance. In this case, a 1,200-watt inverter would handle the power tools or coffee maker, and would also run the microwave oven and blender simultaneously.

Your inverter should have adequate surge capability for starting appliances with electric motors. The initial-surge requirement can be several times the rated output of the appliance. Check with your supplier to make sure you properly match inverter output with AC appliance surge demand.

Battery capacity. The second thing you must calculate is how much battery capacity you need to supply DC power adequately to the inverter. It is all too easy to ignore where the inverter's power is actually coming from. You may want a few high-power AC appliances,

FIGURE 11-7. **Schematic of a shipboard electrical system having multiple charging options. Components relevant to use of DC-to-AC inverter are highlighted.**

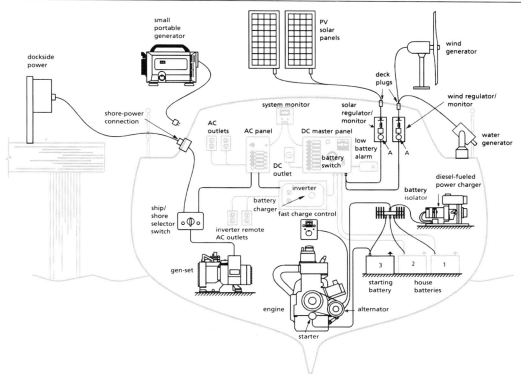

even though your DC loads on board are moderate. The batteries must be capable of supplying full instantaneous current to the inverter, and also have enough capacity to supply all AC and DC loads between normal charging cycles. For large inverters, the amount of instantaneous current required can be substantial. A 90-percent-efficient 2,000-watt inverter under full load draws more than 175 amperes at 12 volts DC. This load may be on for only a very short time, and thus the total energy consumed might be fairly low, yet the batteries must supply this short-term current without being harmed. Some batteries are better able to supply high current than others. As a general rule, the battery capacity in ampere-hours should be at least four times the maximum current draw in amperes. For example, a 100-ampere-hour battery can handle a current draw of 25 amperes without harm. This means that a 2,000-watt inverter requires a battery bank of over 700 ampere-hours.

Selection

When selecting an inverter, you will probably weigh power output, efficiency, and other features against cost. More-efficient units will pay for their difference in cost over time. Be realistic about your needs. If you have the money to invest, get a unit that allows for future loads. If possible, select an inverter that can charge batteries. Figure 11-8 lists a few of the most popular inverters on the marine market.

FIGURE 11-8.   **Comparison chart for DC-to-AC inverters.**

Model	Rating (watts) Surge	Continuous	No-load standby current (amps)	Output wave form	Battery charging option (amps)
Heart Interface					
HF 12-600	1500	600	.025	MSW	No
EMS 1800	?	1800	.065	MSW	65
EMS	?	2800	.070	MSW	100
PowerStar					
380/700/1,300	3,000 (all 3)	380/700/1,300	.065	MSW	No
Professional Mariner					
QuietWatt	6800	2300	.003	MSW	No
Statpower					
PC 100	200	100	.060	MSW	No
ProWatt 250	500	250 → 150	.060	MSW	No
ProWatt 600	1500	800 → 500	.120	MSW	No
Trace Engineering					
612	600	400	.025	MSW	25
2012	6000	2000	.030	MSW	110
Tripp-Lite					
PV 100	110	100	2.500	SqW	No
PV 500 FC	550	500	3.500	SqW frequency controlled	No
SB 1000 FC	1100	1000	3.500	SqW frequency controlled	Yes

12

Direct AC Power Systems

════

I t is often necessary or convenient to have circuits on board for operating AC appliances directly from an AC source. This applies in particular to boats that spend time at a dock or marina or have very large AC loads or limited battery capacity. Inverters are practical for loads up to 2,500 watts when adequate battery capacity is available, particularly if the larger loads are intermittent. A microwave oven is a good example of a large intermittent load easily handled by an inverter. The microwave may consume up to 1,500 watts, but it typically operates for only 15 minutes or less at a time. Marine inverters can provide 2,800 watts of AC power, but a direct source of AC power makes more sense for large AC loads that are on for longer periods.

There are two ways to achieve direct AC power on a boat: buy it from the utility company when you are dockside, or generate it yourself. If you can get by with having direct AC power only when you're at a dock, the shore-power connection is much more practical. It is fairly inexpensive to install and operates quietly. If you need direct AC power when under way, or at anchor or mooring, then some means of onboard generation is your only alternative.

High-capacity AC generating equipment comes in one of three forms:

1. Gen-sets or large portable generators that couple a gasoline- or diesel-fueled engine with an AC generator;

2. AC generators driven off the boat's engine shaft with pulleys and a drive belt;

3. Specialty alternator/control systems that allow your marine alternator to operate in an AC-only mode.

The first type closely matches engine horsepower with the electrical output of an AC generator for maximum efficiency. The second and third alternatives require no additional engine, relying instead on the main engine for power.

THE SHORE-POWER CONNECTION

The simplest and least expensive way to get direct AC is to install a shore-power connection, taking advantage of the electricity already available dockside. With this system you can operate AC circuits anytime you have access to a dock with power. You eliminate the need to own, operate, and maintain costly generating equipment. An inverter can then supplement your needs by providing AC power away from the dock, as long as AC use during those times is moderate.

Marina AC power is supplied to waterproof distribution boxes at the slips. The system is metered, in watt-hours, if there is a charge for the electricity. The electric service at the distribution boxes is supplied through circuit breakers typically rated at 15, 30, or 50 amperes. The circuit breakers protect the system by "tripping"—opening the circuit after an overload.

Shore-Power Components

A complete shore-power system brings power to the boat and distributes it to the individual circuits on board. The system's components are each described below.

Shore-power cord. Similar to outdoor extension cords, marine shore-power cords differ in a few important ways. Like standard cords, they have a male plug on one end and a female receptacle on the other. Unlike straight-blade ends found on standard cords, marine cords incorporate twist-lock devices at each end so the cords can't be unplugged accidentally. This is desirable, since the cords are often in areas of foot traffic. Shore-power cords also are coated to resist ultraviolet rays, salt, and moisture. Setup cords complete with end plug and receptacle are available in 12-, 25-, and 50-foot lengths, with either a 30-ampere or 50-ampere rating. Amperage ratings are applicable for both 125-volt and 250-volt services. The end plugs on 250-volt cords have a slightly different configuration to keep the two services separate. Adapters are available to connect between 125- and 250-volt cords, and between systems with straight-blade and twist-lock ends. End connectors and insulated wire can be purchased separately to make your own cords.

Power inlet. This is where the shore power enters your boat. The inlet consists of a male plug mounted in a waterproof box with a tightly sealed cover similar to those of outdoor electrical outlets for homes. The box is placed at a convenient location on the boat's topsides or cabin. It should be as close as possible to the boat's AC electrical panel.

Isolation transformer. Incoming AC from the dock should be electrically isolated from the boat's AC circuits for safety, and from the boat's DC circuits to prevent electrolysis. You can use an isolation transformer (see Chapter 3), to transfer power through the unit via an electromagnetic field, without direct wire connections. Transformers can also be used to step the voltage up or down. Incoming 220-volt AC can be stepped down to 110 volts with an isolation transformer. When changing voltages, the energy transferred is always a little less due to minor losses in the transformer.

Ship-to-shore selector switch. This "double pole, double throw" switch allows you to select either shore power or output from your on-board gen-set to supply the boat's AC circuits. You may elect to install one of these switches for future use if you don't have an AC gen-set in the system. The switch cuts power from one source before engaging the other, thus preventing the two systems from mixing. Some ship-to-shore switches include a remote-start generator switch (see Chapter 3). The switch shown in Figure 3-15 comes in 60- and 120-ampere ratings for 120- and 240-volt operation. A similar switch can be used to select either gen-set or inverter for your on-board AC source.

AC master control panel. The master control panel distributes the power to individual circuits, including 110-volt refrigeration, water heater, and groups of AC outlets. The panel is equipped with a master breaker that disconnects the entire AC system on board, and individual breakers for each circuit. Some panels have a safety feature that indicates faulty shore-power wiring. Marinco offers a polarity tester that plugs into any AC outlet and warns of such common AC wiring problems as reversed hot and ground, reversed hot and neutral, open safety ground, and open hot conductor. This $30 tester, widely available, is well worth the investment.

AC outlets. Outlets for marine use are almost identical to those used on land. Outlets with ground fault interrupt (GFI) protection should be used near head and galley, and can be used throughout the boat for added protection. One GFI outlet can protect "downline" outlets on the same circuit. Marine outlets are available with teak or stainless steel cover plates.

System Efficiency

How efficient is the shore-power connection at converting energy into usable AC electricity? There is no appreciable energy loss from the dockside outlets to the outlets on the boat, so the system efficiency depends on how efficiently the power utility manufactures electricity and transports it to the marina or dock. Typically, about 25 percent of the energy available in the fuel used at the power plant ends up at the dock or in our homes.

GEN-SETS AND LARGE PORTABLE GENERATORS

Any generator that is coupled with an internal combustion engine could reasonably be called a gen-set. Industry practice, however, is to call units with handles and 3,600 RPM operation "portable generators," and to reserve the term *gen-set* for permanently mounted units without handles and operating at 1,800 RPMs (although some gen-sets, like the Kohler gasoline-fueled 6.5 CZ, operate at 3,600 RPMs). In this book we make a further distinction between "small portables," which are typically used for battery charging and occasional AC power (see Chapter 7), and "large portables," which are primarily used for providing direct

AC power. We categorize large portable generators as weighing more than 75 pounds, with a rated output generally over 1,400 watts. Rated output for gen-sets starts at around 3,000 watts. Gen-sets and large portable generators can be powered by either a four-stroke gasoline-fueled engine or a diesel-fueled engine. The engine and generator shafts are directly coupled, so the engine RPMs are also that of the generator. Engine RPMs are governed so the frequency of the AC output is held fairly constant. Large portables operate at 3,600 RPMs and are similar in construction to the small portables described in Chapter 7. Gen-sets have AC generators designed to operate at 1,800 RPMs for 60-hertz output, or around 1,500 RPMs for 50-hertz output. On these larger units, the lower engine speed reduces vibration.

Large Portable Generators

Large portable generators are rated according to their continuous AC output capabilities, from around 1,500 watts up to 10,000 watts. These units typically house the engine-generator assembly and wiring-control box in an open, sledlike tubular frame as shown in Figure 12-1. The frame supports and protects the various components and provides handles for carrying. The engine is typically air-cooled. Most large portables come with an integral fuel tank like the smaller portables, and both electric and manual starting capability. The engine and AC generator are larger versions of those used on smaller portables. The AC output is supplied to two or more 15-ampere outlets on the control panel. Some of the larger units have four 20-ampere AC outlets. Minimal DC output of 8 to 10 amperes for battery charging is supplied to a pair of polarized terminals. As with smaller portables, the DC output is fine for giving the batteries a small boost when you're also using the AC side, but the only efficient method of charging is to operate a properly sized AC-to-DC battery charger off one of the AC outlets (see AC-to-DC Battery Chargers, Chapter 7).

FIGURE 12-1.   **Large portable generator. (Courtesy Gen-Pro)**

Installation. No installation is required with a portable generator. The unit can be stored and brought out when needed. Gasoline-fueled units should be used only above decks, where there is adequate ventilation. Make certain to place the unit where there is no chance for the exhaust fumes to be pulled down into the cabin. Diesel-fueled units can be operated below decks with proper ventilation both for cooling the engine and venting the exhaust gases. These units should be operated only when the boat is in port, or in calm conditions when the boat is under way. The unit should be well secured during operation.

Portable generators can be connected to the boat's AC electrical system in several ways. Diesel-fueled units that are operated below decks can be directly connected through a transfer switch that selects either shore power or the boat's on-board generator for AC supply. Gasoline-fueled units that operate above decks can simply be connected to the shore-power inlet plug (power inlet) if available, or appliance power cords can be connected directly to the AC outlet plugs.

Noise. Portable generators are noisy. Gasoline-fueled units that must be operated above decks can be particularly annoying. Not much can be done about airborne noise unless you

FIGURE 12-2. **Schematic of a shipboard electrical system with multiple charging options. That portion of the system relevant to on-board AC power production from a dockside outlet, a gen-set, or a portable generator is highlighted.**

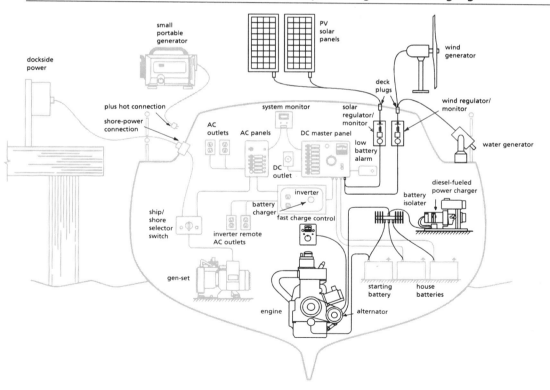

FIGURE 12-3.   **Comparison chart for large portable generators.**

Model	Fuel	Rating (watts)		Output voltage	Fuel capacity (gallons)	Hours of operation	Weight (pounds)
		Surge	Continuous				
Yanmar YDG-2000	diesel	2,200	2,000	120 V AC 12 V DC	2	9	130
Robin D2500	diesel	2,500	2,200	120 V AC 12 V DC	2	7.1	121
Gen-Pro GP-38	gasoline	3,850	3,500	120 V AC	5	8	126
Onan K3200	gasoline	3,000	2,500	120 V AC 12 V DC	3.4	5.9	132

use a well-ventilated compartment lined with sound-deadening material. Noise transmitted through the structure can be reduced by placing the unit on a rubber mat to absorb vibration and sound.

There is a wide choice of large portable generators. Figure 12-3 shows specifications for several gasoline- and diesel-fueled units.

Gen-Set Specifications

Like large portable generators, gen-sets are rated according to their continuous AC output capability. This ranges from around 3,000 watts for the smaller units to more than 15,000 watts. Gen-sets, which look like auxiliary engines, are permanently installed below decks, and therefore come as a complete package (see Figure 3-12). The engine shaft couples directly to a specially designed AC generator. Engine RPMs are typically 1,800. Fuel is supplied from a separate tank or from the main-engine fuel tank. Marine gen-sets are water-cooled in one of three ways: by seawater pumped through the cooling system and into the exhaust system; by a heat exchanger, in which heat is exchanged between captive water in the gen-set and seawater; or by keel or skin cooling, in which pipes in the keel or a section of the hull act as the heat exchanger. You'll find a comparison of these three cooling systems in Figure 12-4.

Gen-sets are wired directly into the boat's AC electrical system. The AC output connects to a ship-to-shore transfer switch that selects either shore power or on-board generator to supply AC power. The two systems remain isolated, since one source is disconnected before the other is engaged. The transfer switch can be operated manually or through an automatic load-transfer control. The automatic version transfers the supply whenever shore power is plugged in, at which time the gen-set cannot be started. Gen-sets can be started manually at the unit, manually by remote switches, or automatically. More than one remote switch can be wired in parallel, making it possible to have a start switch in several locations on the boat. The automatic demand control starts the unit whenever a load is switched on, and stops the unit when all loads are switched off.

FIGURE 12-4. **Advantages and disadvantages of various marine cooling systems. (Courtesy Onan Corporation)**

Cooling System	Advantages	Disadvantages	Areas of use
Sea Water	direct simple lowest initial cost	seawater through cylinder block leaves deposits increased thermal shock due to cold water entering block unable to use rust inhibitor or anti-freeze	freshwater lakes
Heat Exchanger	eliminates seawater in cylinder block allows use of rust inhibitor and anti-freeze in captive water system lower water temperature differential reduces thermal shock on cylinder block improves temperature control of engine	more costly than seawater cooling chance of clogging heat exchanger filter, strainer, etc., in contaminated water (seawater side) extra plumbing on unit	seawater inland lakes or rivers where the water contains debris or is heavily silted
Keel or Skin-Cooling	single captive water system, no seawater—no chance of clogging engine water passages in dirty water eliminates seawater in cylinder block allows use of rust inhibitor and anti-freeeze in captive water system lower water temperature differential reduces thermal shock on cylinder block improves temperature control of engine	extra plumbing inside craft increased drag reduced cooling capacity when vessel not moving extra water system needed to provide seawater for exhaust cooling external keel cooler subject to damage boat must be dry-docked to service external keel cooler	river where the water contains debris or is heavily silted seawater

Installation. Installation of a gen-set should follow Coast Guard regulations as well as those of the American Boat and Yacht Council (ABYC) and the National Fire Protection Association (NFPA). According to the Onan Corporation, manufacturers of marine portable generators and gen-sets, the following points should receive special attention:

- adequate air to cool generator
- discharge of circulated air
- adequate fresh air for combustion
- adequate water to cool engine
- discharge of circulated water
- discharge of exhaust gases
- electrical connections and bonding
- fuel connection
- sturdy, flat mounting base
- accessibility for operation and service

Gen-sets must be on rubber isolation mounts, like an auxiliary engine, to control vibration. The exhaust gases should be water-cooled except for vertical dry-stack installations. In the latter case, the exhaust system must have spark arresters and be water-jacketed or effectively heat-shielded between manifold and spark arrester. The cooling-water and fuel systems should be installed according to the manufacturer's recommendations. Adequate ventilation must be provided to remove dangerous gases. The Coast Guard and NFPA have stringent ventilation requirements to prevent the accumulation of flammable gases. Proper ventilation is also important because it helps cool the unit during operation.

Noise. Gen-sets, like portable generators, create a considerable amount of noise, transmitted through the air and the hull. On large boats, these units usually are installed where the mechanical equipment can be isolated from the living spaces, but additional steps can be taken to improve the noise isolation. Most manufacturers offer some type of "sound shield," or sound-deadening panels. This greatly reduces noise transmitted through the air. Additionally, rubber mounting feet and the use of flexible water, fuel, exhaust, and electrical connections reduces hull-transmitted noise.

Figure 12-5 shows specifications for several marine gen-sets.

System Efficiency

How efficient are these units at converting fuel energy into usable electricity? The overall system efficiency for gen-sets and large portable generators is typically around 15 or 20 percent when you are using all of the electricity they are capable of producing. When a gen-set or

FIGURE 12-5.   **Comparison chart for gen-sets.** **217**

Model	Fuel	Rating (watts)	Output voltage	Output amperage	Weight (pounds)
Ensign 4500	gasoline	4,500 @1,800 RPMs 1 phase	120	38.0	335
6500	gasoline	6,500 @1,800 RPMs 1 phase	120	54.0	335
4.0 MDKC 3R/1	diesel	4,000 @1,800 RPMs	120 240	33.0 16.7	480
Kohler 6.5 CZ	gasoline	6,500 @3,600 RPMs	120	54.2	218
16 CCO	diesel	16,000 @1,800 RPMs	120 240	133.0 67.0	760

portable generator is operating, AC power is available but not necessarily being used. A gen-set's fuel consumption is usually proportional to its load, so there is some fuel savings at loads less than rated output. If a 4,000-watt gen-set is operating and only 1,000 watts of AC electricity are being consumed, the overall efficiency drops to around 10 or 15 percent. AC generators are not like DC charging systems, in which useful energy is being stored or consumed every time they operate. System efficiency can be increased by closely matching output to electrical needs; operating your AC loads together when possible to make full use of unit capacity; turning off the unit anytime it is not needed; and operating an AC-to-DC battery charger that stores unused available energy for later use.

ENGINE-DRIVEN AC GENERATORS

AC generators that run off the boat's main-engine drive shaft also produce direct AC power. They are simple to install and eliminate the need for a costly, space-consuming gen-set. There are two types available for boats. The first is a separate AC generator that connects to the main-engine drive shaft. It can operate simultaneously with the marine alternator whenever the engine is in use. In fact, this is when system efficiency is the greatest, since you are taking best advantage of the engine power available. The second is a modified marine alternator. This unit actually replaces the standard marine alternator with one that can produce either full AC or DC output.

Separate AC Generator

Separate AC generators are capable of producing 2,000 to 6,500 watts of power. They are most useful for AC loads that are too large for inverters, but not on long enough to justify the expense of a gen-set. They are a good alternative to a large portable generator if you don't need to take the unit off the boat. The power that drives the generator is taken off the main-engine drive shaft by a belt-and-pulley arrangement. Because of the high power output of these units, strong drive belts are required. Before purchasing this type of system, make sure that there is sufficient clearance around the engine to install the unit—on many boats there just isn't enough free space in the engine compartment.

Like high-output alternators, AC generators that run off the main-engine drive shaft consume some of the available engine power when they are operating. For example, a 4,000-watt unit may require 7 to 8 horsepower, and a high-output alternator operating at the same time another 3 to 4 horsepower. A total of 10 to 12 horsepower is required just for producing electricity. If the AC power is used only in port, this presents no problem, but the engine must be large enough to handle the extra load if AC power, high-output DC battery charging, and boat propulsion are all expected at the same time. To eliminate unwanted power drain, AC generators can be turned off by a cut-out switch when not in use. The AC output can be wired directly to an AC master panel for distribution.

Figure 12-6 shows specifications for several types of engine-driven AC generators.

Modified Marine Alternator

The other direct AC power system that is driven by the main engine uses a modified marine alternator and control intended to replace the standard alternator or operate as a secondary unit. If you are considering upgrading your alternator and also want occasional high-capacity AC power, investigate this system. Kestrel offers three versions of a modified marine alternator system: 2,000-watt AC with 65-ampere DC; 3,500-watt AC with 95-ampere DC; and 5,000-watt AC only. The alternator output is wired to an external control box. A switch allows you to select 120-volt AC power, fast-charge DC power, or normal-charge DC power (DC power is not available on the 5,000-watt version).

With this system, your engine must be running to supply AC power, and there is no DC power supply when the unit is switched to AC. This means the engine has to run double-time to supply both AC and DC loads. As with all engine-driven direct AC sources, you must

---

FIGURE 12-6.   **Comparison chart for AC generators driven off the boat's main engine.**

Model	Rating (watts)	Output voltage	RPMs required	Weight (pounds)
Auto-Gen M-2501	2,500	120	1,500	102
Auto-Gen M-4002	4,000	120 240	1,750	125
Auto-Gen M-6502	6,500	120 240	1,750	155
Winco 2B-200W	2,000	120	3,600	56

tolerate some noise while using the AC appliances. If this is unacceptable, the only solution is to use an inverter for "quiet time" loads.

System Efficiency

How efficient are engine-driven AC generators at converting fuel energy into usable electricity? Running the main engine to produce electricity is not as efficient as operating a gen-set or portable generator. The overall system efficiency is typically around 10 to 15 percent for the AC output under maximum load. If the unit is producing 4,000 watts of power, but only 1,000 watts are being used, the overall efficiency drops to 5 to 8 percent.

13

Estimating Your Electrical Load

===

$\mathbb{A}$ t this point you should have enough information to become your boat's energy manager. Your first order of business is to begin sizing and selecting your on-board energy system.

Step one is to come up with a reasonably accurate estimate of how much electricity you need on a daily or weekly basis. If you know how much you use, you can determine how much you need to produce, and from which charging sources. I say *reasonably* accurate because there are a great many variables associated with producing and using electricity on a boat. It's difficult, and not really necessary, to attain a high degree of accuracy. Make an educated guess of your expected electrical load, then size your system with a margin of safety for the unexpected and, if your bank account permits, future plans. Think ahead; if funds don't permit, you can still make provisions in the system to accommodate equipment you might buy later.

Your energy consumption is determined by the nature and size of the electrical appliances you have or plan to have. A list of the electrical equipment usually found on pleasure boats, with the draw in amperes and average daily hours of use for each, is given in Figure 13-1. We'll discuss ways to reduce demand without sacrificing comfort and safety. It's an accepted fact that energy conservation is the most practical energy resource we have available. This chapter concludes with six hypothetical shipboard electrical loads ranging from very small to very large. In Chapter 14 we'll see how to match an appropriate energy system to an anticipated demand.

ELECTRICAL LOAD OF MARINE APPLIANCES

The electrical load for each appliance shown in Figure 13-1 is an average. The power draw in watts will vary slightly with battery voltage. Remember that watts = volts ×

FIGURE 13-1.   **Electrical load of marine appliances.**   **221**

Appliance	Electrical load (amps)	Typical daily hours of use	Total daily consumption (amperes)
Cabin lights (incandescent or fluorescent)			
6 Watt	0.50		
8 Watt	0.60	3.5 hours of cabin lighting each night	Depends on number and combination of lights
12 Watt	1.00		
25 Watt	1.20		
25 Watt	2.00		
40 Watt	3.20		
Running lights			
Steaming light	1.00	11.0	11.0
Masthead tricolor	2.00	11.0	22.0
Port/starboard/stern	1.00 each	11.0	33.0
Anchor light			
Small draw (see later this chapter)	0.05	11.0	0.55
Regular masthead	1.00	11.0	11.00
Bright masthead	2.00	11.0	22.00
Spreader lights (2)	5.00		
Sealed spotlight beam 300,000 candle power	12.00		
Sealed spotlight beam 200,000 candle power	7.50	Intermittent	Depends on use
Halogen bulb 110,000 candle power	4.00		
Strobe light	0.75		
Instruments			
Radar	10.00		
Depth sounder	0.50		
Knotmeter	0.10		
Knotmeter w/log	0.10	Depends on the sailing you do	Depends on use
Wind speed indicator	0.10		
Wind direction	0.10		
Instrument lights	0.10		

Appliance	Electrical load (amps)	Typical daily hours of use	Total daily consumption (amperes)
Bilge pumps			
400 gallon per hour	2.00	0.5	1.00
800 gph	4.00	0.5	2.00
1750 gph	8.00	0.5	4.00
3500 gph	15.00	0.5	7.50
Water pressure pump	4.00	0.5	2.00
Shower pump (on demand)	2.00	0.5	1.00
Seawater intake pump (clear)	4.00	0.5	2.00
Seawater intake pump w/ barnacles covering the opening	up to 15.00	0.5	7.50
Electronics			
Stereo	2.00	0.3	6.00
Tape deck large draw	2.00	2.0	4.00
small draw	1.00	2.0	2.00
AM-FM receiver	0.50	3.0	1.50
TV B/W	1.25	2.0	2.50
color	4.00	2.0	8.00
CB receiver	0.50	2.0	1.00
VHF receiver	0.50	2.0	1.00
transmitter low	1.00	2.0	2.00
transmitter high	5.00	0.5	2.50
SSB receiver	1.00	0.5	0.50
transmitter	20.00	0.5	10.00
Loran standard	0.50	4.0	2.00
with memory	1.00	4.0	4.00
Sat-Nav standard	0.50	4.0	2.00
with memory	1.00	4.0	4.00
12-volt motors			
Refrigeration compressor	5.50	10.0	55.00
Autopilot	0.50	12.0	6.00
Anchor windlass	20.00	0.1	2.00
Engine compartment blower	2.50	1.0	2.50
Cabin fan (oscillating)	1.20	4.0	4.80

Appliance	Electrical load (amps)	Typical daily hours of use	Total daily consumption (amperes)
12-volt tools			
Drill	10.00	Depends on the work you do	Depends on the work you do
Saber saw	15.00		
Soldering iron (small)	5.00		
Miscellaneous			
Horn	2.00	0.5	1.0
Bell	1.00	0.5	0.5
VCR	2.00	Depends on use	Depends on use
12V microwave	45.00		
12V blender	2.50		
12V vacuum	11.00		
12V mini washing machine	5.00		

amperes. If your appliance is rated in watts, use that and battery voltage to solve for amperes. If the rating is in amperes, solve for watts. Check the rating of your equipment to get exact numbers. If there is no power rating, use an ammeter to measure actual current use. Alternatively, check the size fuse used if available, or use Figure 13-1 with an added margin for good measure. Equipment such as autopilots might have a 4- or 5-ampere rating, yet their average draw is typically less, since the motor operates intermittently. With this type of equipment, you need to determine the average electrical draw. The goal is to find your daily or weekly power consumption in watts, then match this with the potential power output of a marine generating system.

WAYS TO REDUCE YOUR ELECTRICAL DEMAND

You are the sole arbiter of which appliances you need or would like to have and which ones you can do without. Before determining your electrical load, take a close look to see if you can reduce the load comfortably, without feeling as though you are missing out on things you really want. A few luxuries on board a boat can make life much more pleasant.

Efficient appliances decrease your load, making the task of supplying energy less difficult regardless of the type of generator you use. Land-based utility companies encourage energy efficiency and conservation for the same reason.

Lighting

One of the easiest and most effective methods of reducing electrical demand is through energy-efficient lighting.

Cabin lights. Even though the warm glow of a kerosene lantern is hard to beat for ambience, electric lighting is truly one of the simple luxuries of our times. It provides much better illumination for reading, cooking, and navigation work, and it's much easier and safer to use, especially with children on board. In addition, the warm glow of a kerosene lamp is much less appreciated in the tropics or in the heat of the summer.

Cabin lighting usually accounts for a large part of your total electrical load, but you can reduce this draw by up to 80 percent if you use energy-efficient fluorescents. Lighting efficiency is measured in lumens per watt, or the light output in relation to the energy consumed. A typical 8-watt fluorescent cabin light, delivering 60 lumens per watt, will give the same light output, or lumen level, as a 40-watt incandescent bulb yielding 12 lumens per watt. The incandescent bulb produces the same amount of light but uses five times the power, losing the balance of the energy as heat. Standard incandescent bulbs are notoriously inefficient.

Incandescent lights operate similarly to heating elements. A tungsten filament is suspended between two metal contacts inside a vacuum bulb. The resistance of the filament determines the current flow. Only about 10 percent of the electricity used is turned into light, while 90 percent is dissipated as heat. This is why incandescent bulbs become too hot to touch. PV solar cells, which transform light into electricity, are more efficient at energy conversion than the common light bulb, which transforms electricity into light. Yet the former is still considered in the development stage, while the latter is used in every household without a second thought.

Fluorescent lights operate quite differently. They use a *ballast*—a starter at the end of the fixture—to spark an electrical charge that flows through cathodes in either end of the fluorescent tube. This charge excites gaseous atoms inside the tube. As they discharge, they cause the phosphor coating on the inside of the tube to "fluoresce," emitting a large quantity of visible light. It's often been said that fluorescents give off a "different" light that is not suitable for cozy living areas. Incandescent lights bring out the warm tones of red, orange, and yellow, while fluorescents have traditionally produced cooler blue and green tones. A bare fluorescent bulb can be harsh on the eyes, but most lights come with a light-diffusing plastic cover that makes them more acceptable. They also now have much better color rendition, and electronic ballasts eliminate the flicker of older bulbs. If you still find the lighting too harsh, you can recess the fixture by placing it behind a small wooden frame with a reflective surface. Fluorescent bulbs last about ten times as long as the incandescent bulbs.

We have eleven 8-watt fluorescent cabin fixtures on our boat, and if all were used at once, the total draw would still be less than one 100-watt incandescent bulb. On a typical evening we operate the equivalent of four cabin lights for about 4 hours, so our average cabin lighting load is 8 watts per hour per light x 4 lights x 4 hours per night = 128 watts per night, or about the same as using one 30- or 35-watt incandescent bulb. At 12 volts, the total current draw is about 10 ampere-hours per night.

Running lights. You can also greatly reduce the total electrical draw of your running lights by switching to a masthead tricolor fixture. It uses only one 25-watt incandescent bulb instead of three separate bulbs for port, starboard, and stern. Your deck-mounted running lights can be left in place for use in areas of heavy traffic. Make sure your energy system is sized so that you always have enough energy for running lights. We've met a number of boaters who conserve electricity at the expense of running lights. One night of operation can consume 60 ampere-hours of current if three 25-watt fixtures, each drawing 2 amperes, are used for 10 hours. The risk of "going without" seems irrational and irresponsible. The load can be reduced to 30 ampere-hours if 12-watt bulbs are used, and to 20 ampere-hours if a tricolor is used. Even a modest energy system can handle this load. If you prefer, good-quality kerosene running lights can be used.

Anchor lights. Most masthead anchor lights, including those incorporated into a masthead tricolor light, have a sizable electrical load. They consume between 10 ampere-hours (if a 12-watt bulb is used) and 25 ampere-hours (if a 25-watt bulb is used) in one night. One alternative is a kerosene anchor light, although such lights are prone to going out in strong winds and are more difficult to use than electric lights. A better alternative is a low-drain anchor light. These are available commercially, or you can make your own (see Figure 13-2). We made one for our boat that gives off at least as much light as a kerosene lantern, uses only 100 milliamperes of electricity (equivalent to 1 ampere-hour for 10 hours of use), and costs under $10.

Making a low-drain anchor light. To make a low-drain anchor light, take a small, fractured-glass preserve jar with a metal canning lid. Punch a hole in the center of the lid, large enough to pass through a two-conductor, 14-gauge insulated wire. Insert the wire through the lid and tie a knot on the inside. Bare the ends of the two leads and solder them to the wires of a 100-milliampere-at-12-volts-DC high-intensity lamp available from Radio Shack. Rustproof and waterproof the metal lid with urethane or silicone caulking, making sure to double-seal the hole where the wire passes through. Make a loop in the wiring outside the jar to receive a small lanyard with which to hoist the light to the spreaders. Wrap a few bands of clear cellophane tape around the outside of the jar to strengthen the glass and to keep the pieces in place should it ever break. You can substitute a plastic jar for the glass one. Larger bulbs can also be used if you prefer a brighter light. This anchor light requires only an occasional airing to release any trapped condensation.

A low-drain anchor light is also available from Conch Research, of Marathon, Florida. The unit hangs in the rigging and plugs into any 12-volt socket. Current draw is about $1/10$ ampere per hour. It has an easily replaceable long-life bulb and retails for about $25. Another option is to purchase a Guest "temporary anchor light," which hangs from a lanyard and runs off a 6-volt lantern battery. Instead of using the lantern battery, you can supply this light with 6 volts from your boat battery (through a 12-volt auto adapter described in Eliminating Disposable Batteries, below). This light is rugged and completely waterproof, and its automatic model comes with a photoelectric switch.

An energy-saving device that works well with anchor lights is a marine-grade photoelectric switch that automatically turns lights on at sunset and off at sunrise. It helps to avoid unnecessary battery drain from leaving the anchor light on, a common occurrence. On unattended boats, the switch takes care of the anchor light requirement posted by many coastal towns. These switches are available from Real Goods Trading Company.

FIGURE 13-2.   **A homemade low-drain anchor light.**

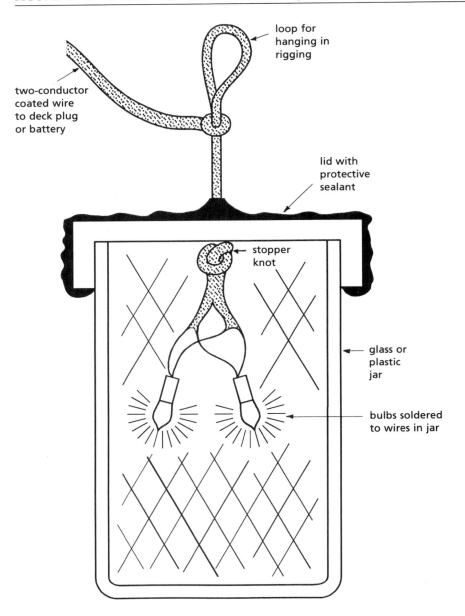

loop for
hanging in
rigging

two-conductor
coated wire
to deck plug
or battery

lid with
protective
sealant

stopper
knot

glass or
plastic
jar

bulbs soldered
to wires in jar

Refrigeration

Although most of the world lives without it, refrigeration is a wonderful modern convenience. On land we take it for granted, yet on a boat it can be one of those much-appreciated simple luxuries, particularly in warmer climates. The decision to have refrigeration on board inevitably places you in a higher energy category, with a need for a more formidable generating capacity. On smaller boats it often represents more than half of the total electrical load. There are simple techniques for reducing the amount of electricity a refrigeration system requires.

Following is a brief review of the marine refrigeration systems available, an estimate of the electrical load you can expect, and recommendations for keeping this load to a minimum.

Types of marine refrigeration.   Marine refrigeration systems are similar to those in the home. Both employ a motor-driven compressor in a vapor-compression cycle to pressurize a working fluid (usually Freon 12). The fluid travels between the evaporator, where it absorbs large amounts of latent heat of evaporation from its surroundings, dropping the icebox temperature sharply, and the condenser, where it returns to liquid form and gives up its excess heat. (See Figure 13-3 for a typical engine-driven refrigeration system schematic diagram.) While basic operating theory is the same for all marine refrigeration systems, there are several options from which to choose. Your choice of unit determines how much of an additional electrical load you will have.

FIGURE 13-3.   **Schematic of engine-driven refrigeration system. (Courtesy Sea Frost)**

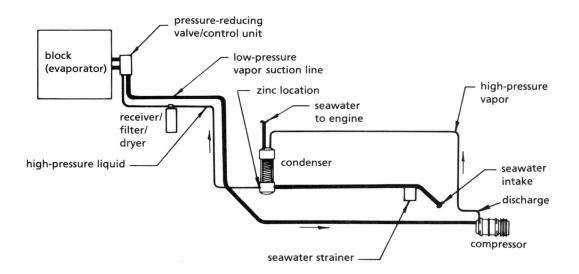

One exception to the above system is called *thermoelectric refrigeration*. Rather than a compressor and Freon, it uses 12-volt-powered solid-state circuitry in a small cooling module. These units are compact and reliable, but their effectiveness on a boat is limited, especially in warm climates when they are forced to run most of the time. They can cool only a small portable ice chest to 40 or 50 degrees below the temperature outside. They draw 4 or 5 amperes when running. For these reasons we have not included them as a preferred marine refrigeration option.

Cooling system. Refrigeration systems can have an air-cooled condenser, as have household systems and many boat systems, or it can have a water-cooled condenser, which takes in seawater and uses it as the cooling fluid. Air-cooled systems are typically less expensive and less involved to install. These systems work well in temperate or cool climates. They can be, however, less efficient than water-cooled systems. Air-cooled refrigeration systems tend to heat up the locker or cabin where the condenser is installed, and are not recommended for tropical climates.

Drive system. The compressor is the driving force of a refrigeration system and the system's main energy consumer. To power the compressor, the system may incorporate a small to medium 12-volt electric motor drawing from the battery banks, or a larger 12-volt motor that operates only when the engine is on and the alternator is supplying electricity. The compressor may also be powered directly by the main engine via a belt-and-pulley drive. Engine-driven units are the most powerful, and are not a drain on the electrical system. The maximum load of an engine-driven system is around 2 HP, easily supplied by any small-boat engine. You can even charge your batteries while operating the refrigeration, preferably with a high-output alternator. Engine-driven systems are usually more expensive, though, and some small-boat engine compartments don't leave room to house one. Systems that have 12-volt motors to drive the compressor are less expensive but also less efficient, and are a large drain on the electrical system if the motor is supplied by the batteries. Many marine refrigeration systems, either 12-volt motor-driven or engine-driven, can also use 110-volt power to drive the compressor when at a dock.

Method of operation. Some marine refrigeration systems are constant cycling, like a household unit; others use holding plates (also known as cold plates). A constant-cycling unit employs a small compressor and electric drive motor that are turned on and off by a thermostat inside the refrigeration box. These units can be small, since they supply only small amounts of cooling on a continuous basis. How often the compressor and motor cycle, and how much electricity they consequently demand, is determined by the size of the box, how well insulated it is, and the ambient temperature. In the other type of system, cold plates are filled with a "eutectic" solution that freezes at a lower temperature than water. The idea is to use a large compressor to freeze the plates as quickly as possible, much as a high-output alternator charges a battery bank as quickly as possible. In both cases energy is stored for later use. The energy is eventually used up, and a new charging cycle is needed. How frequently you must charge the plates is determined by the factors listed above with constant-cycling systems, as well as the size of the compressor and the holding plates.

Method of installation. The final variable is how the unit is installed. Some small 12-volt motor-driven, air-cooled, constant-cycling systems come preassembled, as either slide-in

FIGURE 13-4. **Components of a Sea Frost refrigeration system.**

229

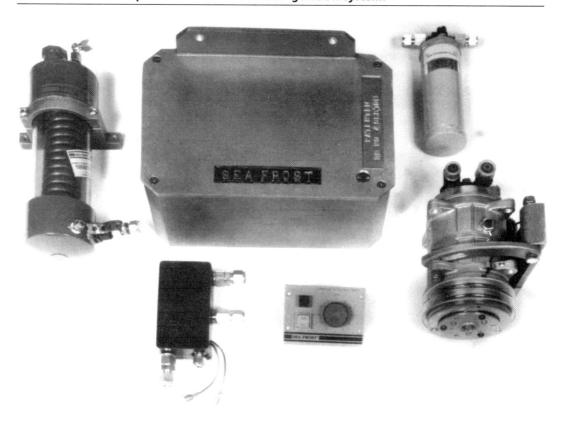

boxes or as top-loading units similar to large portable iceboxes. In most cases all they require is setting in place and plugging into a 12-volt source. These units are simple and inexpensive, but are less efficient because of air-cooling, front-loading access door, and/or lack of insulation. Permanently installed constant-cycling or cold-plate systems, with custom-made, superinsulated boxes are much more efficient. They almost always have top-loading doors with double seals.

Selecting a refrigeration system. Commercially available marine refrigeration systems comprise some combination of the variables listed above. More detailed descriptions follow.

Engine-driven system. These systems, like the Sea Frost shown in Figure 13-4, are always water-cooled, use holding plates, and are permanently installed. They can be powerful and do not impose an extra load on your 12-volt electrical system, making them also suitable for small boats. Engine-driven systems are fairly costly to install, and require that you run your engine every day or so to charge the plates. (An engine-driven system may be interfaced with a 12-volt compressor, or a 110-volt compressor through an inverter, to use renewable engery gains.) The charging cycle depends on plate and compressor size, box size, amount of insulation and tightness of access door seals, and ambient temperature. If you are in a warm climate, and have a well-designed and well-constructed system with a moderately sized box, you can figure on running the engine for the equivalent of 1/2 to 1 hour a day.

12-volt motor-driven, cold-plate system. This system is also water-cooled and permanently installed. The 12-volt motor must be large to drive a compressor sized for quick charges of holding plates, drawing 40 amperes or more (depending on system size) when running. A large bank of deep-cycle batteries is needed, plus a high-output generating system (or combination of systems) to handle refrigeration plus other boat loads on a regular basis. Though the current draw is high, the motor runs efficiently by not cycling on and off. It is turned on until the holding plates are charged, then turned off. If you are in a warm climate, and have a well-designed and well-constructed system of moderate size, you can figure on the 12-volt motor running 1 to 2 hours per day, for a daily load of perhaps 40 to 60 ampere-hours—less than that with a constant-cycling system.

12-volt motor-driven, constant-cycling, water-cooled system. A system of this type is permanently installed because of the water-cooling, and is most efficient if you have a superinsulated box of moderate size with top-loading access door and tight seals. A constant-cycling system can be much smaller, lighter, and less expensive to install than an equivalent system with holding plates. Manufacturers' claims of current draw when running are a little misleading. A constant-cycling DC motor runs less efficiently because of high start-up, or "surge," loads every time it comes on. The surge load can be appreciable. If you operate this type of unit in a warm climate, and have a well-designed and well-constructed system of moderate size, you can figure on a daily load of around 75 ampere-hours from refrigeration.

12-volt motor-driven, constant-cycling, air-cooled system. This system can be permanently installed in a superinsulated box of moderate size with top-loading access door and tight seals, or can come complete in a preassembled package as a slide-in unit or portable ice chest. Although these systems are the least expensive to purchase and install, they are also the least efficient to operate. There are many things you can do, however, to increase system efficiency (see recommendations below). They are fine for use in temperate and cool climates. Total current draw will be about the same for permanently installed units with superinsulation and portable units with much less capacity and insulation. For comparison with the above units, with similar conditions, you can figure on a daily load of 75 to 100 ampere-hours. Note on current draw of this system: The above figures for each system are for comparison only. Your refrigeration load might be more or less, depending on system efficiency and how you use it, as well as ambient temperature.

Reducing your refrigeration load. There are a few simple things you can do to reduce your load and stretch your electrical energy supply no matter what system you have.

1. Keep the size of your box modest. It will be much easier to cool and will allow more room for insulation.

2. Superinsulate your refrigerator box. Don't skimp on this important aspect of construction. From 3 to 4 inches of urethane insulation are recommended, and up to 6 inches is not out of the question. The pieces of insulation should fit together snugly without voids. Urethane foam spray can be used to seal any small gaps.

3. Have a top-loading access door, despite its inconvenience. A front-loading door allows all of the cold air to spill out every time you open it.

4. Make sure the access door has a double layer of tight seals. Warm air leakage into the box is a major cause of inefficiency. For the same reason, keep your trips into the box and time of door opening to a minimum.

5. Have a thermal blanket or extra insulation that you can encase your food in if the box is not full. This reduces further the space you are keeping cool, increasing efficiency. Make sure to include the evaporator plates in the area to be cooled!

6. Allow your cooked food to cool completely before placing it inside the box.

7. If you have an air-cooled condenser, locate it in a well-vented locker with plenty of access to fresh air.

Energy-Efficient Appliances

Try to purchase the most efficient appliances with the least current draw. Other than lighting, this applies especially to such things as autopilots and electronics. Items such as tape decks and personal computers vary widely in energy consumption. After a determined search, we found a reasonably priced laptop computer for word processing with one-tenth the current draw of our Apple MacIntosh, yet with equivalent memory. Twelve-volt fans range from 0.2 ampere to 2 amperes or more when running. The higher-draw units aren't necessarily more effective.

You can also increase the efficiency of 12-volt motor-driven pumps on board by keeping waterways clear of obstructions. This is especially important for seawater intakes and bilge pumps. The current draw of a seawater pump can triple if the opening is clogged with barnacles. A good friend of ours almost destroyed his battery before realizing that the seawater inlet was all but closed due to marine growth. His first indication of this condition was the dimming of lights when the pump came on!

Eliminating Disposable Batteries

By choosing energy-efficient appliances, you make the job of supplying electricity on board much easier, with no lessening of comfort or performance. At the same time you can eliminate the expense and waste of disposable batteries in one of several ways.

12-volt auto adapter. Almost any battery-operated appliance can be made to run directly from your 12-volt boat battery. This includes radios, tape decks, flashlights, and spotlights. Most battery-operated equipment runs on less than 12 volts, determined by the voltage and number of the batteries (cells) connected in series. Examples are given below:

- two C size at 1.5 volts each = 3 volts

- four AA size at 1.5 volts each = 6 volts

- four D size at 1.5 volts each = 6 volts

- one "lantern battery" at 6 volts = 6 volts

- six D size at 1.5 volts each = 9 volts

- one "radio battery" at 9 volts = 9 volts

If your appliance does not come with a separate 12-volt DC adapter plug, purchase a universal DC auto adapter from Radio Shack. This adapter plugs into a 12-volt socket and has several output voltages to choose from, typically 3, 4.5, 6, 7.5, and 9 volts (refer to Figure 3-8). You will also need an adapter cord to the appliance. We soldered this cord to an internal connection on our 6-volt SW/AM-FM radio to allow it to be operated by either four D-size rechargeable batteries or our 12-volt boat battery.

Rechargeable batteries. An easier way to go is simply to use Nicad rechargeable batteries. These can be recharged from the boat batteries by means of a 12-volt charger, or even a solar-powered DC charger, both available from Real Goods Trading Company. Alternatively, you could use a regular 110-volt battery charger run off a small inverter. The initial cost is higher for rechargeables, but they make sense and pay for themselves quickly.

Tabulated below are load calculations for six hypothetical boats with electrical requirements ranging from small to large. These show how to define the parameters of the problem and make the relevant calculations, and you may find that one of them closely matches your own electrical needs. In Chapter 14 we design a charging system for two such sample loads.

Appliance	Watts	Amps	Hours	Total ampere-hours
Boat One: 10 Ampere Hours Per Day Average				
Cabin lights	16.0	1.33	2.50	3.30
Anchor light	1.2	0.10	11.00	1.10
SW/AM-FM rec.	2.0	0.17	2.00	0.34
VHF receive	6.0	0.50	0.17	0.09
VHF transmit	60.0	5.00	0.02	0.10
Tape deck	18.0	1.50	2.00	3.00
Bilge pump	48.0	4.00	0.50	2.00
			Total:	10 ampere-hours
Boat Two: 25 Ampere-Hours Per Day Average				
Cabin lights	30.0	2.50	4.00	10.00
Anchor light	1.2	0.10	11.00	1.10
Short-wave/ AM-FM rec.	2.0	0.17	2.00	0.34
VHF receive	6.0	0.50	4.00	2.00
VHF transmit	60.0	5.00	0.25	1.25
TV/VCR comb.	72.0	6.00	0.50	3.00
Cabin fan	12.0	1.00	4.00	4.00
Bilge pump	48.0	4.00	0.33	1.32
Running lights	25.0	2.00	1.00	2.00
			Total:	25 ampere-hours

Appliance	Watts	Amps	Hours	Total ampere-hours
Boat Three: 50 Ampere-Hours Per Day Average				
Cabin lights	48.0	4.0	4.0	16.0
Anchor light	10.0	0.8	11.0	8.8
Instruments	12.0	1.0	4.0	4.0
Tape deck	18.0	1.5	2.0	3.0
Cabin fan	12.0	1.0	5.0	5.0
Small inverter	120.0	10.0	1.0	10.0
Autopilot	36.0	3.0	1.0	3.0
			Total:	50 ampere-hours
Boat Four: 80 Ampere Hours Per Day Average				
Cabin lights	48.0	4.00	4.0	16.0
Anchor light	10.0	0.80	11.0	8.8
Running lights	25.0	2.00	2.0	4.0
SW/AM-FM rec.	2.0	0.17	4.0	0.7
SSB receive	12.0	1.00	2.0	2.0
SSB transmit	240.0	20.00	0.7	14.0
Instruments	12.0	1.00	4.0	4.0
Tape deck	18.0	1.50	2.0	3.0
Cabin fans (2)	24.0	2.00	4.0	8.0
Small inverter	60.0	5.00	4.0	20.0
			Total:	80 ampere-hours

Appliance	Watts	Amps	Hours	Total ampere-hours
Boat Five: 120 Ampere-Hours Per Day Average				
Cabin lights	48.0	4.0	4.00	16.0
Anchor light	10.0	0.8	11.00	8.8
Running lights	25.0	2.0	6.00	12.0
Instruments	12.0	1.0	4.00	4.0
Tape deck	18.0	1.5	2.00	3.0
TV/VCR comb.	72.0	6.0	0.50	3.0
Cabin fans (2)	24.0	2.0	3.00	6.0
Small inverter	150.0	12.5	0.80	10.0
12-V refrig.	60.0	5.0	10.00	50.0
Elec. water pump	48.0	4.0	0.50	2.0
Elec. windlass	240.0	20.0	0.17	3.4
			Total:	120 ampere-hours
Boat Six: 180 Ampere-Hours Per Day Average				
Cabin lights	72.0	6.0	4.00	24.0
Anchor light	10.0	0.8	11.00	8.8
Running lights	25.0	2.0	2.00	4.0
Instruments	24.0	2.0	1.50	3.0
Radar	48.0	4.0	8.00	32.0
Tape deck	18.0	1.5	4.00	6.0
TV/VCR comb.	72.0	6.0	0.50	3.0
Cabin fans (3)	36.0	3.0	4.00	12.0
Inverter	150.0	12.5	1.00	12.5
12-V refrig.	60.0	5.0	12.00	60.0
Elec. windlass	240.0	20.0	0.17	3.4
Autopilot	36.0	3.0	4.00	12.0
			Total:	180 ampere-hours

14

Selecting Your Energy System

===

Selecting an energy system for your boat should involve sorting through practical information and research, tempering what you read and hear with your own needs and preferences, then making a well-informed decision. While we highly recommend this analytical approach, and provide a detailed account of it in this chapter, you may be more inclined by nature toward a "seat of the pants" approach using trial and error. There is nothing wrong with this method as long as you don't mind making a few potentially costly mistakes along the way. Perhaps for you that is all part of the fun. If your electrical load is light and your system costs modest, by all means try the empirical approach. If your load is larger, however, or you want be certain of selecting the right components first time around without wasted money or effort, follow the selection procedure outlined below.

Each of the sections that follow represents one step in the process of designing an energy system for your boat. Keep in mind that your total energy system includes the appliances that consume energy as well. Purchasing more efficient appliances is the equivalent of adding generating capacity to your system. Near the end of the chapter we'll see how all the decisions and calculations come together in two hypothetical case studies.

ESTIMATED DAILY ELECTRICAL LOAD

In this section you should come up with an estimated daily electrical load for your boat as described in Chapter 13. Try to be as complete as possible. If you find the system required to satisfy the projected load is too costly, or the charging cycles too frequent, reduce your load accordingly. Conversely, after working through the selection process you may find you have extra capacity in the system to handle additional loads.

By now you may have a preliminary concept of the energy system you envision for your boat. You know which charging systems appeal to you, both operationally and aesthetically; what components you feel a good energy system ought to include; and what appliances you want on board. As a first step, put your ideas and preferences on paper. Your concept may be modified by later considerations, but at least you'll have a starting point. It's especially helpful to combine a written description with a rough sketch of the proposed system.

FINANCIAL BUDGET

There is little point in selecting equipment you can't afford to purchase. If current realities depress you, come up with two budgets: a realistic one to meet present needs, and one for the future.

One approach to purchasing energy equipment is to buy standard components that are initially less expensive and usually less efficient. What you lack in efficiency you'll have to make up in increased energy consumption and inconvenience. Consider an energy system comprising a standard marine alternator and voltage regulator, a tired set of batteries, and inefficient lights and other appliances. The budget required for these is small, or nothing at all if they already exist on your boat. The electrical output is lower and electrical consumption higher than with a more efficient system, so you must run your engine longer to keep the batteries sufficiently charged. More engine running means greater fuel costs, more wear and tear on the engine, more hours of enduring the noise. You have chosen regular maintenance costs and added inconvenience over a larger initial investment. Almost always, a less expensive battery, appliance, or generating device is less efficient and imposes higher monthly maintenance costs.

This leads obviously to a second approach, which is to consider more efficient equipment an investment that will eventually pay for itself by reducing costs of maintence and use. One prime example is a PV solar panel. It has about the highest initial cost per watt of any generating device, yet it has a long life expectancy with no maintenance costs. If you invest in PV solar panels you are investing in energy savings and convenience, and, with enough use, your investment will be returned. The same applies to wind and water generators, high-output alternators with fast-charging controls, high-quality batteries, and energy-efficient appliances.

As energy manager you'll have to decide how much of an investment you can afford. Try to be realistic; one can always start with a modest system and add to it as money becomes available. In this case, come up with a two- or three-year investment plan. For example:

Year 1: Two 40-watt solar panels, efficient lighting $850

Year 2: High-output alternator, new batteries $850

Year 3: Wind generator and controls $850

total cost $2,550

After working through the balance of the selection process you may find that this budget or your overall design needs revision. Alter as necessary.

NOTES ON TYPE OF BOAT

Write down any characteristics of your boat that seem relevant to the type of energy system you want. How much mounting space is available for PV solar panels, wind generators, or both? Does the stern configuration lend itself to mounting a water generator? What type of engine, prop, alternator, and regulator does your boat have? Is there room for a larger alternator or additional battery storage? Is there storage space for a portable generator or a rigging-suspended wind generator? What is the typical cruising speed and range of your boat? What other equipment—such as a bimini, davits, or a self-steering vane—might interfere with mounting a generator?

NOTES ON HOW THE BOAT IS USED

Do you use your boat mainly on weekends, with an occasional extended cruise? Do you live aboard? Do you work while living aboard? Are you a racer? How much time do you spend motoring? How often do you make long passages? Do you spend more time at anchor or mooring than underway? Do you spend much time at a dock? Do you ever charter your boat? Do you often have guests aboard? How important are amenities such as refrigeration to you and your guests? Do you often have children on board?

Questions such as these will affect your energy system choices. Be as complete as possible in your answers, and refer to them as you proceed. Take a moment now to review your initial system concept. It may already be time to make some changes.

NOTES ON WHERE THE BOAT IS USED

This information is relevant to the renewable sources of energy such as solar, wind, and water generators. Their output is more location dependent than generators using fossil fuels. If you cruise only one area, write down some notes concerning available sunshine, average wind speed, your average sailing speed, and how suitable the waters are for towing a water generator. If you expect to be cruising through a variety of climates and conditions, include this information as well. All of this helps to determine the average output you can expect from your renewable generators. Also include information relevant to engine-driven generators, such as how much time you spend sailing versus motoring.

Refer to this information as you continue the selection process.

AC ELECTRICAL NEEDS

Make a list of all the appliances you expect to have on board requiring 110-volt alternating current. Before you do, though, remember that you can handle these loads in four different ways.

1. The first is to have an inverter sized so you can power AC appliances from your boat batteries. This requires no additional generating equipment, although your existing generator and battery capacity may have to be modified to handle larger AC loads.

2. The second is to use AC only when you can plug into shore power at a dock.

3. The third is to have a gen-set or large portable generator on board with AC output equivalent to your needs. The larger the output, the more weight and space required for the generator.

4. The final method for handling AC loads is to eliminate them by restricting appliances to those that run off 12-volt DC. It's extraordinary how many appliances are now available for 12-volt operation—televisions, VCRs, computers, blenders, microwaves, vacuums, power tools, even small washing machines!

Your list of AC equipment and its associated power requirements determines the need for AC power on board. Once the need is established, decide how you are going to handle it: DC-to-AC inverter, shore-power connection, or onboard AC generator. These decisions also affect total battery capacity required.

CHARGING GENERATOR OUTPUT

The next step in the selection process is to determine the realistic average electrical output from the generators you expect to have on board. Average output takes into account variable engine speeds, battery state of charge, available sun, wind, and boat speed. Refer to the table on page 240–241.

TOTAL BATTERY CAPACITY REQUIRED

Your needed battery capacity is in part determined by how much time you'd like to see elapse between engine-driven recharges. For systems with deep-cycle batteries, the objective is to generate until the batteries are full, use this stored electricity to supply your load until the batteries are about 50 percent discharged, then generate again. The length of time between charges depends on two things: load and battery capacity. If your load is light and battery capacity sufficient, you can go many days between generating periods. As load increases, it makes sense to generate more frequently, thus avoiding the need for a very large battery capacity.

As an example, let's assume your electrical load is 25 ampere-hours per day, and you would like to have four days between generating periods. What is the appropriate deep-cycle battery capacity? From Chapter 5 we know that deep-cycle batteries operate most efficiently and without harm when discharged only to the 50 percent level before recharging. We also

Generator	*Average output at typical engine RPM*
Standard marine alternator	**Hourly output (amps)**
35-amp unit with standard voltage regulator	15
35-amp unit with fast-charge control	25
50-amp unit with standard voltage regulator	20
50-amp unit with fast-charge control	35
High-output alternator	**Hourly output (amps)**
100-amp unit with standard voltage regulator	75
100-amp unit with fast-charge control	85
160-amp unit with standard voltage regulator	120
160-amp unit with fast-charge control	140
Small portable generator	**Hourly output (amps)**
600-watt unit coupled with 30-amp battery charger	30
Tanaka QEG 250	20
Power Charger 100	85
Battery charger	**Hourly output (amps)**
10-amp	10
20-amp	20
40-amp	40
PV solar panels	**Daily output (ampere-hours)**
20-watts total capacity	6
40-watts total capacity	12
80-watts total capacity	24
160-watts total capacity	48
Wind generators	**Daily output (ampere-hours)**
small prop—moderate winds	25
strong winds	50
large prop—moderate winds	50
strong winds	100

Generator	Average output at typical engine RPM
Water Generators	**Daily output (ampere-hours)**
± 4 knots avg. boat speed	50
± 5 knots avg. boat speed	100
± 6 knots avg. boat speed	150

know that it is a slow generating process to get that last 10 percent of capacity, and in fact it isn't necessary to do this every charging cycle. It would be appropriate to routinely use the battery between 50 and 90 percent of full charge. In other words, usable battery capacity is 40 percent of total capacity. (Note: Individual energy system suppliers have their own recommendations for battery use and sizing, which may vary slightly from those presented here.)

Remember from Chapter 6 that if you only discharge your deep-cycle batteries to the 50 percent level before recharging, an alternator (or other engine-charging source) with a rated output of about 25 percent of total battery capacity is recommended. A somewhat larger alternator rating is fine, it just means that the alternator won't be fully utilized. (Note: Prevailer gelled-electrolyte batteries can accept higher levels of current, utilizing a larger alternator.)

Calculate your needed battery capacity as follows:

25 ampere-hours per day × 4 days = 100 ampere-hours usable capacity required

100 ampere-hours usable capacity = 40% of total capacity

Total capacity is therefore 100 ampere-hours/.4 = 250 ampere-hours

Recommended alternator rating = 60 amperes

In this case one 250-ampere-hour battery or two 125-ampere-hour batteries would do the job.

Suppose you feel that a two-day charging cycle is adequate. The usable capacity required then drops to 50 ampere-hours, and the total capacity required is 125 ampere-hours. For a total capacity of 125 ampere-hours, however, an alternator rated at around 35 amperes would be appropriate. This means you would have to run the engine the same amount of time every two days instead of every four days. Viewed in this light, the larger battery capacity makes more sense.

When sizing battery capacity for a larger load, follow the same procedure. Assuming a daily load of 100 ampere-hours and a three-day charging cycle:

100 ampere-hours per day × 3 days = 300 ampere-hours usable capacity required

$$300 \text{ ampere-hours usable capacity} = 40\% \text{ of total capacity}$$

$$\text{Total capacity is therefore } 300 \text{ ampere-hours}/.4 = 750 \text{ ampere-hours}$$

$$\text{Recommended alternator rating} = 160 \text{ amperes}$$

Note: Storage capacity can be supplied by 12-volt batteries in parallel, six-volt batteries in series and parallel, or even two-volt batteries in series. The batteries can be connected as one large bank or in two or three smaller banks.

Hybrid Systems That Include Renewable Generators

Battery sizing becomes a little more complicated if you have a hybrid system incorporating PV solar panels and a wind or water generator, which may be generating to some extent most of the time. Their daily output varies with available sunshine, wind speed, or boat speed. You no longer have a well-defined charging routine. What you do have is an opportunity to save fuel, reduce total battery capacity, and extend the intervals between engine charges. The following is a suggested battery selection process when renewable energy is available:

Step 1. Select a desired interval between engine charges and size your battery capacity as if you have no renewable generators on board (as would be the case if for some reason the renewable generators were out of commission). Let's assume a daily electrical load of 100-ampere-hours and a three-day charging cycle. Ignoring the contribution from renewable generators, your requisite battery capacity would be sized as follows:

$$\text{Daily electrical load} \times \text{desired charging cycle} = \text{usable battery capacity required}$$

$$100 \text{ ampere-hours/day} \times 3 \text{ days} = 300 \text{ ampere-hours usable capacity required}$$

$$\text{Usable battery capacity}/.4 = \text{total battery capacity required}$$

$$300 \text{ ampere-hours usable capacity}/.4 = 750 \text{ ampere-hours}$$

Step 2. Now take the renewable generator output into account and make a revised estimate of the total battery capacity required. Let's assume an average daily output from renewable generators of 50 ampere-hours. This effectively reduces your average daily electrical load to 50 ampere-hours/day, which means total battery capacity can be reduced. The greater the contribution from renewables, the more the total battery capacity can be lowered (to a required minimum). Let's estimate that 500 ampere-hours would be sufficient battery capacity for this system.

Step 3. Now make sure this capacity is adequate for all conditions as follows:

- With 500 ampere-hours of battery capacity, what does the engine charging cycle become if the renewable generators are out of commission? *(Answer: 2 days.)* Is this accepable? *(Answer: Since the original request was for a three-day cycle, this is probably acceptable.)*

- When sun and wind conditions are optimal, is there enough battery capacity to store daily renewable generator output? Output in very good conditions is at least twice the average. Using this estimate (at times the output might be higher, but some portion of the energy is used directly to satisfy the daily electrical load), we find that the daily output in optimal conditions is approximately 100 ampere-hours, while the usable battery capacity is 200 ampere-hours, more than sufficient.

- Under average conditions, what is the interval between engine charges when renewable energy is accounted for?

Since renewable generator output, in effect, lowers the average daily electrical load to only 50 ampere-hours a day, the routine time between engine charging becomes:

200 ampere-hours / 50 ampere-hours/day = 4 days

The average length of charging cycle is twice that when no renewable generator output is considered, and one day longer than originally requested.

All conditions seem to be satisfied, so a total battery capacity of 500 ampere-hours is selected.

Summary
Batteries should be sized according to average daily electrical load and desired engine-charging interval. Any contribution from renewable sources will pleasantly reduce the need for engine-driven generator charging, and can reduce the total required battery capacity. If the output from renewable sources is sufficient, routine engine charging can be eliminated altogether. Battery capacity should still be large enough for these eventualities:

- When little or no renewable energy is available, and you are forced to rely totally on engine-driven generators for charging, you'll still want a decent interval between engine charges.

- When conditions for renewable energy are very good and high levels of energy are produced, you'll want to be able to store it. Any energy that is not either used directly or stored is lost.

EQUIPMENT SELECTION AND COST

Finally, make a list of needed equipment. The list may have to be revised several times before it conforms to all the above considerations. Include approximate initial cost and estimated installation cost, if applicable.

SAMPLE ENERGY SELECTION FORM (FOR BOAT A)

Now let's work through the steps outlined above with a hypothetical 31-foot auxiliary cruising catamaran, which we'll call Boat A. Step one is to estimate daily electrical load, just as we did for six hypothetical boats back in Chapter 13.

Estimated Daily Electrical Load

Appliance	Watts	Amps	Hours	Total ampere-hrs
Cabin lights	36.0	3.00	4.00	12.00
Running lights	25.0	2.00	1.50	3.00
Low-drain anchor light	1.2	.10	10.00	1.00
Instruments	12.0	1.00	2.00	2.00
Short-wave/ AM-FM	2.0	0.17	2.00	0.34
Tape deck	18.0	1.50	1.00	1.50
VHF receive transmit	6.0 60.0	0.50 5.00	1.00 0.25	0.50 1.25
Cabin fans (2)	12.0	1.00	4.00	4.00
Small inverter	60.0	5.00	2.00	10.00
Small 12-volt refrigerator	60.0	5.00	10.00	50.00
			Total:	85 ampere-hours

Initial System Concept

Boat A wants the bulk of its electrical power to come from renewable sources. A hybrid system incorporating several large solar panels and a combination wind/water system seems to make the most sense for the boat, its cruising grounds, and its regular crew. The large-prop wind unit should be rigging-suspended for times in port, and the water generator employed for passages. The solar panels should have mounting brackets, but should also be movable to follow the sun. There should be adequate renewable output and battery storage to last at least three days before the engine must again be used for recharging. The skipper wants a 100-ampere high-output alternator to keep engine running time to a minimum, saving his old 35-ampere standard alternator as a backup. He feels this should handle any future electrical loads. Proper system monitoring equipment is important to him. A small inverter should be available for operating a personal computer along with future light AC loads. The refrigeration system is a 12-volt, constant-cycling, water-cooled variety with a small, super-insulated box. Refrigeration load varies with outside temperature.

Financial Budget

Boat A's owner/skipper estimates that his entire system will cost around $3,500. He has $2,000 to spend in the first year, and $750 in each of the following years.

Notes on Type of Boat

Boat A is a 31-foot cruising catamaran set up for living aboard, with adequate cabintop space forward for solar panels. A flexible bimini shades the entire cockpit/back deck area most of the time in harbor. The foretriangle area with its roller-furling jib is big enough for a rigging-suspended, large-prop wind unit. The wide transom is suitable for a trailing-log water generator, without interfering with steering vane and taffrail log. The auxiliary engine has, as mentioned, a 35-ampere, small-frame, standard marine alternator and voltage regulator.

Notes on How the Boat Is Used

Boat A is used for extended family cruising by a husband, wife, and two children. They often have friends on board. The auxiliary engine is used as little as possible. Almost no time is spent at a dock. The boat is never chartered.

Notes on Where the Boat Is Used

The boat is used mainly on the U.S. East Coast, in the Bahamas, and in the Caribbean. These areas have good average sun and wind conditions for renewable energy. The family plans to cruise farther afield within a few years.

AC Electrical Needs

The personal computer (to be run off an inverter) requires 60 watts. The few small power tools that will be used, such as a soldering iron need 140 watts or less. No AC generator is needed to meet this modest demand. A 140-watt pocket DC-to-AC inverter will do nicely. No AC-to-DC batter charger is contemplated.

Charging Generator Output

Generator	Expected Average Output
Alternator with fast-charge control	100 amperes/hr
Solar panels (80 watts total)	25 ampere-hrs/day
Wind generator (large-prop unit in moderate winds)	50 ampere-hrs/day
Water generator (used in place of the wind generator when under sail)	Assume at least equivalent to wind unit output
Total average output from renewable: 75 ampere-hrs/day	

Total Battery Capacity Required

Ignoring the contribution from renewable sources, Boat A's battery capacity should be as follows:

Daily load × desired charging cycle = usable capacity needed

85 ampere-hours/day × 3 days = 255 ampere-hours

Usable battery capacity / .4 = total battery capacity needed

255 ampere-hours / .4 = 638 ampere-hours

When renewable sources contribute on a daily basis, in effect the daily electrical load is reduced. This means that total battery capacity can be reduced. With that revision in mind, the owner of Boat A estimates that 400 ampere-hours will suffice for his system. He then tests that estimate as outlined previously:

- With 400 ampere-hours of capacity, what is the engine-charging cycle during periods of poor renewable generator output? *(Answer: 400 ampere-hours capacity × .4 = 160 ampere-hours' usable capacity, enough for a two-day charging cycle. This is acceptable to Boat A's crew.)*

- When sun and wind conditions are optimal, is there enough battery capacity to store the daily output from these sources? *(Answer: Output under optimal conditions is at least twice the average, or 150 ampere-hours per day. The usable battery capacity is 160 ampere-hours. Thus, 400 ampere-hours of total battery capacity would be sufficient, although some energy may be lost during periods of sustained high output.)*

- Under average conditions, how long can Boat A go between engine charges when renewable energy is accounted for? *(Answer: the usable battery capacity is 160 ampere-hours. Since renewable generator output, in effect, lowers the average electrical load to only 10 ampere-hours per day, the average time between engine charges will be 16 days! The owner of Boat A decides that 400 ampere-hours of battery capacity will suffice.)*

Equipment	Estimated Cost
Generators	
100 ampere-hour high-output alternator with fast-charge control	$ 650
80 watts of standard-grade PV solar panels	$ 700
large-prop wind/water combination generator	$1,000
Controls and Monitors	
ammeters and battery state-of-charge monitors	$ 200
Batteries	
400 ampere-hours of capacity	$ 600
AC System	
DC-to-AC inverter, 140 watts	$ 150
Installation, labor, miscellaneous parts	$ 150
Total System Cost	$3,450

Boat A's afterdeck (husband and wife) examine their joint bank account and the other expenses on their horizons, and decide to buy the alternator, regulator, monitors, batteries, and inverter in year 1. They'll buy the solar panels and wind/water generator in years 2 and 3 respectively, living with more frequent engine charging cycles in the meantime.

SAMPLE ENERGY SELECTION FORM FOR BOAT B

Boat B is a trawler yacht with a substantially larger energy appetite than Boat A. Let's work the problem.

Estimated Daily DC Electrical Load (when cruising)

Appliance	Watts	Amps	Hours	Total ampere-hrs
Cabin lights	72	6.0	4.50	27.0
Anchor light	10	0.8	11.00	8.8
Running lights	25	2.0	2.00	4.0
Instruments	24	2.0	1.50	3.0
Radar	48	4.0	4.00	16.0
Tape deck	18	1.5	4.00	6.0
Cabin fans (3)	36	3.0	4.00	12.0

(*continued on page 248*)

Appliance	Watts	Amps	Hours	Total ampere-hrs
*Inverter (avg.)	336	28.0	1.00	28.0
12-volt DC refrig.	480	40.0	1.50	60.0
Elec. windlass	240	20.0	0.17	3.4
Autopilot	36	3.0	4.0	12.0
			Total:	180 ampere-hrs

*(refer to section on AC electrical loads)

Estimated Daily DC Electrical Load (when living in port)

Appliance	Watts	Amps	Hours	Total Ampere-hrs
Cabin lights	72	6.0	4.5	27.0
Anchor light	10	0.8	11.0	8.8
Tape deck	18	1.5	4.0	6.0
Cabin fans (3)	36	3.0	4.0	12.0
*Inverter (avg.)	150	12.5	1.0	12.5
**110-volt refrig.	(no DC load; gen-set or shore power to supply AC loads)			
Elec. windlass	240	20	0.17	3.4
			Total:	70 ampere-hours

*(for "quiet-time" AC loads)
**(refer to section on AC electrical loads)

Initial System Concept

Boat B's system should be capable of handling two different types of loads, one when cruising and one when staying in port. When cruising, the bulk of the AC loads will be handled by an inverter. In port, the inverter will handle "quiet-time" loads when no shore-power connection is available, while a small gen-set will take care of larger AC loads at times, providing supplemental battery charging at the same time. A high-output engine alternator will supply the bulk of the energy needs when cruising, since the main engine will be operating daily. Engine running just for charging batteries could be kept to a minimum through the use of some type of alternate energy. There is space on board for large battery banks if necessary. The refrigeration system has holding plates and utilizes a large electric motor to drive the compressor. It can be operated on 12 volts DC when cruising or 110 volts AC in port. Proper system monitoring equipment should be included.

Financial Budget

Boat B's husband-and-wife owners estimate the additions to their existing engine/alternator system to be approximately $7,500, with the gen-set representing about half that cost. They are just retiring and have the money to invest in the complete system in year 1.

Notes on Type of Boat

Boat B is a Grand Banks 36 trawler yacht set up for a liveaboard couple. The boat is powered by a 6-cylinder Lehman diesel main engine (135 HP) with space and capacity to operate a large, high-output alternator. The boat currently has 500 ampere-hours of battery capacity, and the batteries are in good condition. There is a complete 12-volt DC electrical system, and an AC circuit with a shore-power connection and several AC outlets. The AC system, until now used only at dockside, would have to be upgraded to accommodate the gen-set.

Notes on How the Boat Is Used

The boat will be used as a seasonal home for a retired liveaboard couple. Occasionally, other family members or guests will spend time on the boat.

Notes on Where the Boat Is Used

Pacific Northwest USA.

AC Electrical Needs

When cruising, the inverter will handle all of the AC loads. It should be capable of a continuous output of around 600 watts to handle loads such as the computer, TV and VCR, small power tools, blender, etc. It should also be able to run a small microwave oven drawing 800 watts for up to 10 minutes, and have an initial surge capability of up to 1,500 watts for starting motors. The smallest unit that would do the job is the Statpower Pro Watt 600, since it can produce 800 watts for up to 10 minutes. It does not have a battery-charging option, so a separate battery charger would have to be purchased. A 1,000-to-2,000-watt inverter with battery-charging option would also be suitable. The gen-set will provide backup AC power if necessary.

In port, small AC loads can be handled by the inverter (if no shore-power connection is available), but large AC loads will be handled by a gen-set or shorepower connection. The gen-set should be capable of producing 3000 watts (3 kw), to handle the loads of 110-volt refrigeration with holding plates, a small vacuum cleaner, increased use of the microwave oven, and the operation of a battery charger. (The inverter could have a battery-charging option.) The recommended battery-charger output is 50 to 100 amps. The gen-set would only have to run 1 to 2 hours each evening to handle these short-term loads.

Charging Generator Output

Generator	*Expected Average Output*
Alternator—high-output type with its standard voltage regulator.	130 amperes/hr
Gen-set (3 kw minimum) used with battery charger (possibly on inverter) and manual ship/shore selection switch	50–100 amperes/hr
Solar panels—Two 40-watt panels to be mounted on the cabintop	16 ampere-hrs/day, since average sunlight levels are only fair.

Total Battery Capacity Required

The desired time between engine charges is just one day; the main engine or the gen-set could be run for a short period each day without difficulty.

The output of Boat B's solar panels will be low compared with electrical load and the output of other charging sources, so the solar panels can be ignored while sizing the system. The batteries should be sized for cruising, since that is when the largest DC load occurs. Thus, 180 amp-hrs × 1 day = 180 amp-hrs usable battery capacity required. Then, 180 amp-hrs/.4 = 450 amp-hrs total battery capacity required.

The existing 500 ampere-hr battery bank will meet Boat B's future needs.

Equipment Selection and Cost

Equipment	Estimated Cost

Generators
    Alternator—high-output w/ control
    PV solar panels—(2) 40-watt panels, no
        voltage regulation needed
	$ 400
	$ 650

Controls and Monitors Digital monitoring system	$ 300

AC System
    Generator—3 kw gen-set with manual
        ship/shore selector switch
    Inverter—800 to 2,000 watts battery
        charger—50- to 100-amp (could be
        included with inverter)
	$4,000
	
	$1,300 (combined cost)

Installation labor, miscellaneous parts Mostly for gen-set installation	$ 750
Total System Cost $7,400	

Boat B's owners spend the remaining $100 of their budget on charts for next year's cruising!

Appendix A
Glossary of Energy and Electrical Terms

Alternating Current. The electric current found at your dock or in your home. In this case, the current travels first in one direction and then in the other. Each reversal is a cycle. The number of cycles per second is the frequency of the alternating current. The most common frequency in the United States is 60 cycles per second, or 60 hertz. In Great Britain it is 50 Hz.

Alternator. A generator that produces alternating current; this is then rectified, by diodes in the unit, into direct current that may be used to charge a storage battery. Current is created by rotating a magnetic field on a rotor inside a series of wire windings (the stator).

Ammeter. An instrument for measuring

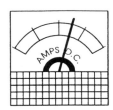

the current in an electrical circuit. Many different scales are available.

Ampere. A measure of the current in an electrical circuit. One ampere is equivalent to the flow of 6.24×10^{18} electrons per second.

Ampere-Hour. A measure of total current draw. If a lamp drawing one amp was left on for one hour, it would consume one amp-hour of electricity. This term is primarily used to rate batteries. A typical marine battery has 100 amp-hours of capacity (often referred to as ampacity).

Appliance. Anything on board a boat powered by electricity.

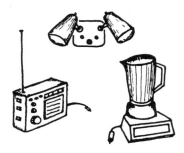

Battery. A group of two or more cells that produces electrical current (DC) due to a chemical action. The lead-acid type, rated at

12 volts (6 cells in series a 2 volts each), is widely used on boats and in automobiles.

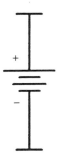

Circuit. A simple circuit comprises a source of voltage (battery), a resistance to current flow (an appliance or load), and a conductor (copper wire) connecting the two. Usually included in a boat circuit are a switch for on/off control and a fuse or circuit breaker as a safety device in case of overload.

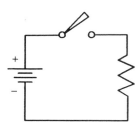

Closed Circuit. Often a source of confusion to students of electricity, it refers to a circuit that is continuous, or complete, and allows electrons to flow freely. A closed switch is ON, an open switch is OFF!

Circuit Breaker. A safety device, often an automatic switch, that opens or disconnects a circuit if more than a set amount of current flows. Unlike a fuse, which must be re-placed, a circuit breaker may be reset once the trouble is corrected.

Conductor. Any material that contains many available drifting electrons. When under the influence of voltage from a battery, the direction of electron drift is from the negative pole to the positive pole. Metals are very good conductors, and copper wire is the usual conductor in an electrical circuit because of its superior performance and low cost.

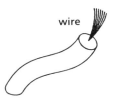

wire

Continuity. A complete, or closed, circuit where electrons flow freely. Continuity is lost if a switch is opened, wires loosen, or an appliance is faulty (e.g., a light burns out).

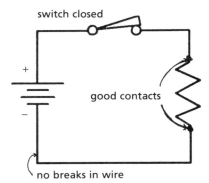

switch closed

good contacts

no breaks in wire

Current. The rate of drift or flow of electrons through a conductor. It is measured in amperes (amps) and is analogous to the flow of water inside a pipe. Current is governed by the voltage pressure and the resistance to its flow in the circuit (see Ampere).

Diode (Blocking Diode). A diode is a small solid-state device that allows current to flow only in one direction. A diode is rated by the maximum current it will safely accept and by peak inverse voltage (PIV), the highest voltage it can effectively block in the other direction. A diode acts both as a conductor, allowing (for example) generated electricity to flow into the battery, and as an insulator, preventing the flow of current into the generating equipment, where it is simply lost or where it can damage equipment.

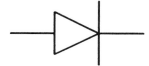

Electricity. The net drift or flow of electrons through a conductor. When a voltage induces electron drift, an energy wave is produced, moving through the conductor near the speed of light.

Electrolyte. A material whose atoms or molecules become ionized in solution (see Ion). In a lead-acid battery, the electrolyte is a sulfuric acid and water solution. When ionized, sulfuric acid gives rise to one sulphate ion carrying two negative charges, and two positively charged hydrogen ions.

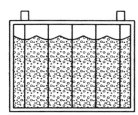

Electron. A subatomic particle that orbits rapidly around the nucleus of an atom. The positive charge of the nucleus determines how many electrons are in orbit. Each electron carries one negative charge. Electrons revolve in various orbits; those in the outer orbit, or shell, can drift from atom to atom. These electrons cause conductivity as they move under the influence of voltage. The movement of electrons is known as electricity. Conductors have three electrons or fewer in the outermost shell; insulators have five or more.

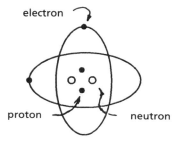

Energy. The amount of power produced by a generator or consumed by an appliance in a given time (typically an hour). It is often measured in watt-hours.

Frequency. The number of times an event recurs in a given period. In alternating current it is the number of times that the electrons reverse direction in one second.

Fuse. A safety device that protects an electrical circuit or appliance from too much current draw (overload). When the current through the fuse exceeds the rating of the fuse (ratings are in amperes or decimal amperes) the metal wire inside the fuse melts, opening the circuit before more damage occurs.

Generator. A rotating electromechanical device that produces electricity by rotating wire windings (armature) inside a magnetic field emanating from a stationary housing (stator). The motion of the wire inside the magnetic field initiates a force (voltage) that pushes electrons down the wire, creating electrical current.

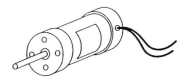

Hydrometer. A device used to measure the specific gravity of a liquid, such as battery electrolyte. Some units measure specific gravity with floating balls. Others give direct numerical readings on a float.

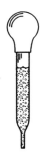

Insulator. Any material that does not allow electricity to flow freely, such as wood, rubber, plastics, and glass. Insulators have five or more electrons in the outer orbit of each atom. They isolate the electrical charge in wires and electrical components, preventing them from leaking electricity, damaging each other, or injuring anyone coming in contact with them.

plastic/rubber

Ion. An ion is an electrically charged atom or molecule formed when a neutral atom loses or gains one or more electrons. The loss of an electron results in a positively charged ion called a cation. The gaining of an electron results in a negatively charged ion called an anion.

Load. The power (in watts) consumed by an electrical device. It is related to the resistance of the device. The more devices or appliances connected in parallel, the lower the total resistance and the greater the load.

Magnetic Field. The force that surrounds magnets, and all current-carrying conductors. If there is relative motion between a conductor (e.g., copper wire) and a magnetic field, an electrical pressure, or voltage, is produced in the wire, causing electrons to flow. This is the principle on which the generator is based.

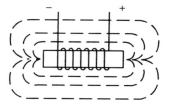

Multimeter. An instrument that functions as an ammeter (usually low amperage), voltmeter, ohmmeter, and continuity tester.

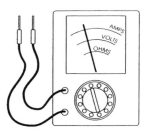

Negative. One kind of electrical charge, refers to an atom that has gained one or more electrons to become a negatively charged ion, and to the terminal on the battery from which electrons flow in an electrical circuit.

Ohm. The measure of resistance (R) in an electrical circuit. It is related to the voltage (V) and current (I) by the relationship $V = I \times R$. Appliances have an inherent resistance, and some components are rated in ohms. Corroded wiring or contacts or loose connections cause excess resistance in a circuit.

Ohmmeter. An instrument for measuring the resistance of an electrical circuit or device. An internal battery supplies a small voltage that creates a current proportional to the resistance in the item being measured. The resistance readings may be taken on one of several scales.

Open Circuit. An electrical circuit that does not allow current to flow because of an open switch, loose wires, or an appliance that has been removed from a plug or socket (e.g., a light bulb).

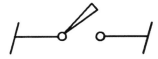

Overload. An excessive amount of current draw in an electrical circuit.

Parallel Circuit. Connecting electrical devices "head to head" and "tail to tail." If two 12-volt batteries are connected in parallel (positive terminals together, negative terminals together) the voltage will remain the same but the capacity (amp-hours) will be the sum of the two. The boat's instrument panel represents electrical appliances wired in parallel. Each appliance has its own switch and safety fuse or circuit breaker.

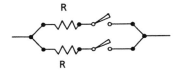

Permanent Magnet. A magnet that does not require electrical circuitry to maintain its magnetism. Such magnets are installed, for example, inside some generators.

Photovoltaic Conversion. The process that converts light (radiant energy) directly into electrical energy by means of a solar cell.

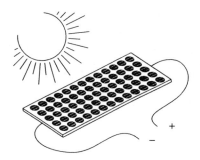

Polarity. The property of an object containing opposite forces. A magnet has north and south magnetic polarity. A battery that supplies direct current has a polarity due to its positive and negative terminals. All DC circuits have positive and negative leads, and are thus polarized.

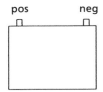

Positive. Refers to the electrical charge of a proton, or to the charge of an atom or group of atoms that has lost one or more electrons and thus has become a positive ion. The battery terminal to which electrons flow in an electrical circuit.

Power. The rate at which work is done by electricity. It is a function of voltage (V) and current (I); $P = V \times I$, and is expressed in watts. Generators are rated in watts according to their power output, and appliances are rated in watts according to the power they consume.

Rectifier. An electrical device, usually consisting of a configuration of diodes, that converts alternating current (AC) into direct current (DC). Alternators have a built-in rectifier since they must supply direct current to the battery.

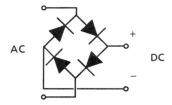

Resistance. The opposition to the drift, or flow, of electrons along a wire. It is measured in ohms, and is analogous to the opposition to water flow due to pipe diameter and friction. The larger the diameter, the less the opposition. Large pipes or wires

offer low resistance. All electrical components and appliances place a resistance on an electrical circuit.

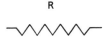

Revolutions Per Minute (RPM). The number of times in one minute that an object revolves 360°. Used to describe the rate of rotation of an engine, generator, or propeller shaft. It is measured with a tachometer.

Series. Refers to electrical devices that are installed "head to tail" in an electrical circuit. If two 6-volt batteries are connected in series, positive terminal of one to negative terminal of the other, the voltage will increase to 12 volts, but the capacity in amp-hours will remain the same as one battery. If a switch is opened in a series circuit, current will stop flowing to all devices in the circuit.

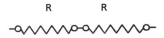

Solar Cell. A thin wafer, usually a slice of a silicon crystal, that has been deliberately treated with impurities to create an excessive negative or positive charge. The size of the cell determines the amperage (typically .063 amp for 4-inch cell). Solar cell voltage, regardless of size, is about one-half volt.

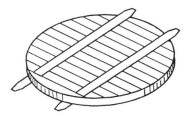

Solar Panel. A thin, rigid frame that houses solar cells connected in series to yield the rated power in watts. The size of the solar cells determines the amperage, and the number of cells determines the voltage, typically 16 to 18 volts in a battery-charging application. For example, a 35-watt panel may have 36 cells of 4-inch diameter producing approximately 2.2 amps.

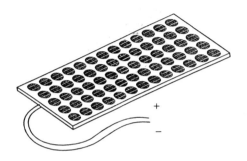

Specific Gravity. The ratio of the weight or mass of a given volume of a substance to that of an equal volume of another substance. For liquids, water is used as a reference with a specific gravity of 1.0. The specific gravity of the electrolyte in a fully charged lead-acid battery is between 1.26 and 1.3.

Switch. An electrical device that opens or closes electrical circuits. Many varieties and ratings are available.

Volt. The measure of the electrical pressure (or voltage) in an electrical circuit.

Voltage. The force that moves electrons along a wire in one direction. It is measured in volts, and is analogous to the pressure that moves water through a pipe. Voltage on boats comes from one or more lead-acid batteries that usually are rated at 12 volts.

Voltage Regulator. An electrical control device that adjusts the output voltage from a generator before it reaches the battery. On car and marine engines, it drops the charging amperage from the alternator soon after start-up so that the batteries will not be overcharged. A purpose-designed voltage regulator may be used with an alternate energy generator (although not necessary) so that batteries will always be protected from excessive charge.

Voltmeter. An instrument used for measuring the voltage in an electrical circuit or battery.

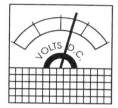

Water Generator. A device that converts the motion of a boat through water into electrical energy. In one common type, a water propeller (similar to a propeller on a small outboard motor) rotates a tightly wound line as it is pulled through the water. The rotary motion of the prop and line is transferred to the shaft of the generator.

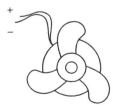

Watts. The measure of power being generated or consumed in an electrical circuit. Watts (P) is related to the voltage (V) and current (I) by the relationship $P = V \times I$.

Watt-Hour.   A measure of electrical energy generated or consumed: 1000 watt-hours = 1 kilowatt-hour.

Watt-Hour Meter.   An instrument that measures the energy produced or consumed in an electrical circuit. It is the electric meter outside your house or at a dock that indicates the number of kilowatt-hours of energy you consume. Not a practical device for on-board use.

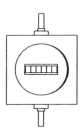

Wind Generator.   A device that converts the mechanical energy of the wind into electrical energy. A propeller transforms the horizontal movement of an airstream into rotary motion. The greater the propeller/generator shaft speed, the higher the electrical output.

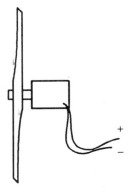

Appendix B
Useful Tables

Note: *the source for Tables B-1 through B-7 is* Boatowner's Mechanical and Electrical Manual *by Nigel Calder* (*International Marine, 1990*).

FIGURE B-1. **Conductor sizes for 3 percent drop in voltage.**

(Total current on circuit in amps.) (Length of conductor from source of current to device and back to source—feet)

amps	10	15	20	25	30	40	50	60	70	80	90	100	110	120	130	140	150	160	170
12 volts																			
5	18	16	14	12	12	10	10	10	8	8	8	6	6	6	6	6	6	6	6
10	14	12	10	10	10	8	6	6	6	6	4	4	4	4	2	2	2	2	2
15	12	10	10	8	8	6	6	6	4	4	2	2	2	2	2	1	1	1	1
20	10	10	8	6	6	6	4	4	2	2	2	2	1	1	1	0	0	0	2/0
25	10	8	6	6	6	4	4	2	2	2	1	1	0	0	0	2/0	2/0	2/0	3/0
30	10	8	6	6	4	4	2	2	1	1	0	0	2/0	2/0	3/0	3/0	3/0	3/0	
40	8	6	6	4	4	2	2	1	0	0	2/0	2/0	3/0	3/0	3/0	4/0	4/0	4/0	4/0
50	6	6	4	4	2	2	1	0	2/0	2/0	3/0	3/0	4/0	4/0	4/0				
60	6	4	4	2	2	1	0	2/0	3/0	3/0	4/0	4/0	4/0						
70	6	4	2	2	1	0	2/0	3/0	3/0	4/0	4/0								
80	6	4	2	2	1	0	3/0	3/0	4/0	4/0									
90	4	2	2	1	0	2/0	3/0	4/0	4/0										
100	4	2	2	1	0	2/0	3/0	4/0											
24 volts																			
5	18	18	18	16	16	14	12	12	12	10	10	10	10	10	8	8	8	8	8
10	18	16	14	12	12	10	10	10	8	8	8	6	6	6	6	6	6	6	6
15	16	14	12	12	10	10	8	8	6	6	6	6	6	4	4	4	4	4	2
20	14	12	10	10	10	8	6	6	6	6	4	4	4	4	2	2	2	2	2
25	12	12	10	10	8	6	6	6	4	4	4	4	2	2	2	2	1	1	1
30	12	10	10	8	8	6	6	4	4	4	2	2	2	2	1	1	1	1	
40	10	10	8	6	6	6	4	4	2	2	2	2	1	1	1	0	0	0	2/0
50	10	8	6	6	6	4	4	2	2	2	1	1	0	0	0	2/0	2/0	2/0	3/0
60	10	8	6	6	4	4	2	2	1	1	0	0	0	2/0	2/0	3/0	3/0	3/0	3/0
70	8	6	6	4	4	2	2	1	1	0	0	2/0	2/0	3/0	3/0	3/0	3/0	4/0	4/0
80	8	6	6	4	4	2	2	1	0	0	2/0	2/0	3/0	3/0	3/0	4/0	4/0	4/0	4/0
90	8	6	4	4	2	2	1	0	0	2/0	2/0	3/0	3/0	4/0	4/0	4/0	4/0	4/0	
100	6	6	4	4	2	2	1	0	2/0	2/0	3/0	3/0	4/0	4/0	4/0				
32 volts																			
5	18	18	18	18	16	16	14	14	12	12	12	12	10	10	10	10	10	10	8
10	18	16	16	14	14	12	12	10	10	10	8	8	8	8	8	6	6	6	6
15	16	14	14	12	12	10	10	8	8	8	6	6	6	6	6	6	6	4	4
20	16	14	12	12	10	10	8	8	6	6	6	6	6	4	4	4	4	4	2
25	14	12	12	10	10	8	8	6	6	6	6	4	4	4	4	2	2	2	2
30	14	12	10	10	8	8	6	6	6	4	4	4	4	2	2	2	1	1	1
40	12	10	10	8	8	6	6	4	4	4	2	2	2	2	1	1	1	1	
50	12	10	8	8	6	6	4	4	2	2	2	2	1	1	0	0	0	0	
60	10	8	8	6	6	4	4	2	2	2	2	1	1	0	0	2/0	2/0	2/0	
70	10	8	6	6	6	4	2	2	2	1	1	0	0	0	2/0	2/0	2/0	3/0	3/0
80	10	8	6	6	4	4	2	2	1	1	0	0	0	2/0	2/0	3/0	3/0	3/0	3/0
90	8	6	6	6	4	2	2	2	1	0	0	2/0	2/0	2/0	3/0	3/0	3/0	4/0	4/0
100	8	6	6	4	4	2	2	1	0	0	2/0	2/0	2/0	3/0	3/0	3/0	4/0	4/0	4/0

(Wire sizes in AWG)

FIGURE B-2. **Conductor sizes for 10 percent drop in voltage.**

(Total current on circuit in amps)	10	15	20	25	30	40	50	60	70	80	90	100	110	120	130	140	150	160	170
12 volts																			
5	18	18	18	18	18	16	16	14	14	14	12	12	12	12	12	10	10	10	10
10	18	18	16	16	14	14	12	12	10	10	10	10	8	8	8	8	8	8	6
15	18	16	14	14	12	12	10	10	8	8	8	8	8	6	6	6	6	6	6
20	16	14	14	12	12	10	10	8	8	8	6	6	6	6	6	6	4	4	4
25	16	14	12	12	10	10	8	8	6	6	6	6	6	4	4	4	4	4	2
30	14	12	12	10	10	8	8	6	6	6	6	4	4	4	4	2	2	2	2
40	14	12	10	10	8	8	6	6	6	4	4	4	2	2	2	2	2	2	2
50	12	10	10	8	8	6	6	4	4	4	2	2	2	2	2	1	1	1	1
60	12	10	8	8	6	6	4	4	2	2	2	2	2	1	1	1	0	0	0
70	10	8	8	6	6	6	4	2	2	2	2	1	1	1	0	0	0	2/0	2/0
80	10	8	8	6	6	4	4	2	2	2	1	1	0	0	0	2/0	2/0	2/0	2/0
90	10	8	6	6	6	4	2	2	2	1	1	0	0	0	2/0	2/0	2/0	3/0	3/0
100	10	8	6	6	4	4	2	2	1	1	0	0	0	2/0	2/0	2/0	3/0	3/0	3/0
24 volts																			
5	18	18	18	18	18	18	18	18	16	16	16	16	14	14	14	14	14	14	12
10	18	18	18	18	16	16	16	14	14	14	12	12	12	12	12	10	10	10	10
15	18	18	18	16	16	14	14	12	12	12	10	10	10	10	10	8	8	8	8
20	18	18	16	16	14	14	12	12	10	10	10	10	8	8	8	8	8	8	6
25	18	16	16	14	14	12	12	10	10	10	8	8	8	8	8	6	6	6	6
30	18	16	14	14	12	12	10	10	8	8	8	8	6	6	6	6	6	6	6
40	16	14	14	12	12	10	10	8	8	8	6	6	6	6	6	6	4	4	4
50	16	14	12	12	10	10	8	8	6	6	6	6	6	4	4	4	4	4	2
60	14	12	12	10	10	8	8	6	6	6	6	4	4	4	4	2	2	2	2
70	14	12	10	10	8	8	6	6	6	6	4	4	4	2	2	2	2	2	2
80	14	12	10	10	8	8	6	6	6	4	4	4	2	2	2	2	2	2	2
90	12	10	10	8	8	6	6	6	4	4	4	2	2	2	2	2	2	1	1
100	12	10	10	8	8	6	6	4	4	4	2	2	2	2	2	1	1	1	1
32 volts																			
5	18	18	18	18	18	18	18	18	18	18	18	16	16	16	16	14	14	14	14
10	18	18	18	18	18	18	16	16	14	14	14	14	14	12	12	12	12	12	12
15	18	18	18	18	18	16	14	14	14	12	12	12	12	10	10	10	10	10	10
20	18	18	18	16	16	14	14	12	12	12	10	10	10	10	10	8	8	8	8
25	18	18	16	16	14	14	12	12	10	10	10	10	10	8	8	8	8	8	8
30	18	18	16	14	14	12	12	10	10	10	10	8	8	8	8	8	6	6	6
40	18	16	14	14	12	12	10	10	8	8	8	8	8	6	6	6	6	6	6
50	16	14	14	12	12	10	10	8	8	8	6	6	6	6	6	6	6	4	4
60	16	14	12	12	10	10	8	8	8	6	6	6	6	6	6	4	4	4	4
70	14	14	12	10	10	8	8	8	6	6	6	6	6	4	4	4	4	2	2
80	14	12	12	10	10	8	8	6	6	6	6	4	4	4	4	2	2	2	2
90	14	12	10	10	10	8	6	6	6	6	4	4	4	2	2	2	2	2	2
100	14	12	10	10	8	8	6	6	6	4	4	4	4	2	2	2	2	2	2

(Wire sizes in AWG)

Conductor Size (AWG)	Minimum Acceptable Circular Mil (CM) Area (ABYC specs)[1]	Conductor Diameter (mm)	Conductor Cross-sectional Area (mm²)
25		0.455	0.163
24		0.511	0.205
23		0.573	0.259
22		0.644	0.325
21		0.723	0.412
20		0.812	0.519
19		0.992	0.653
18	1537	1.024	0.823
17		1.15	1.04
16	2336	1.29	1.31
15		1.45	1.65
14	3702	1.63	2.08
13		1.83	2.63
12	5833	2.05	3.31
11		2.30	4.15
10	9343	2.59	5.27
9		2.91	6.62
8	14810	3.26	8.35
7		3.67	10.6
6	25910	4.11	13.3
5		4.62	16.8
4	37360	5.19	21.2
3		5.83	26.7
2	62450	6.54	33.6
1	77790	7.35	42.4
0 (1/0)	98980	8.25	53.4
00 (2/0)	125100	9.27	67.5
000 (3/0)	158600	10.40	85.0
0000 (4/0)	205500	11.68	107.2
00000 (5/0)	250000	13.12	135.1
000000 (6/0)	300000	14.73	170.3

1. 1 circular mil (CM) = 0.0005067 mm²

FIGURE B-4. **Common electric cables and their designations (USA).**

TW: *Thermoplastic[1] Insulation* (usually PVC), suitable for *Wet* locations (60°C/140°F heat-resistance rating)

THW: *Thermoplastic Insulation* (usually PVC), *Heat Resistant* (75°C/167°F rating), suitable for *Wet* locations.

THWN: Same as for THW except *Nylon* jacket over reduced insulation thickness. Also rated THHN.

THHN: *Thermoplastic Insulation* (usually PVC), *High Heat Resistant* (90°C/194°F rating), dry locations only, *Nylon* jacket. Also rated THWN.

TFFN: *Thermoplastic Insulation* (usually PVC), *Flexible Fixture* wire, *Nylon* jacket. Also rated MTW and AWM

XHHW: *Crosslinked Synthetic Polymer[2] Insulation*, *High Heat Resistant* (90°C/194°F rating) for dry locations only, suitable for *Wet* locations but de-rated to 75°C/167°F.

RHH: *Rubber Insulation* (commonly crosslinked polyethylene because it qualifies for rubber), *High Heat Resistant* (90°C/194°F rating) for dry locations only.

RHW: *Rubber Insulation* (commonly crosslinked polyethylene, as in RHH), *Heat Resistant* (75°C/167°F rating), suitable for *Wet* locations.

USE: *Underground Service Entrance.* Most utilize crosslinked polyethylene insulation rated for 75°C/167°F in direct burial applications. Product is usually triple-rated RHH-RHW-USE.

MTW: *Machine Tool Wire.* Usually thermoplastic insulation (PVC) or thermoplastic insulation with nylon jacket. Moisture, Heat, and Oil Resistant. Most MTW is rated 60°C/140°F. Much stranded copper type THHN is also rated MTW (see AWM).

AWM: *Appliance Wiring Material.* Usually thermoplastic insulation (PVC) or thermoplastic insulation with nylon jacket. Thermosetting[3]. Much stranded copper type THHN in AWG sizes 14 through 6 is also rated AWM. As AWM, the product carries a 105°C/221°F rating.

Key: W = moisture resistant
H = heat resistant, 75°C/167°F
HH = high-heat resistant, 90°C/194°F
M = oil resistant
T = thermoplastic

1. A plastic that can be softened by heating.
2. A plastic formulation in which polymers are linked chemically by polymerization.
3. A plastic that is heat-cured into an insoluble and infusible end product.

FIGURE B-5. **U.S. wiring color codes for marine engine installations.**

Color	Application
Purple	Ignition switch controlled
Black	Grounds
Red*	Unprotected battery wires
Red/purple	Overcurrent protected battery wires
Yellow	Alternator AC output and alternator field
Green	Bonding
Brown and brown/stripe	Alternator starter to ignition module
Orange	Alternator DC output and accessory feeds
Light blue	Oil pressure
Tan	Water temperature
Grey	Tachometer
Green/white	Engine trim in and/or tilt down
Green/orange	Engine independent trim down
Blue/white	Engine trim out and/or tilt up
Blue/orange	Engine independent tilt up
White	Must not be used in under 50v wiring
Yellow/red	Starting circuit
Yellow/black	Choke
Black/yellow	Ignition stop
Brown/white	Trim position sender
Manufacturer's discretion	Ignition triggering and color/stripe for functions not designated

*Red/purple may be used for overcurrent protected wires.

FIGURE B-6. Degrees fahrenheit to degrees celsius/centigrade conversion table.

°F	°C	°F	°C	°F	°C	°F	°C	°F	°C	°F	°C	°F	°C	°F	°C
−454	−270	−31	−35	19.4	−7	70	21.1	120.2	49	171	77.2	225	107.2	660	348.9
−450	−268	−30	34.4	20	−6.7	71	21.7	121	49.4	172	77.8	230	110	662	350
−440	−262	−29.2	−34	21	−6.1	71.6	22	122	50	172.4	78	235	112.8	670	354.4
−436	−260	−29	−33.9	21.2	−6	72	22.2	123	50.6	173	78.3	239	115	680	360
−430	−257	−28	−33.3	22	−5.6	73	22.8	123.8	51	174	78.9	240	115.6	690	365.6
−420	−251	−27.4	−33	23	−5	73.4	23	124	51.1	174.2	79	245	118.3	693	370
−418	−250	−27	−32.8	24	−4.4	74	23.3	125	51.7	175	79.4	248	120	700	371.1
−410	−246	−26	−32.2	24.8	−4	75	23.9	125.6	52	176	80	250	121.1	710	377
−400	−240	−25.6	−32	25	−3.9	75.2	24	126	52.2	177	80.6	255	123.9	716	380
−390	−234	−25	−31.7	26	−3.3	76	24.4	127	52.8	177.8	81	257	125	720	382
−382	−230	−24	−31.1	26.6	−3	77	25	127.4	53	178	81.1	260	126.7	730	388
−380	−229	−23.8	−31	27	−2.8	78	25.6	128	53.3	179	81.7	265	129.4	734	390
−370	−223	−23	−30.6	28	−2.2	78.8	26	129	53.9	179.6	82	266	130	740	393
−364	−220	−22	−30	28.4	−2	79	26.1	129.2	54	180	82.2	270	132.2	750	399
−360	−218	−21	−29.4	29	−1.7	80	26.7	130	54.4	181	82.8	275	135	752	400
−350	−212	−20.2	−29	30	−1.1	80.6	27	131	55	181.4	83	280	137.8	760	404
−346	−210	−20	−28.9	30.2	−1	81	27.2	132	55.6	182	83.3	284	140	770	410
−340	−207	−19	−28.3	31	−0.6	82	27.8	132.8	56	183	83.9	285	140.6	780	416
−330	−201	−18.4	−28	32	0	82.4	28	133	56.1	183.2	84	290	143.3	788	420
−328	−200	−18	−27.8	33	0.6	83	28.3	134	56.7	184	84.4	293	145	790	421
−320	−196	−17	−27.2	33.8	1	84	28.9	134.6	57	185	85	295	146.1	800	427
−310	−190	−16.6	−27	34	1.1	84.2	29	135	57.2	186	85.6	300	148.9	806	430
−300	−184	−16	−26.7	35	1.7	85	29.4	136	57.8	186.8	86	302	150	810	432
−292	−180	−15	−26.1	35.6	2	86	30	136.4	58	187	86.1	310	154.4	820	438
−290	−179	−14.8	−26	36	2.2	87	30.6	137	58.3	188	86.7	320	160	824	440
−280	−173	−14	−25.6	37	2.8	87.8	31	138	58.9	188.6	87	330	165.6	830	443
−274	−170	−13	−25	37.4	3	88	31.1	138.2	59	189	87.2	338	170	840	449
−270	−168	−12	−24.4	38	3.3	89	31.7	139	59.4	190	87.8	340	171.1	842	450
−260	−162	−11.2	−24	39	3.9	89.6	32	140	60	190.4	88	350	176.7	850	454
−256	−160	−11	−23.9	39.2	4	90	32.2	141	60.6	191	88.3	356	180	860	460
−250	−157	−10	−23.3	40	4.4	91	32.8	141.8	61	192	88.9	360	182.2	870	466
−240	−151	−9.4	−23	41	5	91.4	33	142	61.1	192.2	89	370	187.8	878	470
−238	−150	−9	−22.8	42	5.5	92	33.3	143	61.7	193	89.4	374	190	880	471
−230	−146	−8	−22.2	42.8	6	93	33.9	143.6	62	194	90	380	193.3	890	477
−220	−140	−7.6	−22	43	6.1	93.2	34	144	62.2	195	90.6	390	198.9	896	480
−210	−134	−7	−21.7	44	6.7	94	34.4	145	62.8	195.8	91	392	200	900	482
−202	−130	−6	−21.1	44.6	7	95	35	145.4	63	196	91.1	400	204.4	910	488
−200	−129	−5.8	−21	45	7.2	96	35.6	146	63.3	197	91.7	410	210	914	490
−190	−123	−5	−20.6	46	7.8	96.8	36	147	63.9	197.6	92	420	215.6	920	493
−184	−120	−4	−20	46.4	8	97	36.1	147.2	64	198	92.2	428	220	930	499
−180	−118	−3	−19.4	47	8.3	98	36.7	148	64.4	199	92.8	430	221.1	932	500
−170	−112	−2.2	−19	48	8.9	98.6	37	149	65	199.4	93	440	226.7	940	504
−166	−110	−2	−18.9	48.2	9	99	37.2	150	65.6	200	93.3	446	230	950	510
−160	−107	−1	−18.3	49	9.4	100	37.8	150.8	66	201	93.9	450	232.2	960	516
−150	−101	−0.4	−18	50	10	100.4	38	151	66.1	201.2	94	460	237.8	968	520
−148	−100	0	−17.8	51	10.6	101	38.3	152	66.7	202	94.4	464	240	970	521
−140	−96	1	−17.2	51.8	11	102	38.9	152.6	67	203	95	470	243.3	980	527
−130	−90	1.4	−17	52	11.1	102.2	39	153	67.2	204	95.6	480	248.9	986	530
−120	−84	2	−16.7	53	11.7	103	39.4	154	67.8	204.8	96	482	250	990	532
−112	−80	3	−16.1	53.6	12	104	40	154.4	68	205	96.1	490	254.4	1000	538
−110	−79	3.2	−16	54	12.2	105	40.6	155	68.3	206	96.7	500	260	1004	540
−100	−73.3	4	−15.6	55	12.8	105.8	41	156	68.9	206.6	97	510	265.6	1022	550
−94	−70	5	−15	55.4	13	106	41.1	156.2	69	207	97.2	518	270	1050	566
−90	−67.8	6	−14.4	56	13.3	107	41.7	157	69.4	208	97.8	520	271.1	1100	593
−80	−62.2	6.8	−14	57	13.9	107.6	42	158	70	208.4	98	530	276.7	1112	600
−76	−60	7	−13.9	57.2	14	108	42.2	159	70.6	209	98.3	536	280	1150	621
−70	−56.7	8	−13.3	58	14.4	109	42.8	159.8	71	210	98.9	540	282.2	1200	649
−60	−51.1	8.6	−13	59	15	109.4	43	160	71.1	210.2	99	550	287.8	1202	650
−58	−50	9	−12.8	60	15.6	110	43.3	161	71.7	211	99.4	554	290	1250	677
−50	−45.6	10	−12.2	60.8	16	111	43.9	161.6	72	212	100	560	293.3	1292	700
−40	−40	10.4	−12	61	16.1	111.2	44	162	72.2	213	100.6	570	298.9	1300	704
−39	−39.4	11	−11.7	62	16.7	112	44.4	163	72.8	213.8	101	572	300	1350	732
−38.2	−39	12	−11.1	62.6	17	113	45	163.4	73	214	101.1	580	304.4	1382	750
−38	−38.9	12.2	−11	63	17.2	114	45.6	164	73.3	215	101.7	590	310	1400	760
−37	−38.3	13	−10.6	64	17.8	114.8	46	165	73.9	215.6	102	600	315.6	1450	788
−36.4	−38	14	−10	64.4	18	115	46.1	165.2	74	216	102.2	608	320	1472	800
−36	−37.8	15	−9.4	65	18.3	116	46.7	166	74.4	217	102.8	610	321.0	1500	816
−35	−37.2	15.8	−9	66	18.9	116.6	47	167	75	217.4	103	620	326.7		
−34.6	−37	16	−8.9	66.2	19	117	47.2	168	75.6	218	103.3	626	330		
−34	−36.7	17	−8.3	67	19.4	118	47.8	168.8	76	219	103.9	630	332.2		
−33	−36.1	17.6	−8	68	20	118.4	48	169	76.1	219.2	104	640	337.8		
−32.8	−36	18	−7.8	69	20.6	119	48.3	170	76.7	220	104.4	644	340		
−32	−35.6	19	−7.2	69.8	21	120	48.9	170.6	77	221	105	650	343.3		

FIGURE B-7. **Kilowatts to horsepower conversion table.**

Kilowatts (kW) into Horsepower (HP)
1 kW = 1.3596 HP

kW	0	1	2	3	4	5	6	7	8	9	kW
0	0	1,3596	2,72	4,08	5,44	6,80	8,16	9,52	10,88	12,24	0
10	13,60	14,96	16,32	17,67	19,03	20,39	21,75	23,11	24,47	25,83	10
20	27,19	28,55	29,91	31,27	32,63	33,99	35,35	36,71	38,07	39,43	20
30	40,79	42,15	43,51	44,87	46,23	47,59	48,95	50,31	51,66	53,02	30
40	54,38	55,74	57,10	58,46	59,82	61,18	62,54	63,90	65,26	66,62	40
50	67,98	69,34	70,70	72,06	73,42	74,78	76,14	77,50	78,86	80,22	50
60	81,58	82,94	84,30	85,65	87,01	88,37	89,73	91,09	92,45	93,81	60
70	95,17	96,53	97,89	99,25	100,61	101,97	103,33	104,69	106,05	107,41	70
80	108,77	110,13	111,49	112,85	114,21	115,57	116,93	118,29	119,64	121,00	80
90	122,36	123,72	125,08	126,44	127,80	129,16	130,52	131,88	133,24	134,60	90
100	135,96	137,32	138,68	140,04	141,40	142,76	144,12	145,48	146,84	148,20	100

Horsepower (HP) into Kilowatts
1 HP = 0.7355 kW

HP	0	1	2	3	4	5	6	7	8	9	HP
0	0	0,7355	1,47	2,21	2,94	3,68	4,41	5,15	5,88	6,62	0
10	7,36	8,09	8,83	9,56	10,30	11,03	11,77	12,50	13,24	13,97	10
20	14,71	15,45	16,18	16,92	17,65	18,39	19,12	19,86	20,59	21,33	20
30	22,07	22,80	23,54	24,27	25,01	25,74	26,48	27,21	27,95	28,68	30
40	29,42	30,16	30,89	31,63	32,36	33,10	33,83	34,57	35,30	36,04	40
50	36,78	37,51	38,25	38,98	39,72	40,45	41,19	41,92	42,66	43,39	50
60	44,13	44,87	45,60	46,34	47,07	47,81	48,54	49,28	50,01	50,75	60
70	51,49	52,22	52,96	53,69	54,43	55,16	55,90	56,63	57,37	58,10	70
80	58,84	59,58	60,31	61,05	61,78	62,52	63,25	63,99	64,72	65,46	80
90	66,20	66,93	67,67	68,40	69,14	69,87	70,61	71,34	72,08	72,81	90
100	73,55	74,29	75,02	75,76	76,49	77,23	77,96	78,70	79,43	80,17	100

This table is very simple to use. Read off the tens in the vertical scale and the units in the horizontal scale. The answer is where the two lines meet.

Example (above): convert 63 kW into HP. Go down the first column until you find 60 and the across until you come to 3. The result is where the two rows join.
63 kW = 85.65 HP.
For values of over 100, the decimal point should be adjusted.

Example (below): Convert 65 HP into kW. Go down the first column until you find 60 and then across until you come to 3. The result is where the two rows join.
63 HP = 46.34 kW.
For values of over 100, the decimal point should be adjusted.

To Convert From	To	Multiply By
Btu	Horsepower hours	.0003927
Btu	Kilowatt hours	.00029287
Btu/square foot	Langleys	.271
Horsepower	Kilowatts	.7457
Horsepower	Watts	745.7
Horsepower hours	Btu	2546.14
Kilowatts	Horsepower	1.34102
Kilowatt hours	Btu	3414.43
Langleys	Btu/square foot	3.69
Lumens (at 5,500 Å)	Watts	0.0014706
Months (mean Calendar)	Hours	730.1
Watts	Btu/hour	3.4144
Watts	Btu/minute	0.05691
Watts	Calories/minute	14.34
Watts	Horsepower	0.001341
Watts/square centimeter	Btu/sq feet/hour	3172.0
Watt-hours	Btu	3.4144
Watt-hours	Calories	860.4
Watt-hours	Horsepower hours	0.001341

Appendix C
Directory of Energy-System Suppliers

This appendix lists only suppliers of complete energy systems who also offer assistance in the design and setup of a system tailored to the needs of a boat and its crew. Contact them for catalogs and current prices. The information given here was correct at the time of printing, but is of course subject to change. Energy-system components are of course sold through many outlets not listed here, including chandleries and cataloguers.

Ample Power Co. 4300 11th Avenue, N.W., Seattle, WA 98107.
Design and supply of marine energy systems. Manufacturer of 3-Step Deep-Cycle Regulator.
High-output alternators, alternator controls (including 3-Step Deep-Cycle Regulator), Prevailer batteries, battery chargers, fans, Genie portable generators, Heart Interface inverters, lighting, solar panels, system components, system monitors, tools, watermakers. Ample Power products are carried by other energy system suppliers.

Balmar Products. 1537 N.W. Ballard Way, Seattle, WA 98107
Manufacture and supply of marine energy system components. Manufacturer of Power Charger portable diesel generator, and monitoring systems.
Lestek high-output alternators, alternator controls (including ABC control), battery chargers, inverters, Power Charger portable generators, system components, system monitors. Balmar products are carried by other energy system suppliers.

Cruising Equipment. 6315 Seaview Ave. N.W., Seattle, WA 98107.
Design and supply of marine energy systems. Manufacturer of Quad-Cycle Regulator/Monitor.
Silver Bullet high-output alternators, alternator controls (including Quad-Cycle Regulator/Monitor), batteries, Dynamote battery chargers, inverters, Hydrocap catalyst battery caps, PV solar panels, system components, system monitors, Four-Winds wind and water generators and controls, watermakers. Cruising Equipment products are carried by other energy system suppliers.

Everfair Enterprises. 723 S 21 Ave., Hollywood, FL 33020.
Design and supply of marine energy systems. Manufacturer of Four Winds wind and water generators.
Silver Bullet high-output alternators, alternator controls (including QuadCycle Regulator/Monitor), batteries, battery chargers, inverters, PV solar panels, system components, system monitors, Four Winds wind and water generators, wind/water combination systems, watermakers. Everfair products are carried by other energy system suppliers.

F.E.I. 1308 51 St., Marathon, FL 33050.
Design and supply of high-output alternators and charge controls.
High-output alternators, alternator controls, monitoring systems.

Greenwich Corporation. 9507 Burwell Rd., Nokesville, VA 22123.
Design and supply of marine water generators. Manufacturer of Power Log water generator.
Power Log water generator systems; trailing log and short flexible lead systems.

Hamilton Ferris Company. P.O. Box 126, Ashland, MA 01721.
Design and supply of marine energy systems. Manufacturer of Neptune Supreme wind and water generators.
Lestek high-output alternators, alternator controls (Including AutoMAC and Auto-CHARGE), batteries, battery chargers, engine-driven AC generators (Auto-Gen), inverters, portable generators and gen-sets (Kawasaki, Power Charger, Tanaka, Yanmar), PV solar panels, system components, system monitors, Neptune Supreme wind and water generators, wind/water combination systems, wind and water generator kits.

Generator Superstore. 1617 Broening Hwy., Baltimore, MD 21224.
1-800-243-6738.
Systems design and supply of portable generators and gen-sets for marine systems.
Onan and Robin portable generators, gensets, and system components. PV solar panels.

Jack Rabbit Marine. 56 Harrison St., New Rochelle, NY 10801.
Design and supply of marine energy systems. U.S. distributor for Ampair wind generator and Aquair water generator.
Ample Power high-output alternators, alternator controls (including 3-Step Deep Cycle Regulator), Prevailer batteries, battery chargers, inverters, solar panels, system components, system monitors, Ampair wind generators and Aquair water generators, wind/water combination systems.

Neilson DC Power. 337 West River Road, Orange, CT 06477.
Design and supply of marine energy systems. Lestek high-output alternators, alternator controls (including ABC control), Professional Mariner battery chargers and inverters, Balmar Power Charger portable generators, system components, system monitors.

OMS. 836 Ritchie Hwy. (#19), Severna Park, MD 21146.
Design and supply of marine energy systems. Wholesaler for Solarex PV solar panels. Balmar high-output alternators, alternator controls (including AutoMAC, Auto-CHARGE, and ABC), batteries, inverters, Power Charger portable generator, PV solar panels (Solarex), system components, system monitors.

Perrin Industries. 21 Chemin des Vignes, 92380 Garches, France.
Manufacture and supply of Hydrobat water generator and Windbat wind generator.
Wind generators, water generators (outboard-leg and short flexible lead types), system components.

Real Goods Trading Company. 966 Mazzoni St., Ukiah, CA 95482.
Design and supply of energy systems.
12-volt appliances, batteries, battery chargers, inverters, lighting, portable generators

and gen-sets, PV solar panels, system components, system monitors.

Richard L. Gaudio II. 4985 Riveredge Dr., Titusville, FL 32780.
Manufacture and supply of a large-prop wind generator systems.
Wind generators and wind system components, wind-to-water conversion kits.

Seelye Equip. Specialists. 913 State St., Charlevoix, MI 49720.
Design and supply of PV solar systems for marine use.
PV solar systems, system components, system monitors.

Sunnyside Solar. P.O. Box 808, Brattleboro, VT. 05301.
Design and supply of PV solar systems and other energy equipment. Manufacturer of energy-efficient 12-volt lighting.
Batteries, battery chargers, inverters, 12-volt lighting, PV solar systems, system components, system monitors.

Weems & Plath. 222 Severn Ave., Annapolis, MD 21403.
Manufacture and supply of AutoMAC, AutoCHARGE, and other electrical system equipment.
Alternator controls, electrical panels, system components, system monitors.

Windbugger. P.O. Box 259, Key Largo, FL 33037.
Design and supply of marine energy systems. Manufacturer of Windbugger wind generator.
Pole-mounted or rigging-suspended wind generators and system components.

INDEX